# PERFIDY IN THE BALKANS -
# THE RAPE OF YUGOSLAVIA

First published in Greece in 1993 by
PSICHOGIOS PUBLICATIONS
1, Mavromichali Street
10679 Athens
Tel. 01/3602535 - 3618654
Telefax: 01/3640683

ISBN 96-274-055-8

Printed and bound in Greece

# ARNOLD SHERMAN

# PERFIDY
## —IN THE—
# BALKANS

★

# THE RAPE OF
# YUGOSLAVIA

ΨΥΧΟΓΙΟΣ

**PSICHOGIOS PUBLICATIONS**

# BY THE SAME AUTHOR

**I. War**
In the Bunkers of Sinai 1971
When God Judged and Men Died 1973
The Splintered Cedar 1981

**II. Aviation**
To The Skies 1972
Lightning in the Skies 1973
Gabriel Was No Angel 1974
Challenging the Skies 1978

**III. Humor**
Impaled on a Cactus Bush 1971
Impaled on a Rhino's Horn 1974

**IV. Travel**
Blue Skies, Red Sea 1974
Going My Way Israel 1974
Pomeranz Connection 1976
Israel on $10 A Day 1976
Israel on $15 A Day 1978
Israel on $20 A Day 1980
Holyland Guide Book 1988

**V. High Technology**
Israel High Tech 1984
Alta Tecnologia 1985
Technology Handbook 1986
Into the 21st Century 1986

**VI. Miscellaneous**
Thought in the Night 1950
Search for Rahamim 1974
The Druse 1975
The Ship 1978
Wings of Icarus 1981
Aryeh Ben-Eliezer 1986
Tel Aviv-Jaffa 1987

Dedicated to the Memory of Joseph Sherman

# Contents

# CHAPTER I
# A THOUGHTFUL THANKSGIVING

The approach of the American Thanksgiving festival, for me at least, had taken on bittersweet overtones. Always one of my favorite holidays, even after three decades of expatriation to the Middle East and the Aegean, it was at that time, six years earlier, in 1986, when my father died. So along with chestnuts, turkeys, cranberry sauce, there were the intrusive memories of mourning and death.

In November, 1992, there were other preoccupations besides celebrating the survival of the early American settlers and the unhealing wound of parental loss.

Although never very soldierly, life had somehow contrived for me to spend time either in or on the peripheries of conflict. There was the Korean War in the early fifties which I considered a not very ennobling experience since the nearest I got to combat was a Stateside Ranger course.

War grew a tad closer in 1967 when I followed Israeli combat engineers into the Golan Heights as a reporter. The experience was repeated again in the early seventies when I wrote a book about the War of Attrition between Israeli and Egyptian forces along the Suez Canal. The Yom Kippur War in 1973 was probably the hardest experience of my life — too many of my friends perished, too many shells seemed to be aimed at me personally. I wrote the first book of that war, however, which was in a way not only a journalistic effort, but a personal catharsis. I spent appreciable time in southern Lebanon between 1980–82 which led to what I incorrectly assumed was my last war book. Incorrect because in November, 1992, just before the traditional Thanksgiving banquet, I was finally assured that I not only had permission to enter Yugoslavia and travel freely through the various war zones and potential areas of conflagration, but that there would be neither political nor military censorship and that I would have free access to the Bosnian Serbs who, at that moment in time, were giving the rest of the world a good case of heartburn.

Entirely on another level, in fact as a travel writer, my wife and I set down in Belgrade just two years earlier. There was nothing very official about the trip. The proximity to Greece made it an easy undertaking and the Balkan geography sort of legitimized the writing because my base of writing operation was Athens.

Almost from the very moment I arrived, Yugoslavia surprised me. No one had prepared me for the revelation that Belgrade was truly a beautiful city, that the Yugoslavs were a very handsome and hospitable people, and that the country was not only a patchwork of distinct ethnic groups, but so geographically diverse. In Slovenia, particularly around Bled, the people seemed like the nearby Italians and Austrians and the scenery was strictly Alpine. Zagreb, and indeed all of Croatia, was Middle Europe. Mountainous Montenegro might have been the idyllic setting of a Nineteenth Century operetta and Serbia, the largest of the republics, was a Byzantine tapestry still vibrant with orthodoxy despite decades of communism.

And then too there was Bosnia and Herzegovina, perhaps the most beautiful part of the whole country. I will never forget dinner, one pristine, autumnal day, under the shadow of the old Turkish bridge in Mostar, fated to be damaged three years later. Nor can I forget interviewing the young Jewish artist from Sarajevo who patiently explained that there could be no other home for him in the world, but the lofty Bosnian aerie. "After all," he smiled shyly, "we have been here for five hundred years."

However divergent the scenery, it was the people who fascinated me. There seemed to be so much pride in Serbia, so much determination to keep Yugoslavia intact and whole.

Unlike adjacent Croatia where World War II memories were either forgotten or reshaped — Serbian recollections were patriotic and proud. Under Marshal Josip Broz Tito, the Serbs pinned Hitler's best to the Balkans instead of permitting the Wehrmacht to pivot east in aid of their struggling armies in Russia or west to the Normandy beaches where additional forces were so desperately required.

The Second World War was etched into the mind of every Serb child, no less than the great battle of Kosovo, in 1389, in which Serbia was finally suffocated under the martial weight of the Turkish East. If a Serb can't shoot, he can't marry, I was informed proudly by friends. The feeling in 1990, however, was cautious optimism. For sure, Belgrade would have to pay more attention to the other republics. The central government would have to be more placating, more responsive to ethnic aspirations. Mistakes had been made. Excesses had been committed. Belgrade would have to learn to be more generous and flexible. But the actual breakup of Yugoslavia seemed hardly rational or feasible at that last quiet moment.

In Ljubljana, the capital of Slovenia, the mood was quite different. It was not a matter of more freedom, but freedom itself. Slovenia was Italy, Austria, Germany. What could it possibly share with the bullies of Belgrade who ran their army, dominated the police, mismanaged their economy and stifled their nationalism? But certainly there was still room for compromise? I asked. Perhaps a looser federation and more local autonomy and a new formula for the police and army whereby more Slovenians would be appointed to high ranks and posts? Too late, I was told by the young zealots of Ljubljana, already intoxicated by the heady wine of full freedom, strengthened by tacit and clandestine promises from western Europe, and particularly Germany, and buttressed by the knowledge that Serbia would have to cross Croatia to intimidate Slovenia, the slenderest of all possibilities since while the Slovenians may have chafed over Serb dominance, the sentiments in Zagreb were far more sanguine.

I remember meeting seventy-one-year-old Baron Janko Vranyczany-Dubrinovic, Minister for Tourism of the Republic of Croatia, in his suite in the distinguished Hotel Esplanade in Zagreb. There had been disturbances for weeks between the two largest ethnic components of Yugoslavia. Road and rail movements in the south, particularly in the region of Krajina, were disrupted by Serb irregulars who felt threatened by the possible breakup of the country. Of the 4.5 million inhabitants of this republic, a full 17% were Serbs and this minority became more restive as the clamor for the breakup of the old federation grew more menacing and stentorian.

"This too shall pass," the Baron assured. "You see, we are not reacting to the barricades and the endless provocations of these people. We are not sending our police south to disperse the Serbs — as almost any other sovereign power would do. Of all the hundreds of thousands of Serbs living in Croatia, perhaps 2-3,000 are extremists. Whatever their views, however, Croatia is committed to becoming an integral part of western Europe. Our present government was mandated by the people in the April, 1989 elections to do just that."

There was little likelihood of war, the Baron mused. Belgrade understood that Serb domination of the other republics was a thing of the past. Not particularly anxious to fight, every Croat would stand firm against any type of Serbian military duress. And, of course, Croatia had friends who would not permit a military travesty to occur. Certainly, this included Germany and Austria, but the United States would be expected to help as well.

Although I was not covering politics at the moment, the Baron's remarks were more provocative than he realized. Several journalists whom I had encountered assured me that a steady trickle of military supplies had begun months earlier from Germany. There were also German officers supervising Croat clandestine training and West German-licensed automobiles were arriving in Croatia, usually at night, with cars full of blond, crew-cutted volunteers.

Perhaps, I thought, the mood was merely precautionary. Surely, no one really wanted a war. It wasn't just a matter of Serbs and Croats, Bosnians and Slovenians, ethnic Albanians and ethnic Hungarians. People had been intermarrying for generations. Nearly all the people were of the same South Slav stock. How could a nation like Yugoslavia, so demographically and economically fused, suddenly tear apart? In a nation of 23.5 million inhabitants, there were over four million recorded intermarriages. No one seemed to want war. No one, in 1990, was even talking war. Everyone realized that there would have to be give and take. Slovenia and Croatia would be offered far more local independence. The central powers of Belgrade would have to be somewhat mitigated. But civil war? That was out of the question.

When I returned to Yugoslavia six months later, this time with a more official writing assignment, the platitudes of 1990 were no longer quite so germane. More and more ethnic incidents were recorded. All sides were squirreling away weapons and ammunition. Shadow police forces and armies existed in both Slovenia and Croatia. Large numbers of escaped, convicted Croatian war criminals were clandestinely being smuggled back into the republic from Germany and Austria.

Young Slovenian intellectuals and academicians were hellbent on implementing the obvious will of the constituents which called for a new country facing west and the dismantlement of Yugoslavia well in keeping with world trends as evidenced by ethnic eruptions throughout the old Soviet Union, newly expressed schisms between Czechs and Slovaks which would lead to a bloodless divorce, even Quebec's call for a French Canadian state rather than remaining a mere province.

In Ljubljana, new currency was devised to replace the dinar. Text books and school primers were edited to conform with the new reality. It was already apparent that Slovenia would accept nothing less than full independence. The Yugoslav army was no longer welcome. The police would be ethnically purged to wash out Serbs from key positions.

Although the young Slovenes talked endlessly about an invasion by the Serb-controlled Yugoslav army, the more mature patriots were convinced that civil war would and could be averted. Slovenia was protected by the long buffer of Croatia in the first place. And, while a significant percentage of the Croatian population was Serbian, the Slovenians were much more inclined to add to their gene pool by fraternizing with nearby Italy or Austria. Also, the Slovenes, like the Croats afterward, discovered and capitalized on one of the main defects of the federal government in Belgrade — the near total incomprehension of international public relations as a political tool. Both Ljubljana and Zagreb hired experts to tailor messages and then drive them home with the same uncanny accuracy as smart bombs. The Serbs, to the contrary, couldn't be bothered less. Belgrade was so certain of its moral rectitude, of the correctness and viability of the federation that it seemed superfluous to explain a truism that was so evident.

I sensed that war was inevitable in that spring of 1991. I was invited to a special champagne performance at the Zagreb Music Center which highlighted an aria from Zrinski, an opera dealing with Croatia's fierce resistance against the invading Turks. The Croatian flag was the standard, not the Yugoslav. The music was moving. The entire hall burst into wild applause when it ended. Women wept openly. Men, jaws jutting out, saluted the ancient checkered symbol of an independent Croatia. There was no doubt that the villains were no longer Turkey and Islam, but Belgrade and the central federal government. Beyond the clamor of wild applause was the whisper of war. It was there for the listening and I felt a great sadness and foreboding that night, despite all the tuxedos and evening gowns and free-flowing bubbly.

Before heading back to Belgrade, I traveled south to Dubrovnik, the picturesque, walled city on the Adriatic which had first enticed me to Yugoslavia thirteen years earlier. What was immediately apparent was that tourism, the life's blood of that medieval enclave, was choked out by the welter of political events. Dubrovnik was virtually empty of foreigners. It was like a beautiful girl, dressed in her best finery, jilted.

More by accident than design, I met Danko Atijas, deputy general manager of a Dubrovnik tourist agency and vice president of the tiny Jewish community, numbering twenty souls, which traced its origins back to 1352.

"Worried? Of course, I'm worried," he confided. "Tempers seem to be worsening all the time and no one really knows where this situation will lead — reconcilement, separation, war. I make no bones about it. Being Jewish in Croatia now is not exactly good for my ulcers. I'm always afraid that fighting will start and then somebody a couple of hundred kilometers away will stand up and shout: 'Hey guys, it's all the fault of the Jews'."

Out of the 85,000 Jews who had once comprised the pre-Second World War Yugoslav Jewish Community, there were barely 10% still in the country and only 1,000, mostly in Zagreb, in all of Croatia. The statement by Atijas was depressing, irrational, illogical, but then anti-Semitism was never very strong on reason.

The same gloom filtered to the streets of Belgrade two days later. The economy, in fine-tuned control only a year earlier, was being savaged by the threat (or, as some claimed, the inevitability) of civil war. Unemployment was growing as was inflation. Like Croatia and Slovenia, tourism had withered in Serbia. Serendipitously I think, I met my former guide and part-time *rakija* drinking companion, Jotsa, outside the Yugoslavia Hotel just overlooking the Danube River. As expected the tensions had not been kind to him. There had been virtually no work for months so he had been forced to slowly hock his possessions — from radio and stereo to overcoat and jacket. His young Serb wife, employed in a Dubrovnik travel agency, had fared no better. First she underwent steady and humiliating demotions. Finally, she was told to leave. There was hardly enough work for good Croats, much less displaced Serbs along the Adriatic coastline.

"Sometimes," he told me, "I think it would be better if there was a war. The waiting is a killer. The economy is down. There is no tourism at all. We hear reports all the time about abuses to Serbs in Croatia and probably they hear the same things about us.

"It is hard to believe that the country really is falling apart. Until now, always I considered myself a Yugoslav. That's how I registered my daughter as well after she was born. My generation was trained to think of itself as Yugoslav irrespective of ethnic origins. Since it was all one country, we could settle anywhere. We could seek out work wherever it was available. I guess it must be the way you feel in the United States. What possible problem could there be for a New Yorker settling in Virginia and marrying a girl from Maryland? But that's all changing now.

"My wife lost her job because she was Serb. I am unemployed because some crazy people want to dismantle my country rather than sit down and discuss honest differences of opinion. Serbs who have lived in Croatia for decades are being threatened and beaten up. It doesn't make any sense. I don't see any future."

In June, 1991, long after I was back in Athens and trying to do my own thing from the Greek capital, the prevalent heavy tensions finally rained war. Zagreb and Ljubljana announced their independence on June 25. For all intents and purposes, Yugoslavia was finished. It began in Slovenia with sporadic attacks against Yugoslavian troops before their evacuation could be performed, spreading rapidly to Croatia. Serbs threw themselves against the Croats with a blind rage. Fueled by fear and atavistic distrust Croats responded by eviscerating their captured Slavic cousins. The beautiful Plitvice Forest became a tank staging ground. Villages were razed, homes burned, prisoners tortured, churches plundered. Over 10,000 people perished quickly as the Pandora's Box of latent ethnic hatred and distrust spewed out into the countryside like poison gas caught in the wind. Thousands of Serbs were transformed into instant refugees. And it was obvious that this was only the beginning.

Ironically, and as predicted, the only safe region in the sundered country turned out to be Slovenia which had achieved its coveted independence easily. But, in the meantime, savage fighting erupted throughout the Serbian areas of Croatia, particularly in Krajina. The cauldron of animosity would soon spill over into nearby Bosnia and Herzegovina where some of the worst battles would take place, leaving that republic totally dismembered and buried in death. The ethnic Albanians, forming a huge majority in the autonomous province of Kosovo in Serbia itself, would introduce a new threat not only to the future viability of Serbia, but to the whole Balkans. And then the Yugoslav Republic of Macedonia in the south would soon insist on its own independence and place in the sun although implacably resisted by neighboring Greece which divined a real danger from the upstart nation whose proposed misnomer foretold of big troubles in the future.

While all this was happening and occasional letters arrived from truncated Yugoslavia describing food and fuel shortages, economic chaos, a flourishing black market, uncontrolled thefts and muggings in the formerly quiet streets of the Yugoslav capital, the whole world decided unequivocally that the ensuing drama was really very simple. There were the good guys and the bad guys. The former wanted independent countries, market economies as opposed to Communist strangulation, westward orientation, motherhood, Christmas trees and colored Easter eggs in season. The latter were apostles of "ethnic cleansing", were still unregenerative Communists, were also secret Fascists, organized concentration camps where prisoners, mostly Moslem, were systematically starved to death. They plucked the eyes out of their prisoners, shot up United Nations' food convoys, caused the greatest influx of refugees since the Second World War. They were anti-Catholic, anti-Moslem, anti-Quakers and anti-Boy Scouts.

# CHAPTER II
# BLACK SHADOW OF BALKAN HISTORY

When you are anxious, events never move very rapidly, a fact I discovered a long time earlier as a neophyte scribbler.

In order to perform the role I had assigned myself in Yugoslavia, I knew I needed help — not the kind that is intrusive and censorial, but the type that is strictly practical like interviewing the right people at approximately the correct time, like reaching certain remote destinations without squeezing a mine with a soon-to-be-dismembered leg or having a translator available when some peptic irregular is determined to shoot you for a spy.

All this meant patience which was another way of preparing for delay — not such a terrible alternative considering the welter of events. By December, 1992, only Slovenia seemed immune from the malaise wrecking the country, even insinuating a new Balkan war which might conceivably include such old and untrusting antagonists as Greece and Turkey.

Bosnia and Herzegovina were literally drenched in blood. Serbia and Montenegro were boycotted, embargoed, virtually under seige and threatened by just about every international body with the possible exception of the "Save the Whales Foundation". Kosovo, in Serbia, was restive with ethnic Albanian nationalism fanned to a frenzy by irresponsible promises orchestrated in Washington much in the same manner as Germany had kindled the ethnic fires of Slovenia and Croatia earlier. Croatia was openly planning an attack against the Serbian enclave in Krajina. And the former Yugoslavian republic of Macedonia was threatening to implode unless someone mollified the neighboring Greeks about the harmless political objectives of that nascent state.

Meanwhile, Iran and Turkey were calling for a *Jihad* against the Serbs. Russia was counseling restraint, reminding potential belligerents that Belgrade was not Baghdad and the Serbs were a tad more serious than the Iraqis.

It became apparent that there would be elapsed time before I could reach Yugoslavia. So since the future was beyond predicting, the present almost too explosive to analyze, it was time to peer back a little into the past.

There is nothing more fascinating — and more frightening — than Balkan history.

The anomaly of Yugoslavia was that two irreconcilable pressures united for political reasons to establish a geopolitical reality in the Balkans — South Slav ethnocentricity washed down with a bellyful of old distrust predicated on disparate histories and religious differences. But even that explanation begged for further elaboration because the land of the South Slavs, which was another way of saying "Yugoslavia", was a strong ethnic breeding ground for other peoples as well. Many of the constituents of the independent enclave of Vojvodina in the northeast, for example, were Hungarians, about one-half million. In the autonomous region of Kosovo in south Serbia, 90% of the two million inhabitants were ethnic Albanians whose religion was Islam and not Orthodoxy. And Macedonia in the south was a melange of South Slavs, Bulgarians, Albanians and even some Greeks.

The South Slavs, however, did dominate, having passed into the region in the Sixth and Seventh Centuries. These first tribes comprised Serbs and Croats, joined in separate migrations by Slovenes. They moved as far south as Bulgaria and the region later euphemistically rechristened "Macedonia" by the irrepressible Marshal Tito.

The three major subdivisions diverged from the very beginning. The Slovenes fell under the influence of Charlemagne and were quickly dominated by the Franks. The Croats established a separate state and developed a distinctive culture which reached its apogee under King Tomislav in the Tenth Century. It was short-lived, however, succumbing to the irresistible pull of the Magyars a century later. In the instances of both Slovenes and Croats, the tribes accepted Roman Catholicism, thereby fixing their eyes to the West.

The situation of the Serbs was different. Committed to the Orthodox Church, the Serbs developed a strong national identity which was, for all intents and purposes, free from the Frankish and Magyar influences.

The Serbian state of Nemanjic persisted from the Eleventh to the Fourteenth Centuries, producing seven kings — Stevan, Vladislav, Radoslav, Uros, Dragutin, Milutin and again Stevan — and two emperors, Dusan and Uros. The kingdom was located in Raska and the Vardar River Valley just north of the present borders with Greece. The main centers of the Serbian state were in Prizren and Skopje. Another viable Serbian state existed simultaneously in nearby Montenegro, dating back to the Eleventh Century.

Serbia cried out for help when the Turks invaded the region, but none came — neither from the Christian East nor the kingdoms of the West which were also imperilled by the massive invasion. Until the Serbs were decisively beaten by the Turks, a very specific and durable culture had developed. After the great rout, some of the survivors fled to the mountains of Montenegro where they found sanctuary with fellow-Serbs.

Modern Serbia was hammered into reality in 1804 when patriots around Belgrade, led by Karadjordje Petrovic, began their long fight for freedom against the Turks. Some concessions were granted in 1815. Finally, in 1878 at the Berlin Conference, after Russia defeated the Ottomans, both Serbia and Montenegro were recognized as independent states.

So although there was a common South Slav language and the ethnic factor was identical, over a millenium had irrevocably changed the three peripatetic Slav branches. Religion was a vital factor. The Roman Catholic faith was deeply embedded in both Slovenia and Croatia. Serbia and Montenegro, however, were stubbornly committed to the eastern rites of Christianity. Soon though it was more than religion. It was national values and political orientation.

Interestingly, the initial reference to some sort of South Slavic unity or "Yugoslavism" was produced not by the Serbs, but rather by Croats. It began as a literary indulgence in 1850 when three prominent Croatian writers in Vienna — I. Kukuljevic, F. Miklosic and I. Mazuranic — invited two Serbian linguistic reformers, V. Karadzic and Dj. Danicic, to sign a preliminary agreement for a common literary language. Eventually, these proposed reforms of the further melding together of the two similar tongues, would become the basis for the Serbo-Croatian language spoken by the overwhelming majority of Yugoslavs. In those days, however, the suggested reforms and modifications were merely a literary exercise with only slight popular support among the Serbs and virtually none with the more obdurate Croats who fiercely resisted the very idea of conceding their Latin orthography and adopting the more pondersome Cyrillic alphabet introduced into the region in the Ninth Century.

Slav nationalism in the Balkans was a vibrant feature toward the end of the Nineteenth Century. In one respect, it made sense because only through unity would the respective peoples attain the strength to fend off imperialist attempts to digest them one by one. There were a couple of problems, however. Serbia, already independent and the largest ethnic presence in the region, was more inclined to Pan-Serbism than Pan-Slavism. In other words, it was primarily interested in its own welfare. Equally problematic though, were the sharp differences in religion, vividly highlighted at the time by what was happening in neighboring Bosnia.

Most Bosnians were Slavs, a minority of whom had long since converted to Islam, a few even before the Turkish occupation. Of the remainder, Roman Catholics showed a natural affinity for Croatia while the Orthodox opted for

Serbia. Serbian territorial claims on Bosnia were fiercely resisted by Croats especially after Austro-Hungary captured the little mountain realm from Turkey.

The explosion that finally rended Europe and started the First World War was the culmination of an acute dislike that had developed between Serbia and the Austro-Hungarian Empire, animosity further fueled by Serbian military successes against the Turks and Bulgars during the Balkan War of 1911-13. Already mostly untacked, Europe fell apart totally when Gavrilo Princip, a young Bosnian member of the Serbian nationalist movement, assassinated Austrian Archduke Franz Ferdinand in the streets of Sarajevo in June, 1914. Although Serbia suffered dreadfully during that conflict, Belgrade had the ultimate satisfaction of knowing that both the Austro-Hungarian and Turkish empires were destroyed forever.

"The war to end all wars" transformed "Yugoslavism" from a literary inspiration to a political theme and, once again, it was Croatians who pioneered unification efforts. Three Croatian deputies of the Austro-Hungarian parliament − A. Trumbic, F. Supilo and J. Smodlaka − all incidentally Dalmatians, reacted with alarm and anger over the 1915 Allied London Treaty which was already dividing up Europe three years before the war was destined to end and at a time when the Allied forces were in deep military trouble. Irrespectively, the British and French nonetheless jubilantly carved up Europe with pens and protocols, awarding Dalmatia, a part of Croatia, to Italy for joining the war against the Austro-Hungarian Empire.

Nor were the Slovenes immune from the political hanky-panky of Whitehall which added parts of Slovenia to the largesse offered to Rome for its welcome support. So the dispirited Croat deputies invited some of their equally confused and befuddled Slovenian colleagues to approach the allied Kingdom of Serbia with the enormously provocative suggestion of including all of Croatia and Slovenia in its own postwar indemnification claim. And this based on a strong

ethnic and linguistic kinship with Serbs, not to mention the
common South Slav heritage. The idea was to exploit Serbia's
enormous war prestige as a tool to thwart Italian imperial
ambitions and Anglo-French compliance with the blackmailing
tactics of Rome. Both regions under discussion, it should be
recalled, were in "enemy territory", and thus up for grabs.

By the time the First World War was over, strong
concentric pressures emerged for a nation of South Slavs,
motivated not merely by the imperialist appetites of the big
power winners of the European struggle, but by the realization
that union meant strength. The first tentative merger was in
1918 under the Serb monarch Peter I who reluctantly
acknowledged that bitter differences of opinion continued to
exist between Croatia and Serbia, particularly since the former
claimed Bosnia as part of its own territory. For the next
eleven  years, bickering in the Balkans was the main theme of
the uneasy alliance whereby almost no one trusted anyone
else. In 1929, however, under royal edict, Yugoslavia was
proclaimed a political reality by King Alexander I. Whether
they liked it or not, Slovenes, Croats and Serbs would not
only be eating from the same table for awhile, they would also
be sleeping in the same bed together. So they could either
make love or screw each others brains out. Unfortunately,
they chose the latter.

Despite the royal edict and their early propensities toward
fusion, the strongly nationalistic Croats were not reconciled to
their submersion into a state which was mostly Serb
dominated. There were violent outbursts which finally
culminated in the assassination of the king in Marseille in 1934
by members of an extreme Croatian nationalist movement
called "Ustashe".

The noun "Ustashe" would take on a connotative meaning
expressing two utterly different ideas to a Yugoslavia still
striving to overcome ethnic distrust, strong religious
differences and the unwavering drift of international politics
which often saw in the country a pawn and not a sovereign

state. For the Serbs and Jews and Gypsies who were destined to die in torment in the Jasenovac concentration camp in a puppet Croatian state, the word would be a synonym for hell. For Croatian nationalists, however, frustrated by the centuries old denial of patriotic aspirations and sublimation forced on them by larger and more powerful nations, "Ustashe" became a euphemism for national survival.

The German invasion of Yugoslavia in April, 1941, was the fulcrum by which Yugoslavia would reach both its maturity and doom. The nationalist differences that always seemed to exist would be further highlighted by events that swept over the country like an enormous, suffocating tidal wave. There would be acts of heroism and bravery so numerous that they would be impossible to catalog properly even fifty years later. There would be so much treachery, so many explosions of poisoned ethnic malice, that the wounds would be festering five decades later and would finally spill pus in the green acreage of Plitvice, near the slopes of Sarajevo, in the burning fields of Krajina where the bodies of Serb males were rearranged by sewing their severed testicles to their dead mouths, in the Moslem villages of Bosnia where rape would be elevated to an acceptable tactic of coercion and terror.

So there I was in Athens, waiting to be called back to Yugoslavia, a country which fascinated me. Earlier, I spent a quarter of a century in Israel where I had not only marched under a blue and white banner four times, but where I had sent three children to war as well, and I experienced the deepest of all sadnesses for Yugoslavia.

History was a willful muse. By incinerating, stabbing, mutilating and shooting six million European Jews, Adolph Hitler had succeeded in destroying an entire culture and then through the sheer terror of his achievement, like the aftermath of a rampant forest fire that devours everything within reach, the seeds were sown for the creation of the first Jewish state in 2,000 years. The same madman sent his proud Wehrmacht to the Balkans, not only to subdue but to erase, and the inferno ignited there changed the world forever and created the scene for the fratricide that would be fought by the grandchildren of those caught in the maelstrom.

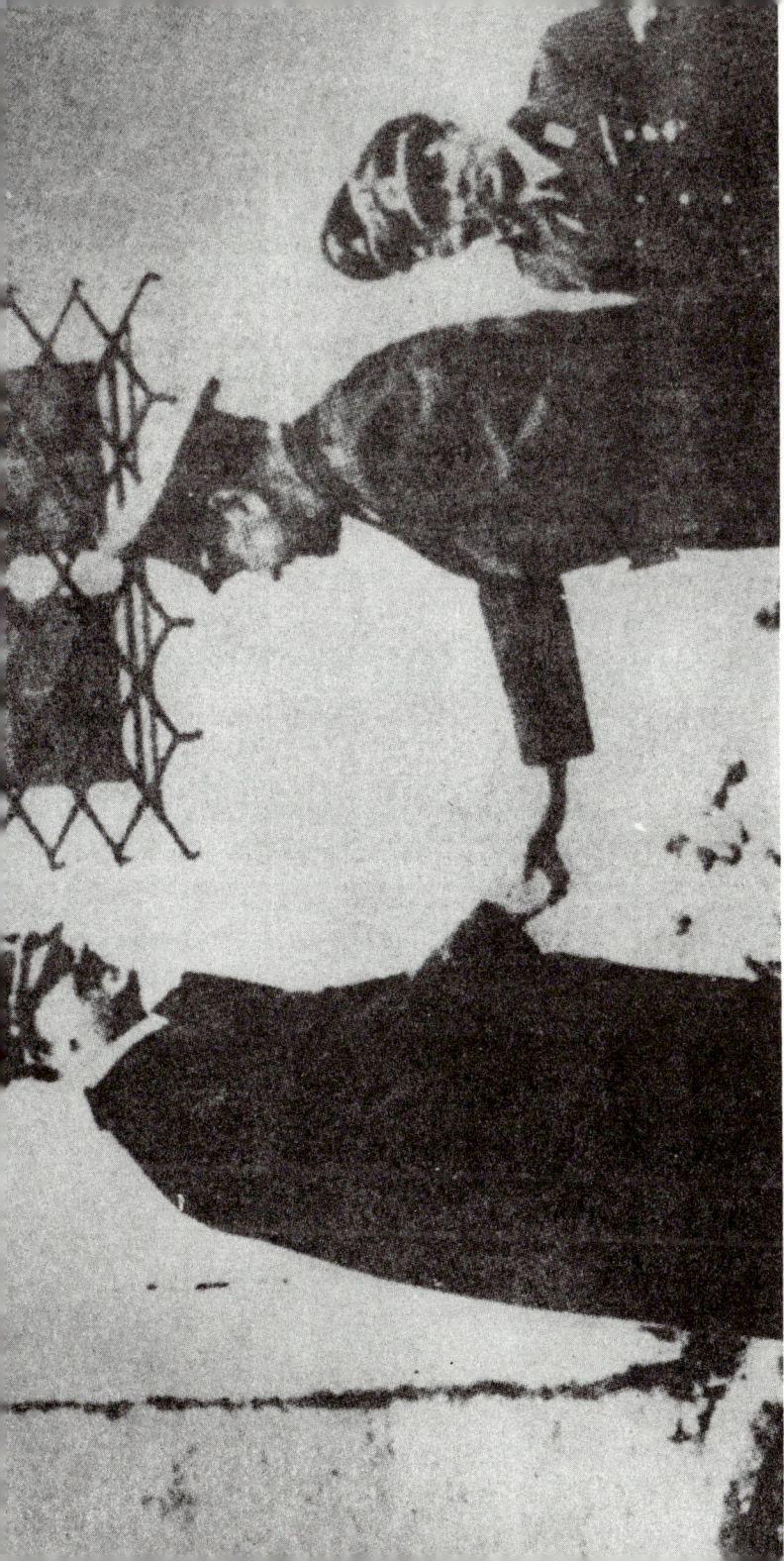

*Ante Pavelic's first visit to Adolf Hitler took place on 16 June 1941. Pavelic met with Hitler on six occasions during World War II.*

*Haji Ali Efendi Aganovic pledged loyalty and all-round coope-*
*ration to the Ustashe movement on behalf of Muslim believers.*

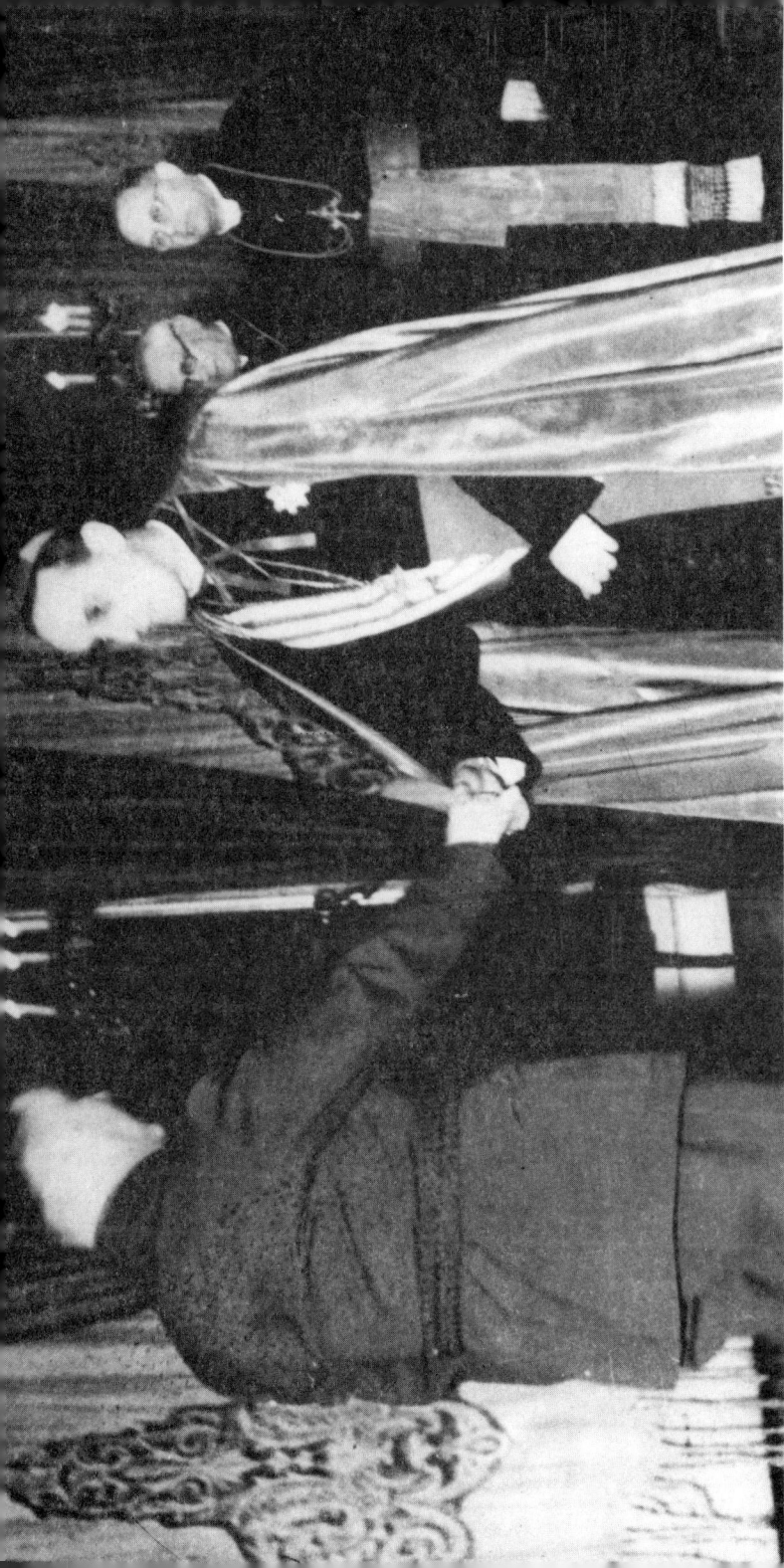

*Stepinac and Pavelic in Zagreb at Pavelic's birthday party.*

*Vlaho Margetic, a Franciscan, converting Serbs into Catholicism in the Slavonian village of Mikleus in 1941.*

*The Ustashe camp of Stara Gradiska, part of the Jasenovac concentration camp where 75,000 men, women and children were killed. The photo was taken on 24 April, 1945.*

*More than 20,000 children were killed in Ustashe concentration camps, 10,340 children in Jasenovac alone. The photo was taken in the summer of 1942 in the children's camp in Sisak*

# CHAPTER III
# UNDER THE NAZI THUMB

The German invasion of Yugoslavia during the early phase of the Second World War was virtually irresistible, an Axis noose consisting of Albania, Italy, Austria, Hungary and Bulgaria, already pulled taut around the strangling kingdom. If, however, the Yugoslavs could not resist the enormous force and numerical superiority of the victorious Wehrmacht, it could and would respond with fierce resistance to the German occupation of their country.

With the Yugoslavian king in self-imposed exile in England, the ethnic mucilage that had barely kept the country together and viable since the end of the last great war quickly dissipated. It was every man for himself and each according to his conscience as tribalism replaced nationhood.

The first to proclaim revolt against the German occupation was a Serbian colonel (later general), Draza Mihailovic, who, at the time of the invasion, was Minister of Defense to the government of King Peter II. It was a fervid plea to a people who had already been more brutalized by internecine war in the region than almost anyone else anywhere else. According to local figures, Serbia alone lost 25% of its total population and 56% of its adult males during the Balkan Wars and up to and including the First World War. This was compared with the American Civil War which was deemed particularly sanguinary and in which casualties for both sides totalled 2%. The accuracy of these figures has been disputed, but no one tried to deny the human carnage suffered by Serbia since the turn of the century.

Mihailovic was in charge of the royal army, later called the "Chetniks", a force supported and partially provisioned by Great Britain which at the time was fighting alone for its very life. Chetnik successes were immediate, but so was the price.

The Germans shot one hundred Serbs for every one of their men killed, halving that number for each German wounded. Yet the first guerilla resistance to Hitler was launched.

The Germans acknowledged early in the occupation that there could and would be no peace with the Serbs whose tradition of resistance was at their core, but other ethnic entities might be mollified and thus turned around.

While Slovenia was simply ingested by the Nazi war machine, Italy invited its Axis partner, Albania, to settle the southern parts of Serbia as a prelude to a complete takeover. These "settlers" were dispatched to Kosovo where a strong minority of ethnic Albanian Moslems had existed side-by-side with their Serb neighbors for generations. The Axis powers expected a double payment from their Moslem colleagues: pacification, the more brutal the better, of the indigenous Serb population; volunteer forces to meld into the Nazi war machine.

Consequently, the newly formed Albanian Fascist militia in western Kosovo violently expelled 70,000 Serbs in short order and "imported" an equal number of non-Serbian speaking Albanians into the region. Between 1941-43, Kosovo was an Italian puppet state. When Italy capitulated to the Allies, however, in 1943, Germany entered. Repressions soon escalated and, in 1944, the SS Skanderbeg Division, manned by Albanian volunteers, massacred thousands of Serbs and forced many of the survivors to flee north.

There was no need to pacify Croatia, the second largest region of the country, where the Germans were greeted not as invaders, but as saviors. There was no need to import racial laws and the technical artifices for extermination because they were already in place on April 10, 1941, when the neo-Nazi Ustashe Party proclaimed the independent state of Croatia, celebrating the event by plotting massacres of Serbs, Jews and Gypsies. As articulated by the new Minister of Education, the formal philosophy of the new nation was "to kill one part of all Serbs living in Croatia, push one part over the border (ethnic cleansing at its best!), and forcibly convert the remainder to Catholicism".

Under the leadership of Ustashe commander Ante Pavelic, the swastika shared honors with the checkered flag of Croatia. The "sieg heil" was adopted along with the German uniform and helmet. Pavelic proudly proclaimed Croatia a full-fledged Axis co-belligerent, declaring war on England immediately and then on the United States on December 12, 1941.

Assembling his elite forces, Pavelic told them that they were the "praetorian guards" of western civilization. The soldiers were then blessed by a Moslem cadi and a Catholic priest. Throughout all formal Ustashe ceremonies in 1941, the Catholic Church was prominent.

Pavelic was offered "technical assistance" to establish his concentration camps by SS Commander Heinrich Himmler, but the Ustashe was already well advanced and facing up to its "Jewish problem".

Almost immediately after the country was declared a state, citizens were asked to donate "any writing that in any way had anything to do with Jews". This comprised books written by Jews, correspondence issued by Jews, pamphlets prepared by anti-Semites. Ustashe wanted to know of any pending court cases by Croats suing Jews for damage while Pavelic personally thanked "the great Croatian people for its systematic analysis of all the sordid details of the Jewish conspiracy".

While all these festivities were taking place in beautiful Zagreb, the Chetniks had taken to the mountains where, despite the terrible toll of retaliation, regions were slowly being liberated from the Germans — but at a terrible price in human suffering and blood. Some Serbian historians aver that fully 15% of the population was killed in the war; others claim less; no one in his right mind denies the horrendous cost of resisting the Nazis years before it became fashionable elsewhere.

Since the Soviet Union had been an ally of Germany at the

onset of the war, sharing the spoils of a desecrated Poland like
a hungry carnivore, the Communist Party was not much of a
factor in the insurrection against Germany at the beginning.
Local Communists were told to lay low by their leader, Josip
Broz Tito, who had returned to Yugoslavia from Moscow in
1937 and was considered a master military theoretician.
Instructions were to stockpile guns and ammunition and be
prepared for all contingencies. Tito, born in Croatia of Croat
and Slovene parents, was quietly establishing the parameters
for his Partisans.

But while Tito was plotting and planning, some serious
flaws became evident in the Chetnik organization. Some of
the recruits, particularly in the leadership, were from the cities
and they found guerilla life, with all its inherent hardships,
unendurable. German intelligence had pinpointed some of
them and their families were being held as hostages. And then
there was a small percentage of turncoats who for favors or
cash were betraying their colleagues. Yet throughout this
entire dark period, it was the Chetniks who carried the banner
of revolt.

When Russia joined the fray, the Partisans began operating
immediately and with great daring. There was a strong
competition between both guerilla armies to determine who
would mostly be benefiting from the British military supplies
which were being air dropped into the mountains to keep the
rebellion alive and flourishing. Mihailovic had long since
established his supply source and Tito was at a decided
disadvantage since Moscow could provide little more than
verbal encouragement and the promise of better days ahead.

Before long, and to the delight of the Germans, open
warfare erupted between Partisans and Chetniks. This new
veneer of fratricide also pleased Pavelic who was personally
singled out by Hitler for praise, his Slavic origins almost
forgiven and forgotten. Throughout the war, Croatia had
proportionately more men under arms than any other Axis
power including Germany. There were 160,000 Domobrani

regulars, 75,000 Fascist militia under the direct control of the Ustashe, 15,000 police auxiliaries divided between the Oruznici and Redarstvo. In addition to its own units, Croatia provided more volunteers to the German army than anyone else in Axis Europe: five full-strength divisions which comprised the Wehrmacht's 369, 373 and 392; the 13th and 23rd divisions of the Waffen SS; a Croat legion of 7,000 volunteers serving under the German command at the Russian front; an anti-aircraft unit of 500 men assigned to protect Austria. Although top commanders were Germans and wore Wehrmacht uniforms and insignias, all also had the Croat national chessboard emblem on the sleeves of their jackets. As a brief postscript to history, most of the Croatian "volunteers" were massacred at Stalingrad. Unlikely to forgive the fleeing Germans for what they had done, the Red Army held the traitorous Slavs in utter contempt.

While Yugoslavia was still in flames and the war remained chaotic — Germany yet presiding over most of Europe — the wiley Tito was preparing not only for victory, but for the creation of a viable Yugoslavia under the banner of communism. In 1943, with the planned exclusion of Serbia which was still under control of either Mihailovic's Chetniks or the German occupiers, he convened a secret meeting of the Yugoslav Communist Party, consisting of five members of the Central Committee over which he presided. The interior borders for the future state were drawn up. Vojvodina in the north with its large ethnic Hungarian community and Kosovo in the south into which Albanians continued to flock under the patronage of Fascist masters, would be given autonomous status at the direct expense of Serbia. An artificial state called "Macedonia" would also be created along the southern border in order not only to assuage the many Bulgarians living there, but more important, and under direct orders from the Comintern in Moscow, to prepare the way for an eventual Communist Yugoslavian expansion to the Aegean — one of the most cherished ambitions of Joseph Stalin.

A loyal and dedicated Communist, Tito knew all about Comintern Protocol 207 which was secretly drafted in Moscow on February 25, 1934, to eventually resolve the "Macedonian problem".

The text blamed the three "imperialist" states of Greece, Bulgaria and Yugoslavia for creating a political impasse in the region and for virtually committing cultural genocide against the "indigenous" inhabitants. Greece was specifically cited for Hellenizing the locals, repressing their national aspirations and forcing Greek civilization on them to the exclusion of their Slavic heritage. Bulgaria was excoriated for trying to dominate the region by employing linguistics as an "imperialist tool".

In general, all three countries were accused by the Comintern of "making slaves of the local Macedonian people" and the working classes of the three "imperialist nations" were called to rise up against the iniquity. For Tito, much later, the message was perfectly clear. Since he was drawing up arbitrary lines anyway and because he understood exactly what his Soviet masters expected of him, he would draw a new border. As both a loyal Communist and a strong Yugoslav nationalist, inventing a new republic might actually lead some day to the very access to the Aegean which both he and Stalin coveted.

To Tito's credit, he was at the time engaged in a life and death struggle with Nazi Germany. There was certainly no fairness about appeasing the Albanians at the expense of the very people who were totally committed to the liberation of Yugoslavia, but Tito was the perfect pragmatist and winning the battle was more important than the future squabbles and ethnic imbalance he was preparing and the betrayal he was committing against the whole Serbian people.

In the meantime, however, "the whole Serbian people" were in imminent danger of being erased — both by the Wehrmacht which was executing Serbs by the tens of thousands and the Ustashe which was achieving levels of brutality constantly praised in Berlin. One observer, however, was a little skeptical of Ustashe claims. Hermann Neubacher, a high-ranking Austrian Nazi serving as special German envoy for southeast Europe wrote petulantly a half-century ago that: "When the leaders of Ustashe boast to have slaughtered one million Orthodox Serbs, that, in my opinion, is a self-glorifying exaggeration. On the basis of reports I have received, I estimate that the number of defenseless Serbs who were slaughtered at three-quarters of a million."

This figure was contested on an important Greek television interview program in the spring of 1993 when a leading scholar claimed that "1,280,000 Serbian skulls were counted after World War II". On the other hand, the Simon Wiesenthal Center in Vienna credited the Ustashe with murdering 77% of the Jews of Croatia, a half-million Serbs and 20,000 Gypsies. Ustashe's Jasenovac, incidentally, was the third largest death camp in all wartime Europe.

One of the great coverups of World War II was the role of the Catholic Church in the extermination of both Serbs and Jews in Croatia. Strongly committed to Croatia from the very beginning as a bulwark of Catholicism against the twin dangers of Christian Orthodoxy and Islam, there was not even an attempt at neutrality (or humanity) while the most unchristian of all deeds were being committed against mostly defenseless, always innocent people. When the Vatican sent an official delegate to Zagreb in April, 1941, to celebrate the creation of the Ustashe state, the Pope was certainly cognizant of the fact that 225,000 Orthodox Serbs were compelled to accept Catholicism under the same enticements employed by Senor Torquemada from his Inquisitorial throne five centuries earlier. Orthodox priests joined rabbis in death and yet there was never a murmur, never a protest from the papacy. Indeed, after the war was over, 692 Catholic criminals were spirited out of the republic by a priest called Beganovic who organized his own "rat canal" for the purpose of protecting convicted Catholic war criminals, many of whom were clergy.

In general, the Catholic Church managed to emerge fairly innocent from the ravages and atrocities of the Second World War, but no coverup could conceal the role of Zagreb Archbishop Alojzije Stepinac whose fealty to the Ustashe finally earned him a red hat.

Edmond Gleise von Horstenau, Germany's plenipotentiary general in Zagreb, wrote on April 17, 1941: "That character (Stepinac) was first a volunteer in the Austrian army, then he deserted and, as a Serbian officer, was engaged in action on the Salonica front where he fought against his former homeland to which he had vowed loyalty. Later on, he became a priest. At the conclusion of the concordat with the Kingdom of Yugoslavia, Stepinac, thirty-two at the time, was appointed the Zagreb Metropolitan. This was one of the tricks the Vatican opportunistically allowed itself from time to time."

Most of the more virulent supporters of Ustashe, including Pavelic himself, were escorted out of the collapsing country through well-prepared underground channels. The first stop for Pavelic was Austria where he was hidden in Roman Catholic churches. Subsequently, he was brought to Rome where he found sanctuary at the San Geronimo Brotherhood, an institution belonging to the Roman Catholic Church of Croatia. Pavelic was finally smuggled out of Rome to Argentina by the Brotherhood. He acted as a security advisor to Argentine President Juan Peron for years, eventually dying peacefully of old age. The Peronist government subsequently provided 35,000 visas to Ustashe criminals sought both by Yugoslavia and the Allies. An interesting footnote of Balkan history was that Tito never even chided the Vatican for its World War II role in Croatia and no collaborator/priest was either tried or punished for the numerous, documented crimes committed under the Nazi/Ustashe banner.

In July, 1941, Friar Djordjije Juricev, personal curate of Pavelic, said that "this is the land of the Croats and only Croats can live here. There is no room for those who won't convert. In these northern parts, I have given orders to do away with every living non-Catholic soul and, if necessary, I will do the same here (the village of Staza), for these days it is not a sin to kill even a seven-year-old child if it gets in the way of our Ustashe movement.

"Today, we should all be Croats and we should expand, and when we do expand and grow stronger we will take from others, if necessary. Don't think because I am in a priest's robe that, when necessary, I won't pick up a machine gun and destroy every living being from the cradle onward who is against the Ustashe state and government."

The Italian daily, Il Tempo, ran an article on September 9, 1953. "On May 21, 1941, three persons reported to the Sassari Division Command in Knin. Among them was the Franciscan priest, Friar Simic. They stated that they had been appointed by the government in Zagreb to take over the civilian government in that region. The Italian general asked them what their policy would be. Friar Simic was the one who answered: 'To kill all Serbs in the shortest possible time'."

An atheist himself, Tito had some very definite ideas about the Jews, particularly the Jews of Yugoslavia. Later, he developed other ideas about the State of Israel and its role in the world.

From the very beginning, the Partisan message to the Jews of Yugoslavia was simple: "You will probably die. The only real choice you have is how. Take a gun and share our lives in the mountains or await betrayal and the journey to the death camps."

History later recorded that eleven of those designated as National Heroes were Jewish, that one hundred and fifty were awarded the Partisan Star 1941, that fourteen Jews became four-star generals, two major-generals and ten brigadiers.

One of Tito's closest wartime friends was Moshe Pijade who was a member of the exalted Supreme Staff of the Army and then president of the National Parliament. Pijade was also a Zionist instrumental in the emigration of 8,000 surviving Jews to Israel, a feat which Tito must have approved.

Later, when it came to Israel, however, Tito was far less sympathetic and much more confrontational. He supported the Arabs almost blindly. He not only permitted the establishment of military training centers for the Palestine Liberation Army, but allowed much more radical terrorist groups into the country. He provided arms, funds and other forms of succor. It was no surprise therefore, years after Tito's death, that Yugoslavia was one of the last countries to open full diplomatic relations with Israel and that a sourness existed between them. All this was made even more anomalous by the centuries of warm and close relations that traditionally existed between Serbs and Jews.

When the war was finally over, Tito presided over a devastated country. The economic infrastructure was destroyed. Along with the millions buried was the old dream of a viable political option for the South Slavs. How could this nation ever possibly work again? The Serbs absolutely despised the Croats and it would take years of deft propaganda, excursions into the twilight zone of reason whereby some bold Croatian deeds against the Nazis were reinterred and then highlighted to the exclusion of other deeds better forgotten, better erased, before the two peoples could even face each other again. Serbia was reeling in alarm as it acknowledged a Kosovo which was suddenly half Moslem and explicitly anti-Serb. The ravaged Slovenians were numbed by their own wartime experiences. They had grown more insular, more indrawn than ever. And by then there was a Macedonia on the drawing board which no one really knew what to do with, the Comintern having presented Yugoslavia with an interesting legacy, but a whole new mythology had to be created in order to make it work.

The world was celebrating the end of World War II, but in Yugoslavia the country was barely alive.

# CHAPTER IV
# THE LEGACY OF TITO

Tito, the Croat, was prepared to pay a heavy price for ethnic Albanian support or at least neutrality during the long conflict with Germany — a price extracted from Serbia.

One of Tito's early acts was legislation passed on March 6, 1945, which inexplicably prohibited Serbs who were expelled by the Axis from returning to their homes. In one of the great paradoxes of modern history, a new law was enacted whereby all land deeds made during the Kingdom of Yugoslavia were annulled while the same transactions performed when the enemy was in power were deemed licit. Eerie, it was only the beginning of a scenario which would have deadly consequences for the region decades later.

Tito next ordered that the border between Albania and the Kosovo region of Serbia be prised open and kept open until 1948 so that another 115,000 Albanian Moslems would be encouraged to find roots in Serbia. It was all almost too good to be true for the impoverished refugees who flocked across the Yugoslavian border where instead of hunger, they received cash subsidies, welfare and child support payments equal to twice the average Yugoslav wage because of the enormous families trailing behind them. And, of course, by presidential edict, the bulk of the largesse was financed, be it ever so reluctantly, by the Republic of Serbia.

In addition to the open borders and attractive benefits offered by the federal government, the immigrants were assured of a large measure of territorial autonomy since Tito was already envisaging a "greater different Yugoslavia" even if it was at the expense of truncated Serbia. This promise of local autonomy was affirmed in the Yugoslav Constitution on January 31, 1946. A year later, it was incorporated into the Serbian Constitution as well — no Serb in his right mind

willing to defy Tito. It was at this juncture in time that the
population of Kosovo was more or less equally divided
between Serbs and ethnic Albanians. It was predictable that
troubles would begin immediately — and they did.

The full name of the province was actually Kosovo-
Metohija which literally meant "monastery land given by the
feudal lord".

The actual decision to "Albanize" part of Serbia was made
by Tito and two other Politburo members — one representing
Croatia and the other Slovenia. One of the signatures was that
of Edvard Kardelj who remarked at the time that the decision
must not be publicized because "it would give powerful
arguments to Serbian bourgeoisie who would accuse us of
breaking up Yugoslavia".

Even before his celebrated break with Moscow in 1948, Tito
was pursuing his own relentless policy of restructuring
Yugoslav society, establishing a tenuous balance between
people who really didn't like each other very much and
certainly didn't trust one another. He was trying to be the
great appeaser, but invariably it was Serbia that suffered the
most.

Kosovo continued to obsess Tito even during the long
years when international attention was focused on the
Yugoslav President as both a Third World leader and a
renegade Communist who preferred nationalism to
Communist Party discipline.

Tito's "Dirty Tricks Department" was run by a close
associate, Fadil Hodza, who pushed through the kind of
legislation that expanded the rights of the ethnic Albanians
and, at the sametime, mobilized ever growing numbers of the
Kosovo Moslems into the Communist Party of Yugoslavia.
On February 23, 1967, at a meeting of the Communist
leadership of Kosovo (predominantly ethnic Albanian by
then), Tito, in the presence of Kardelj, stated: "All you need is
to bring up your share of party membership". It was the
clearest of all invitations for the burgeoning Moslem

population to take political control. Following the meeting, Kosovo Albanians joined the Communist Party in droves, taking over the Provincial Assembly, local government, courts and public enterprises. According to Belgrade sources: "This, in consequence, launched a systematic terror over non-Albanians including Serbs, Moslem Turks and Gypsies. Thousands of the oppressed fled to Serbia."

Obviously, there was resistance to the sellout. Tito understood that Kosovo was not merely real estate. It was virtually holy ground. It was where Serbia, in one final cataclysmic struggle, for awhile resisted the irresistible. Six centuries after the Serbian defeat and the onset of the long Ottoman night, a friend confided: "We Serbs are really a very crazy people. Who else would commemorate the anniversary of their greatest defeat?" Indeed, who else?

Those Serbs, however, who had the temerity or masochism to question Tito's Kosovo policies were quickly removed from the stage and often severely persecuted. In reference to Kosovo, Tito was a monomaniac.

Such a victim was Dobrica Cosic, one of Serbia's greatest writers and later president of Yugoslavia. Years after severe persecution for venting his views publicly about the betrayal of Serbia in Kosovo, he was asked about the recurring injustice that seemed to shadow the Serbian people.

"We do not live in a world of justice and truth," he said sadly in 1991. "The truth about nations and individuals is rare and conditional. Truth is mainly the power of literature and some sciences. Politics does not care about truth."

In order to accelerate the handover of Kosovo to the Albanians and consequently further enervate the largest of the six republics, Tito channeled larger amounts of federal funds to his pet project. As before, the money came from Serbia, thus greatly weakening an economy which began to lag behind Slovenia and Croatia. And, at the sametime, pressures continued from Belgrade to force the remaining Kosovo Serbs out of their homes.

In 1974, six years before Tito's death at the age of eighty-eight and at the zenith of his political power, at a time when he was hailed as a key international leader, with palaces and country homes by then strewn throughout the country, he enacted the legislation that finally turned Kosovo-Metohija into a full-fledged sovereign state of the Republic of Serbia. By then, the Kosovo´population was overwhelmingly Moslem — 85%. It had taken him almost thirty years to complete the "Albanization" of Kosovo, but he had succeeded.

Tito's Kosovo legacy was a decade of turmoil. Between 1980-88 there were five hundred separate ethnic Albanian assaults against the federal army and police installations in the region. Large caches of military hardware were either stolen outright or smuggled into the region from Albania which maintained a long, contiguous border with Kosovo. Police stations and barracks were raided and a call went out from Pristina, the capital of the province, for pan-Islamic support from both the Middle East and North Africa.

Meanwhile, the local Moslems were reproducing proportionately faster than any other ethnic group in Europe — a net annual increment of 46,000 live births compared with 13,800 in Serbia and Vojvodina. But while the population grew, jobs did not. Unemployment was rife throughout the region with somewhere between 50-80% of eligible men perpetually idled. Apparently, Tito's master plan for the region did not take into consideration the lack of mineral resources, the paucity of industrial life and the endemic lack of tourist appeal in an area where wells were being poisoned, cattle blinded and crops burned in order to pressure the remaining non-Moslems into leaving.

By the tail end of the last decade, with the advent of the Slobodan Milosevic government, the Serbian authorities in Belgrade had finally decided to reverse directions. More troops were sent into Kosovo and the local police were strengthened. A call went out to Serbs who had previously lived in the area, promising them not only land but protection if they returned. The local Moslem population was meanwhile placed under heavy stricture. Civil liberties were suspended. Curfews were introduced. Martial law was imposed. The Serbs were accused of "rough tactics" as they often used excessive physical force to intimidate the locals. While demonstrations, strikes and sabotage were taking place in Kosovo and Islamic extremists were galvanized in an illicit, separatist movement called "Greater Albania", government-controlled newspaper and radio reports about an eventual "Islamic system in Yugoslavia" were proliferating out of Tehran. According to Belgrade sources: "It is becoming increasingly clear that an organized Islamization of the Balkans is taking place, and Moslem priests were directly involved in large numbers in the most recent demonstrations of Greater Albanian chauvinists."

Tito's policy of championing Moslem interests was not relegated to Kosovo alone. He was for years the close friend and confidant of Egypt's President Gamal Abdul Nasser who, himself, was one of the most destabilizing factors in the Middle East, having been directly instrumental in causing the civil war in Lebanon which virtually paralyzed that country for over a decade. He was friendly to George Habash who represented radical terrorism at its worst and was an early and staunch supporter of Moslem rights in the Republic of Bosnia and Herzegovina.

Harking back to the German invasion of Yugoslavia in 1941, and recalling Croatia's unrequited appetite for Bosnia and Herzegovina, the Nazis gave the region to the Ustashe government early in the war. Like their Albanian coreligionists in nearby Kosovo, indigenous Moslems were mobilized to assist the Axis war effort. They served in Fascist militias and police, encouraged by such pro-Nazi Arab personalities as the Grand Mufti of Jerusalem who was actually invited to Ustashe-controlled Bosnia during the German occupation. Tito made it a point of personal honor to wean back from the Fascists as many errant Moslems as possible. He had no problems with the Serbs who were deeply committed to the conflict from the beginning, but the wavering Moslems represented a particular challenge for the charismatic leader of the Partisans.

Tito wooed the Bosnian Moslems assiduously, promising he would reward them when Yugoslavia was whole and at peace again. He did, particularly when he recognized Yugoslavia's Moslems "as a nation and not merely a religion" in the mid-seventies. The move was pure Tito — politically clever, myopic and totally unhinged from reality. The Bosnian Moslems, sprigs from the South Slav branch, were ethnically as Slavic as either the Serbs or Croats. They had gradually adopted Islam in order to improve their social status during the Ottoman Empire and to avoid paying taxes for non-Moslems.

Members of the Sunni branch of Islam, half of the Bosnian Moslems were reputed to be atheists. Turning these people into a "nation" when they were clearly a religious bloc was bound to create some fancy problems in the future.

If for no other reason than its sheer, majestic beauty, the part of Yugoslavia that impressed me the most in 1990 was Bosnia and Herzegovina. Because of my own background, my Moslem host, Munir Rasidovic, accompanied my wife and me to the Vraco Liberation and War Memorial Park overlooking Sarajevo. Chairman of the Sarajevo Tourist Association, Rasidovic told us that 9,000 Bosnians, overwhelmingly Jews, were murdered during the Nazi occupation of the region. "It was quite natural that we honor our fallen Jewish comrades. After all, we lived together for centuries. We fought together. We died together. Here, in Bosnia, we are all equals — Moslems, Christians, Jews."

At the time, the ethnic salad which was Bosnia consisted of 41% Moslems, 39% Serbs and 18% Croats. Over the centuries, the people really had learned to live together, to more than tolerate each other. Sarajevo, the capital of Bosnia and formerly host city to the Winter Olympics, was at the sametime both alpine and exotic. A strong Turkish influence prevailed in the old, picturesque part of the city while the luxurious Holiday Inn hotel was a symbol of winter sports and future tourist expectations. In those days, it seemed that Bosnia didn't have a care in the world. Even if trouble erupted in Slovenia or Croatia, those republics were light years away from the top of the ziggurat.

"We Moslems here are not a very religious people." Rasidovic almost apologized. "Turkey came and left. Ancient armies invaded and then disappeared. Only the people endure. Personally, I couldn't care less about a person's religion. The only thing that matters is his humanity and that is why war in Bosnia is inconceivable. Christians and Moslems would never fight each other here. Why should they? We are all friends."

I would remember those words often in the future when Serbs were accused of implementing genocide against the Moslems and the United Nations castigated Bosnian Serbs for committing "30,000" rapes — not 29,417, nor 30,003, but "30,000" authenticated, premeditated, authorized attacks against Moslem women. And I would recall his words when the bodies of tortured, mutilated Serb villagers were excavated from a bog or when the Croats murdered over two hundred Moslem villagers in a single day and during one of those rare ceasefires that seemed to work. I promised myself that when I finally returned to Yugoslavia, and the time was nearing according to what I had gleaned from Belgrade, I would seek out Rasidovic if he was still alive and still in Bosnia and over a *rakija* ask the Moslem who took such pride in his city and his state, how could this have happened? Was Bosnia the dark side of the moon? Were their sinister forces afoot like evil gremlins tripping through the graveyards at midnight which invoked the delirium of national suicide? Was so much hate and spite buried for so long that only a drop of catalyst was needed to explode a world? And if apparently belligerents have to kill, if man is so craven that he can find solutions no other way, then why must he murder with such brutality?

Why the torture and mutilation before the rites of execution? Was this ordained in the Koran or the New Testament or was the Balkans giving birth to a new and terrible religion and was Munir Rasidovic either deceived or a fool?

Whatever might be the case, Rasidovic erred, and erred seriously, on one other point in addition to Balkan brotherly love. Even during my visit, it was apparent that religion was becoming a much more formidable factor in the lives of Bosnia's Moslems than they cared to admit, despite claims of religious indifference. The mosques were full during prayer times – and not with the hoary and bearded. The supplicants were mostly young, mostly unemployed or under-employed. There was a reaching out among the young Moslems and it was not toward Belgrade, but rather in the direction of Mecca.

In the decade before the dismemberment of the old Yugoslavia, but after the encouragement provided to Islamic elements by Tito, strong interest in Bosnia developed in Turkey, which increasingly saw itself as the Moslem protector of the Balkans; in Iran which viewed the region as a testing ground for an expanded Islamic agitation throughout Europe; in Libya where the concept of Moslem revolution was the primary export after oil; in Saudi Arabia which exhibited a proprietary sentiment for small, struggling Moslem groups trying to survive in alien environments e.g. in Europe.

Although these countries accelerated subversions after the 1991 dissolution of the former state, they were alive and active in Bosnia throughout the eighties and this was true particularly of Iran.

The Moslem President of the spinoff country of Bosnia and Herzegovina, Alija Izetbegovic, was sympathetically portrayed by most of the world press and television networks as the moderate leader of a besieged and highly victimized people. But according to the reputable British publication "Defense and Foreign Affairs Strategic Policy", Izetbegovic "has long been an Iranian protégé and member of the Fundamentalist *"Fida'iyane Islam"* organization committed to the conversion of all of Bosnia and Herzegovina into an Islamic republic despite the fact that Moslems number only about one-third of the population".

Izetbegovic, a paternal figure on television, was the author of a seventy-page "Islamic Declaration" which he first wrote in 1970 and then had reprinted twenty years later when I was visiting Bosnia. In the treatise, he expressed deep doubts about a Bosnian secular state, championing instead the more vibrant cause of Islamic unity.

"The Islamic movement must and can take power," he wrote, "as soon as it is morally and numerically strong enough — not only to destroy the non-Islamic power — but to build up a new Islamic one." Two of the inevitable, and certainly unavoidable, conclusions of the document were that a Moslem state must be formed in Bosnia and that no Moslem state can tolerate any other religion.

All the ingredients, but one, were in place to create the savage tragedy of Bosnia: the acquisitorial propensities of both Croatia and Serbia; the near numerical balance between Moslems and Serbs; the strange propensities of Tito; decades of Moslem Fundamentalism quietly proliferating into the region; external influences promoting regional destabilization; and evidently a lot of pent up animosities. The one item missing from the equation was that prior to the breakup fully 60-65% of all the private land in the former republic belonged to Serbs, according to the 1981-91 land books registers. Little wonder then the Serbs felt so threatened and were prepared to react so fiercely.

# CHAPTER V
# TUDJMAN - THE IMPARTIAL HISTORIAN

When Nobel Prize winner Elie Wiesel told guests at the inaugural ceremony of the Holocaust Museum in Washington DC in April, 1993, that he hadn't slept for the six months since personally witnessing the palpable tragedy that had undertaken Bosnia, it was clear who was the victim and who the vanquisher. There was further amplification when U.S. President Bill Clinton, formally dedicating the edifice to the millions martyred by the Nazis, said that the evils portrayed in the building "still find echoes today from the ethnic cleansing in Bosnia". These remarks were addressed to concentration camp survivors, families of victims, heads of state, the President of Israel, Haim Herzog, who had flown in especially for the event.

Strategically located on the dais, near to the Presidents of the United States and Israel, was the head of Croatia, Franjo Tudjman, historian, politician and World War II partisan who was twice convicted later by the Communists for his strong nationalist views. In one of his three published books, he wrote that the Jews, by their international egalitarianism, "directly help and even incite anti-Jewish sentiment". Deeply sensitive to the accusation that his new state continued to nurture anti-Semitism, Tudjman nonetheless described the State of Israel as "Judeo-Nazi" for its treatment of the Palestinians and openly thanked the graces that his wife was "neither a Jew nor a Serb".

This was the same Tudjman who, during early 1991 rallies in Zagreb to gather public momentum for a total split from Yugoslavia, defended the 1941 Nazi puppet state of Croatia as "an expression of the historical aspirations of the Croatian people for an independent state of their own and recognition of international factors — the government of Hitler's Germany in this case".

Even Time Magazine, hardly a mouthpiece for the Belgrade government, could not stifle its amazement over the cynicism of having Tudjman at a ceremony for the victims of Nazi racism. "Standing brazenly among the honored guests," writer Bruce W. Nelan wrote, "personifying the very tragedy Wiesel condemned, was Croatian President Franjo Tudjman. His Croat brethren had just begun a vicious onslaught of 'ethnic cleansing' in western Bosnia, burning villages and villagers in one of the cruelest campaigns of the war." Nelan then went on to quote a British peacekeeper who stated that a whole valley of people had been massacred and that the scene was "horrendous".

· For Tudjman the invitation to the ceremony was no small victory. For the Jews of the world and for the slandered Serbs it was a disgrace. One of the early official acts of the invitee in 1991 was to order the physical erasure of Jasenovac and the burning of all records and artifacts in order to turn the concentration camp area into "a rare bird sanctuary". There was nothing repentant about this man. If anything there was only arrogance.

Tudjman, the historian turned politician, invitee to the most solemn of all ceremonies recalling the Holocaust, wrote on page 149 of Wastelands — Historical Truth "...the fact (was) that German imperialism for geopolitical reasons was oriented primarily to the attainment of domination over Europe. For this reason the establishment of Hitler's new European order could be justified by the need both to remove the Jews (undesirable more or less in all European countries) and to correct the Franco/British sin of the Versailles Treaty."

The Croatian scholar had some other interesting information to impart such as on page 156 of the same book "...the estimated loss of up to six million dead is founded too much on both emotional and biased testimonies and exaggerated data in the postwar reckoning and squaring of accounts with the defeated perpetrators of war crimes... (this) is evidenced, for example, in the highly multiplied data on Jasenovac with the assertion that of the allegedly 770,000 killed there, 20,000 Jews were killed even though it is stated that the Jews from Croatia, under German orders, were deported to the east while some found sanctuary in the Italian zone."

Tudjman continued. "In the mid-eighties, world Jewry still has the need to recall its 'Holocaust' even by trying to prevent the selection of the former UN Secretary-General Kurt Waldheim as president of Austria. And for this there was certainly no reasonable excuse because he... was neither a war criminal nor could he make any decisions on the executions of such orders. And at the sametime one can be deaf and blind to everything that is happening in front of one's face on orders of the Israeli generals and government which demonstrate the inviolable domination of historical unreasonableness and narrowness in which Jewry is certainly no exception.

"...After everything they suffered in history, particularly the hardships in World War II, the Jewish people soon afterward became so brutal and conducted a genocidal policy toward the Palestinians that they can rightly be defined as Judeo-Nazi."

Tudjman launched some of his harshest criticism of Jews and Israel by finding a couple of self-hating Jewish professors who provided him with invaluable quotes. The more anti-Israel the professor, the more revered he was as both scholar and academician by the Croatian president.

Seated on the same stage as the president of the State of Israel, Tudjman blithely accused Israel in his book of committing "spiritual genocide" and then he asked the pithy question: "What does this small historical step from Nazi-Fascism to Judeo-Fascism indicate?"

Summing up his general feelings, Tudjman stated: "The Jews provoke envy and hatred, but actually they are the unhappiest nation in the world, always victims of their own and others' ambitions, and whoever tries to show that they are· themselves their own source of tragedy is ranked among the anti-Semites and the object of hatred of the Jews."

Tudjman became president of the sovereign state of Croatia on May 30, 1990, exactly a decade after the death of Tito. His party had taken control of the Sabor or parliament and he had a clear mandate to declare an independent state, but there was still some flickering hope that an acceptable new confederation could be hammered out that would preserve at least some of the rudiments of old Yugoslavia.

The Croatian ministers and officials I interviewed at the time were, however, fairly adamant that some drastic new arrangements had to be made with Belgrade although no one was yet talking too loudly about divorce. Both the Croatian and Slovenian positions were so similar that they obviously were forged either together or at least thought out together.

Both republics felt that Belgrade was denying them their fair share of the economic pie and inadvertently causing high unemployment although they had to admit that, overall, the Yugoslav economy was flourishing and that inflation had been beaten into the ground. Most intermediate positions in both the police and armed forces were occupied by Serbs — virtually a tradition in Yugoslavia by then — and this rankled. Both Slovenes and Croats wanted their own people in the key army and constabulary positions in their own lands. They also demanded access to caches of weapons and ammunition located in their territories. Croats and Slovenes complained that Belgrade was still too steeped in communism and incapable of making the drastic transition to a market economy which was a prerequisite of dealing with and becoming a part of western Europe. The Serbs, they told me, were a little "too oriental" for their tastes, a euphemism I imagined for Levantine.

Slovenia knew it had little to fear from independence since it was exposed to no serious military threat and was dealing anyway with a fairly homogenous situation at home. Besides, Slovenia by then had a firm promise from Germany's

Chancellor Helmut Kohl and Foreign Minister Hans Dietrich Genscher of immediate recognition, intercession with the European Community on its behalf, loans, commercial transactions and United Nations intervention if required, which was another way of saying if Serbia made trouble.

Matters were a trifle more complicated in Croatia because of a vocal Serb minority. The flash points were Krajina, western Srem, Banija and Slavonija where Serbs had been living for more than five hundred years. These people, 700,000 strong, were not intent on surrendering rights to a new political entity which they regarded as hostile anyway. I recall one angry Serb from Krajina, part of an undisciplined gang that was systematically interrupting communications throughout the southern portions of Croatia. "I promise you one thing," he said bitterly. "I will not become a second-class citizen in my own land. I would rather die first, but before I die I'll take a few Croats along with me."

While troubles were brewing in the south of Croatia, Tudjman was engaged in a characteristic maneuver. Presiding over the first convention of the Croatian Democratic Union (HDZ), which had swept him into office, he invited more than one hundred Ustashe war criminals back to Zagreb, promising them not only a safe haven, but a place in the new Croatian sun. They returned from Australia, Argentina, Paraguay and were hailed as "state heroes".

On the political front solid German assurances to Slovenia and the unequivocal same support promised to Croatia produced a heady atmosphere in Zagreb that virtually precluded any further negotiations with Belgrade. It was at this stage that German skinhead volunteers began arriving in the Croatian capital to provide moral and perhaps brute support. Officials in Belgrade were stunned. Even the worst-case scenario, people thought at the time, would leave some elements of the seventy-two-year-old federation intact. There were so many eco-political hurdles to consider that a total, abrupt divorce seemed inconceivable, although that was exactly what was happening.

But first, on December 22, 1990, with the blessing and complicity of the German government, Croatia's independence and territorial sovereignty was declared. Tudjman introduced a new constitution which divided the world between Croats and "others". Henceforth, non-Croats would be compelled to sign loyalty oaths not to the state, but to the Croatian government, discriminatory taxation would be introduced and Serbs employed in government functions would be dismissed to make room for Croats. Automatic passports would be issued only to "pure" Croats.

As expected the Serb enclaves in the south reacted violently. Positions were hardening. The Serbs saw a great betrayal, the reversal of a federal agreement that should have been immutable.

The Croats, however, were euphoric. They had reached their conclusions through national referendum. Everything had been done carefully and democratically. All over the world there were new expressions of what had been nascent nationalism and so why not in Croatia which, after all, had a long and persistent yearning for nationhood? Tudjman again spoke to Kohl and Genscher and again was guaranteed support and assistance. Austrian and Italian diplomats promised the same. If there were still a few tenuous strands holding the confederation together, it was almost as if the EC was cutting them with a hack saw.

In early 1991, the mood in Zagreb was changing, becoming much more martial. The Yugoslav Armed Forces (JNA) were still in place, negotiations were being carried out when the new Minister of Internal Affairs, a former general in the Yugoslav army, Martin Spegelj, said on January 21, 1991: "We are in a war with the army. Should anything happen, kill them all in the streets, in their homes, throw hand grenades, fire pistols in their bellies...."

Since it was becoming apparent everywhere, except paradoxically in Belgrade, that Yugoslavia was about to die, the Croatian government began scurrying for the arms to defend itself. Because the JNA had been strongly influenced by Serbs, it was clear that most of the heavy weaponry, armored vehicles and aircraft would be "retrieved" by Belgrade. However, new militias and constabulary were already in place and equipment was purchased from the former state of East Germany. Croatia, it would have appeared, was a highly propitious event for Bonn which had just inherited huge stores of East European arms which were non-compatible with its own NATO-equipped forces. There was everything from depots full of automatic assault weapons to roughly 2,000 serviceable tanks. These weapons were placed at the beck and call of Croatia while, at the sametime, Zagreb sent emissaries throughout eastern Europe to negotiate additional arms purchases.

At the sametime, there was a spate of "patriots" returning to the Balkans. Serbs, expatriated to the United States and Canada for years, decided to "revisit" the homeland just in case their services would be required. Croats reacted the same way. Droves entered the country as tensions and a final split appeared more and more inevitable.

Brutal fighting erupted in Croatia in mid-1991, some of the first victims being Orthodox churches which were systematically burned to the ground. The Krajina Serbs were meanwhile accumulating arms — and using them as Croatian militias tried pacifying them. After gleaning Croatia's intention to hold a referendum on secession from Yugoslavia, Serbs in Krajina conducted their own plebiscite on May 14, eleven days before the formal secessions of both Slovenia and Croatia from the Yugoslav federation. The Serbs voted overwhelmingly to secede from Croatia should it break with Yugoslavia. This was termed "illegal and provocative" by Zagreb which conducted its own secessionary referendum immediately afterward.

War, meanwhile, spread to Vukovar where, according to "Defense and Foreign Affairs Strategic Policy" the Ustashe

beat local Serb forces into submission. Fighting also spread to
nearby Borovo-Selo between June 1 and November 23.

"At the Borovo footware factory at the exit from Vukovar,
the Croats established a new concentration camp rounding up
and interning local Serbian civilians. At this site the Croats
interned some 5,000 Serbs, and there, at the Rowing Club of
Vukovar, the almost ritualistic killing of Serbs began again.
The basement of the Borovo-Komoro concentration camp
also housed the headquarters of Marko Filkovia commanding
officer of the ZNG, the official Croatian national guard corps.
More than 1,000 Serbs died in these two facilities, and on the
streets and in their homes, before the JNA fought its way into
Vukovar on November 23, 1991."

Well-rehearsed in public relations techniques, Croatia deftly
used the Vukovar incident as an image manipulator — the first
of many successful excursions into the wondrous world of
Madison Avenue. Wounded Serbs were shown being treated
in Croatian hospitals. Captives expressed gratitude for the
humanity shown to them. According to the British publication, cited earlier, however, and later confirmed by Yugoslav authorities, all the prisoners were subsequently killed.

The Serbs were not blameless either. Croats who stumbled
into the hands of truculent, vengeance-seeking Serb irregulars
were butchered mercilessly.

The Serbs demonstrated that Catholic churches burned with
the same speed and alacrity as Orthodox chapels. Both sides
were accused of "rape", and Zagreb launched a verbal
offensive which indicated, incorrectly as it turned out, that
most of the arms consigned to the Yugoslav army were either
outrightly shipped to Serbia or clandestinely distributed to the
newly formed contingents of Serbs operating in Croatia.

By this time Germany was openly and unequivocally
proclaiming its support of Croatia, insisting upon immediate
EC recognition and entrance into the UN. Later, and in
conformity with Bonn's special sentiments for Croatia, and as
part of an agreement hammered out earlier with Tudjman,

Genscher demanded and got EC agreement of full diplomatic rupture with Yugoslavia.

On July 18, 1991, Tudjman had new secret talks with top German officials in Bonn in which further German support was guaranteed. Tudjman later told Croatian television that his conversation with Helmut Kohl lasted eighty minutes. He then added that he also spent more than an hour with Genscher. "The talks were fruitful and we were all satisfied," he beamed.

It was about that time that a new song emerged out of Zagreb. It was called "Goodbye Yugoslavia, You Paper Tiger". A sample of its lyrics was:

"Your time has run out.
You weren't at home for us.
Now we're not at home for you.
You bastard of war.
Never knock at our door again."

Pulling along both Austria and Italy, also sharing a warm regard for Croatia dating back to 1941 and the victorious march of the Axis into the Balkans, German foreign policy was deftly directed at the future isolation of Belgrade. This propensity proved easy to export to the farside of the Atlantic as well. There was heavy pro-Croat and pro-Slovene public relations activity in the United States which had already charmed key members of the Bush Administration. And, not to be outdone by his Republican rivals, Democratic candidate Bill Clinton began making the kind of political noises that pleased the authorities in Zagreb and Ljubljana.

Although the Yugoslav army was officially mandated by Belgrade merely to assemble its equipment and cross over into the new borders of Yugoslavia, there were frequent incidents of clashes with Croatian forces which were growing stronger and more aggressive. Belgrade gave the impression that the army only responded to attacks, a statement somewhat less than true. By then atrocity stories of Croatian abuses to prisoners, Serb farmers and Orthodox priests were spreading. So Yugoslav regulars, by then preponderantly Serbs and Montenegrins, sought out the opportunities for armed confrontations.

By late 1992, Croatia had evolved into a formidable military entity which counted a force of over 40,000 men distributed in ten to twelve brigades and backed by sixty heavy tanks and eighty artillery pieces which could be dispatched to the "Bosnia front" alone, an indication of how swiftly the Croatian forces had grown. There was an air force and a navy and arms were developed and produced. There were plenty of advisors and volunteers who, despite low-profile instructions, were all too evident.

In tandem with the fighting which included some fierce tank battles and artillery exchanges, the Tudjman government implemented strong press restrictions which resulted in the mass firing of Serbs from media, particularly in Dalmatia.

Whatever constraints Tudjman could shackle his own press with, however, some international journalists and scholars like Nora Beloff, a former chief political correspondent of the Observer and the author of some very trenchant writing about Yugoslavia and the reasons for its dismemberment, continued analyzing the recurring theme of Germany's role in the disintegration of the federal union.

"In the dismemberment of Yugoslavia," she penned, "Germany has played a bigger role than any other outside country. The German government, having turned its back on the past almost to the point of forgetting it, has intervened unilaterally in order to achieve what it hoped would be freedom, democracy and peace. The sequel, indeed to some extent the consequence, has been anarchy, vicious inter-ethnic bitterness and bestial violence...

"Defying British, French and American views, Germany eagerly promoted the collapse of an internationally recognized state, without any apparent concept of the future of the diverse communities scattered like a leopard-skin on Yugoslavia's ethnic map. For two years German policy has been directed toward prompt, unconditional recognition of the independent states of Croatia and Slovenia. Other western powers, anxious not to strain relations with a vital power in the European Community and NATO, and with no clear idea of what to do, meekly followed suit."

Besides his attendance at the ceremonies of the Holocaust Museum, Tudjman experienced some other real successes in 1993 such as a sharp, surprise attack against Serbian forces in Krajina on January 25 in which he scored some notable military gains until stopped, the offensive action against his former Moslem collaborators in Bosnia which added to Croatia's foothold in the region, worldwide diplomatic recognition of the checkered Phoenix risen out of some of the ashes of former Yugoslavia.

He had not done badly in the political realm as well, managing successfully to steer his country away from the ultra-conservative, neo-Fascist elements that would turn Croatia into a reflection of the villainous state it had once been and closer to his own variety of super nationalism. As far as the economy was concerned, however, Tudjman proved to be a slow starter.

One of his major 1990 campaign promises was the drastic reform of the Croatian economy, which, he claimed, had been hobbled in the past by Belgrade. This, he had explained, was the key to the good life, to the western life, to a comfortable future within Europe. In 1993, more than 90% of Croatia's economy was still in state hands and a heavy, tangled bureaucracy continued to stifle the country. Tudjman, however, was secure, virtually untouchable politically as long as "patriotic" wars waged in the southern part of the country and deep in the aeries of Bosnia where the ancient Croat appetite for more "Lebensraum" continued unabated.

# CHAPTER VI
# MEDIA, MACEDONIA AND PANIC

A ssured by both Belgrade and the Yugoslav ambassador for Greece that the estimated time for departure was approaching, I continued scouring and scavenging for material about the old and new Yugoslavia.

Greece, where I was living, was no mere bystander in the drama that was taking place in the north. In May, 1993, Prime Minister Constantine Mitsotakis had taken the bold step of inviting all the belligerents to Athens in the hope that his last-ditch diplomatic effort would forestall some of the smart bombs the Americans were threatening to toss all over the Serbs, both in Bosnia and Yugoslavia proper. He later went to Pale where he addressed the Bosnian Serb assembly, pleading for compromise and patience — two ingredients in very short supply at the moment.

This was not Mitsotakis' first brush with the consequences of the implosion of a neighboring and friendly country. One of the main diplomatic problems of his government since the dissolution up north began was the issue of "Skopje", which was Greek for the little state, spun off from old Yugoslavia and midwifed, once again, by the venerable Tito, which was known to the rest of the world as "Macedonia". And then there was the additional problem of Kosovo, incendiary at the best and close enough to the borders to ignite.

Although the imbroglio had devolved around the name "Macedonia", the northernmost province of Greece, the issue was really much deeper than mere nomenclature. It was a fact of geography that the area comprising the territory presided over by Phillipus first and then his son Alexander was divided unequally between three nations. Over 60% of the original kingdom was in Greece with the rest divided between the former Yugoslav Republic of Macedonia and Bulgaria. It was also a fact, a historical one this time, that both father and son were Greeks, that the language they spoke was Greek, that the gods they worshipped were Greek and that they had performed their military reconnoitering a full millenium before the South Slavs slipped into the region.

A nation, however, needed a bit more than a defined boundary and some citizens to really establish itself. It required some common, identifiable history which, in the case of Yugoslavian Macedonia was lamentably missing. The people were diverse — ethnic Bulgarians, Albanians, Serbs and Greeks.

The Macedonian language they spoke was a not very serious linguistic invention, Bulgarian laced with Serbo-Croatian. It was actually made a state language in old Yugoslavia because to do otherwise would have created a furor among citizens who demanded parity with the rest of the country's relatively independent republics. It should be recalled that "Macedonia" was thought out first by the Comintern which was seeking ways, back in the thirties, of destabilizing the region so that the Soviet Union might one day achieve access to the Aegean. It was picked up next by Tito who knew a good thing when he saw one. Creating the "Republic of Macedonia" opened up a whole new series of political options — placating the citizens of the region with a little undeserved history, establishing a future claim to the whole territory of Macedonia if and when the political climate would be right, exerting a little wholesome pressure on the country to the south.

To the chagrin of Greece, and the disappointment of Belgrade, the former Yugoslav republic declared its independence on January 24, 1991. Kiro Gligorov was elected the first President of the country and, despite assurances to Athens to the contrary, a nervous verbal battle ensued over just who the "real" Macedonians were. The banner of Alexander was adopted as a national symbol. Maps, produced in Skopje, appeared showing Salonika as an integral part of the new country. School books were produced which falsified history so utterly that it was hard to discuss matters on a rational level.

The problem, however, was not merely the fabrication of history — something virtually turned into an art form by Stalin — but the inherent problems of a slice of real estate that probably was never meant to be a country.

Macedonia comprised 25,713 square kilometers of landscape which was mostly poor. Never very developed, the economy collapsed when Skopje sundered itself from the rest of Yugoslavia. There was absolutely no real economic infrastructure, virtually no visible mineral deposits, the most primitive forms of farming.

Demographic statistics were utterly misleading except the bottom line number of two million. Statistics compiled in Skopje indicated that 64% of the population was "Macedonian", 20% Albanian, 8% Turk, 2% Gypsy, 2% Serbs and 4% miscellaneous. Everyone at the time was talking about ethnic cleansing, but this was demographic doubletalk. The Macedonian number actually was just another way of saying that the majority of those calling themselves "Macedonians" were Serbs and Bulgarians simply willing to be rostered as constituents of the new state. The same ethnic problems endemic to Bosnia and Herzegovina were equally apparent in Macedonia. Even the capital city of Skopje, risen from the ruins of a disastrous 1963 earthquake, was already 40% populated by Albanians and there were enough minarets and Byzantine coffee shops in the otherwise newly architectured city to indicate future directions.

And so, despite fervent proclamations and the September 17 Macedonian assembly adoptation of a declaration on strict respect for existing frontiers and the rejection of future territorial claims, Greece was uneasy.

Nor was the situation made any lighter by the strange noises emanating out of the White House about sinister Serbian plans to invade Macedonia along with Kosovo. It was almost as if somebody was trying to provoke a war.

As a matter of fact, Gligorov and Milosevic were old friends and had shared a lot of political and professional history together.

With the United Nations, the United States and the European Community more acrimoniously united against Yugoslavia than ever, the only remaining friend Belgrade really had was Greece. Virginia Tsouderou, Greece's under-secretary for foreign affairs, saw nothing strange in the almost unique position Greece had adopted and despite strong pressures from both the EC and the United States.

"There are many common points between us," she said. "We are both Christian Orthodox. We were both invaded and occupied by the Ottomans and fought back relentlessly and at great expense. We both resisted the Germans during the Second World War. There is a commonality to our people which cannot be changed or suppressed. Also some of the forces which are trying to destabilize Serbia and the rest of the Balkans are equally trying to damage Greece."

Further elaboration? I asked.

None, she smiled.

What really set my teeth on edge while waiting to leave for Yugoslavia was the invidious comparisons the press was making between Nazi Germany and desiccated Yugoslavia. Further boggling the already over-boggled mind was the continuing allusions of Clinton, key members of his administration, NATO luminaries and EC bureaucrats that Serbia would be castigated with steel and fire if it dared "invade" Kosovo.

I wanted to ask some of my esteemed colleagues who carouselled regularly through CNN talk shows how do you "invade" your own country? I wanted to know why atrocities against Serbs were worth less air time than tortured Moslems. Or why half-starved Bosnian Moslems were featured on Time Magazine's cover and Serbia was accused of actuating a death wish in the editorial pages, but nobody really cared very much about children in Belgrade who were perishing for lack of drugs that were not getting through because of an international conspiracy masquerading under the sobriquet of "blockade".

The Fourth Estate, ever sensitive to the underdog and the under-privileged, was the conscience of the world in Bosnia and Herzegovina as Serb forces rolled from victory to victory, leaving behind them the inevitable results of war — dead bodies, charred buildings, slain animals. Yet where were the cameras in 1991 when the 700,000 Serbs in Croatia were threatened with very painful and very permanent extinction? They were on tea break.

The anchormen and women of the world were yet to learn that there was nothing very simple about the Balkans. There were no white knights, pristine truisms, perfect platitudes. If there was a bogeyman, his name was history. If there was recurrent human tragedy, it was because of the capriciousness of geography and the disorderly brains of two-legged animals.

There was no escaping the headlines as little-known and unknown congressmen pontificated to the public and press about a new holocaust foisted on the world by Yugoslavia. There were photos of women and children scavenging for splinters of wood in the destroyed houses throughout Bosnia. Since Saddam Hussein had paled somewhat as an international thug and menace, mighty public relations efforts were launched from New York and Washington to replace the partially defanged Iraqi with Slobodan Milosevic, President of Serbia, as the new criminal of the year. Unsmiling, unrepentant, unremorseful and most certainly unbowed, Milosevic was characterized as a villain by communications media fed a lot of canned pap and oiled by effective public relations' dollars.

There were newsreels and photos of "new Serbian atrocities", mostly against the hapless and helpless Moslem citizens of Sarajevo, in nearly every television network and news magazine. There were ugly stories of fratricide running from the Bosnian capital of Sarajevo to Mostar in Herzegovina, although the latter was "being attended to" by the Croats.

Although Serbia was the undisputed villain of the tragedy and Milosevic the putative architect of the civil war in Bosnia, I was not overly impressed by a diet of daily diatribes. Once, in 1982, I found myself in an uncomfortable position in Lebanon which helped color future judgment.

I was asked to accompany a group of fourteen journalists, all from the West, to the Casbash Quarter of Tyre where a rather strange phenomenon had occurred during an earlier Israeli air raid. A 200-kilo bomb had dropped through the roof and two stories of a home, landed on the blue couch of a living room at ground level, but miraculously had not exploded. The ordnance was simply just sitting there, like a guest who had serendipitously arrived from another planet.

It was a good story and the journalists naturally interviewed the owner of the building, a middle-aged Maronite Lebanese. "I had to evacuate the family," he said. "I couldn't have my wife and children sitting around in a building with a bomb in it. But I want to tell you something. If I had three buildings and if all three were destroyed the same way, I would surrender them all happily. This is the first freedom I have known in seven years. This is the first time I don't fear for my wife and children."

The early part of the interview was scrupulously recorded. During the second statement, cameras were turned off, pens returned to pockets. Was the story that appeared about the ruined building and the homeless family true? I guess so. The results, however, did not make me feel very proud of my profession. Actually, I felt shame. And so I was not willing to prejudge all of Serbia, its President, what remained of Yugoslavia, because of bad press.

Whatever my own reservations might have been, however, the world was not exactly unprejudiced and undecided about who the "heavies" were in the war that tore Yugoslavia apart.

The United Nations had not only excoriated Serbia and Montenegro, but a full-scale blockade was in place, both in the Adriatic and along the Danube River. The new Yugoslavia was booted out of the UN and treated as a pariah by nearly every international body.

By then it was also apparent that American foreign policy was trying to change Yugoslavia both from within and from without. Enter Milan Panic. Serb par excellence. Almost too good to be true. Maybe a Slavic messiah. He was handsome. He was sincere. His middle name might have been Success. And he was available.

Panic had landed in Belgrade like a meteorite hurled out of Washington DC. A naturalized American citizen who had entered the United States as a young man with little more than good looks, high hopes and an inherent belief in free enterprise and hard work, he epitomized the Yankee dream. In other words, he was a successful entrepreneur and consequently a very rich man.

Whether the deal was cut in Washington or Belgrade, and at a time when Yugoslavia was becoming a very sullied expression in the American language, Panic suddenly emerged in Yugoslavia with the blessings of Milosevic as Prime Minister of that highly threatened, embargoed, boycotted republic.

Yet it was evident from the beginning that his real mandate had nothing to do with expressing and implementing the political policies of the government he was sworn to uphold and represent. Panic went his own way which included some very ascerbic remarks about Serbian President Slobodan Milosevic, pronounced criticism of Yugoslavia's approach to the Bosnian conflict, and a call for compromise and rapprochement.

Panic was an immediate success with parts of the Yugoslavian population such as the young men and women who were unemployed because of American and European sanctions and those who were simply looking for an alternate to the old Communist leadership which had been distilled into a more potable socialism, but for them, still had a repressive odor. Certainly, not everyone approved of Milosevic and his government and there were enough people tired of a war that seemed to be going nowhere.

America had a lot of clout. Russia, with its own gargantuan problems threatening its very survival, was in no position to help not even by proffering moral support. The EC had made its will known a long time earlier, with Germany steering and most of the others around for the ride. All of this and more was bound to contribute to the appeal of a man whose simple message was peace will bring prosperity. It was obvious that Panic wore the stamp of American approval and for those who demanded further proof he was accompanied to Belgrade by an entourage of American advisors and counselors.

One interesting feature of Panic's entrance into Balkan politics was the strange, new liberalism suddenly shown by the American State Department. American law was very clear about U.S. citizens running for any form of foreign electoral office or serving in anyone else's government or army or civil service. In the past Americans were stripped of their citizenship for even voting in a foreign election – a very menial sin when compared with being prime minister of another country.

Before long it became apparent that the effervescent Serbo/American was not satisfied with the position of prime minister, but was casting his eyes at Milosevic's office where it appeared the real power lay. And so Panic prepared to challenge the establishment in the national elections of December 20, 1992. With the moral support of the world behind him, the only undetermined facet of the contest was the position of the Yugoslavian people.

Panic cried unfair from the very beginning and he had at least one telling point. Yugoslavia's main television network was government-controlled which was another way of saying that Milosevic owned a lot of the tube. On the other hand, a good part of the Serbian press was in favor of Panic and there seemed to be plenty of money around to organize political events.

There were no obfuscating pre-election messages. A victory for Panic meant moderation, accommodation, a quick end to the blood-letting in Bosnia, dialogue with the Croats, removal of the embargo, reacceptance into the world of nations. A Milosevic win, however, promised further tightening of the naval blockade, more political and diplomatic isolation, the sure destruction of Serbian aircraft caught flying over Bosnia, Tomahawk missile and smart bomb attacks against Serbian air force installations, the possible elimination of important infrastructural facilities such as hydroelectric plants, power stations, railroad depots and the bombing of Belgrade itself.

Primarily, it was the United States ratchetting up both the pressure and the ante. Although many of America's chief military advisors, including the commander of the Joint Chiefs of Staff, were counseling for moderation and diplomatic alternatives, both the retiring Bush and the president-elect Clinton were opting, at least publicly, for military options.

This blind disgust with the Serbs, on both sides of the Bosnia and Herzegovina border, was a direct result of bad reporting, bad understanding and bad will. Thus America made it very clear to the Serbian people, during the pre-Christmas election, that patience was running out and the alternatives were nil.

There were international observers monitoring the election from the beginning and the decision of the people was clear. Milosevic walked away with 56% of the vote. Right wing nationalists grabbed another 10% and Panic ended up with a third of the electorate. Actually, it was not a bad showing for the Serbo/American, but neither Washington nor Panic could disguise their bitter disappointment.

Whether Milosevic won an outstanding victory or not

might be debatable because there were some people, myself included, who were convinced that he had a secret ally assisting him — the United States of America. By blatantly interfering with someone else's national election, by showing so much prejudice in favor' of one candidate against the others, and by threatening the voters, Washington succeeded in appealing to the national sentiments and patriotism of every Serb man and woman. If America really wanted to play the role of honest broker in the region, it had over-played its hand.

CHAPTER VII
ALICE IN BOSNIALAND

The scenario for May, 1993, most certainly was concocted by either Lewis Carroll or Franz Kafka or by some Anglo-Czech consortium specializing in the non-sequitur.

There was a Mad Hatter quality to the events transpiring in and around Yugoslavia which began with the Athens meeting orchestrated by Mitsotakis and featuring the by-then famous libretto written by Great Britain's Lord David Owen and America's Cyrus Vance. The Vance-Owen plan, billed as the last chance to avoid a calamitous Balkan war and the certain punishment of Serbs and Serbia for both truculence and military success, was exhibited with the same sort of awe usually reserved for biblical tractates. Lord Owen pronounced the document sacrosanct – not a syllable would be altered, not a comma changed. It was take-it-or-leave-it time and Slobodan Milosevic had a pretty good idea of what failure to accept the plan could mean to Yugoslavia – at the best, severe tightening of international restrictions against his country, more likely some form of military intervention spearheaded against Serbia by the United States. And so it was that Milosevic joined Mitsotakis in adding further pressure on Bosnian Serbs to accept the controversial peace program.

Stripped of a lot of diplomatic gibberish what the plan really said was that there would never be a free state of Bosnian Serbs and there would be no contiguous, defendable borders with either Yugoslavia or Krajina. Holding by then 70% of the former Yugoslavian republic's territory, the Serbs would withdraw to 41% as a punishment for aggressions. Part of a new, multi-ethnic society dominated by Moslems, the Bosnian Serbs would be relegated to tribal areas surrounded by people who, by then, were openly committed to their erasure. Pale, worried, threatened and harassed, Bosnian Serb leader Radovan Karadzic signed the agreement on May 2, warning the world, however, that his signature meant nothing without the endorsement of the people he represented.

The compliance of Karadzic merely produced a new fusillade of bellicose threats from leading members of Congress and the White House who reacted to Serb acquiescence as a new imperilment to world peace. Both Milosevic and Karadzic were reviled and Serbia was again threatened if it made moves against either Macedonia or Kosovo. Acting to defuse an already incendiary situation Milosevic ordered a total boycott of Bosnia's Serbs which again was greeted by congressional clamor for immediate, military measures against Serbia.

On May 10, with the Belgrade boycott in place against his people and the hermetical isolation of Bosnia's Serbs almost complete, Karadzic, himself turned back at the border, warned: "We are Christians. We are fighting to preserve our Christian way of life. Now we have nothing — nothing but God."

Karadzic's analysis was a bit self-serving. Besides "God" and the nearly universal sentiment that Yugoslavia would never totally cut off its brethren in Bosnia, there were an estimated 35,000 battle-hardened troops backed by 55,000 reservists, 300 tanks, 50 warplanes, and a wide assortment of armored personnel carriers still tipping the war in favor of Bosnia's Serbs. Nearly all this equipment had been "inherited" from departing Yugoslav troops after Bosnia opted for independence, a situation similar to that in Croatia. Karadzic's main worry though was not equipment, but fuel. If Belgrade really turned off the spigot, the air force wouldn't fly and the heavy artillery wouldn't move.

Since the actual plebiscite to determine whether Bosnia's Serbs were willing to accept Vance-Owen as an alternative to Serbian hegemony and perhaps even a Greater Serbia was more than a week away, the cry for military intervention — bulldozed by America, but supported also by Italy and Turkey — was made even more inexplicable. American carrier aircraft in the Aegean were on high alert and there were persistent rumors about American commando units parachuted into Bosnia in order to locate and pinpoint future targets.

Commenting on the situation, the Athens daily Estia had the following editorial statement to make: "Before the ink of the signatures of the Athens conference had dried, there was a decision to take military action against the Serbs, proving beyond any doubt the truth that certain leaders are not interested so much in peace, but in the punishment by war on the Serbs... It seems that peace cannot be achieved unless it comes out of American and Turkish guns."

Even more bizarre in light of the fierce world criticism against Serbia, Karadzic's promise to prohibit all forms of aggressive military action during that interregnum was holding absolutely. There were no Serb guns being fired, no cannons directed at Sarajevo, no snipers plucking triggers in eastern Bosnia. Elsewhere, however, in that battered and brutalized landscape, the situation was not the same.

Croatian forces were mauling their former allies in the ancient citadel of Mostar and throughout central and southern Bosnia. In Mostar, the Moslem radio warned: "The few buildings left whole are burning. The destruction of the town continues." In Ostrozac, in central Bosnia, Croatian artillery shelling was described by victims as of "hurricane proportions". The Croats were providing no respite, their appetite for Bosnia even more insatiable than that of their Serbian cousins.

On May 19, the Mad Hatter presided again over world affairs. The plebiscite results of the Bosnian Serbs had never been in doubt and, when announced from Mount Jahorina, 96% of Bosnia's eligible Serb voters — 1.2 million — had a very explicit message for the rest of the world. They weren't going anywhere. They would not imperil their own existences. They would not ratify national suicide even at the cost of jeopardizing Lord Owen's possible candidacy for a Nobel Peace Prize. They were not guilty of dismembering Yugoslavia and thus causing Europe's most horrific anguish since the end of the Second World War, so why take the heat? Isolated and threatened by everyone, however, could they hold out and for how long? "Why not?" replied Karadzic. "We grow our own food. We are self-sufficient in most important areas. We have stockpiled enough military equipment, spare parts and ammunition to keep us going for quite awhile. Since there are no other alternatives, I guess we will just have to manage."

Haris Silajdzic, Moslem Bosnia's erudite Foreign Minister, took the occasion to express his government's sentiments. "We want the UN out of Bosnia," he said. "They are not doing us any good and they hinder us from defending ourselves." He also wanted an end to the arms embargo which, he claimed, was affecting his nation deleteriously, although the Croats were still selling arms to the Moslems and killing them at the sametime. Lashing out bitterly at world indifference, Silajdzic claimed, perhaps hyperbolically, "that over 14,000 youngsters under the age of fourteen had already been killed, that 200,000 victims had perished and that two million people had been displaced and were wandering the world as refugees".

So now the Yugoslav theatrics were even further enhanced. America still wanted to bomb Serbia which had declared a blockade against its own people. Croatia was murdering Moslems who were supposed to be protected by the United Nations which, in turn, was not wanted by the people it was supposed to defend. Zagreb was exporting death and weaponry at the sametime. And, in a reply to the electoral rebuff of Bosnian Serb voters, U.S. Secretary of State Warren Christopher, addressing the Foreign Affairs Committee, finally induced genuine pandemonium by stating that "there are various ways in which we can safeguard the continued independence of the former Yugoslav republic of Macedonia, and they are presently under careful evaluation". Of course, there were no threats whatsoever against Macedonia at that moment in time. The Skopje government had not been asking for safeguards since no one was threatening. And yet, continued Christopher, "we shall try to ensure that Serbia is fully aware of the grave consequences to the United States of any action toward Macedonia". But since there were no such indications of Serbian intentions, the Secretary of State continued, "we are also concerned about Kosovo".

Not to be outdone by the other participants in the drama, Albania's Prime Minister Aleksandr Meksi, presiding over the poorest and most neglected country in all of Europe, warned that "Serbia and Albania could go to war over Kosovo".

Accusing Belgrade of "ethnic cleansing", Meksi said, "the Albanians of Kosovo have rights and we are obliged, it is our duty, to defend them". Apparently, Christopher had won over at least one more convert. While England and France were cautious and Germany thoroughly guilt-ridden, Italy and Turkey were willing to bomb the hell out of Serbia, now joined by Albania which might not be able to contribute airpower, but at least could shift around some ground troops who might otherwise be fleeing illegally across the border into Greece, already the unhappy recipient of more than 150,000 illegal and destitute Albanian refugees.

Greece, it appeared, was not only concerned about an influx of illegal Albanian immigrants who were grabbing menial jobs at substandard wages, thereby increasing an already serious unemployment problem, and causing, at the sametime, a huge surge of violent crime, but also with what was happening in neighboring Yugoslavia.

In the same month of May, on European Community Day, Greece's President Constantine Karamanlis issued a dour warning to the world about "....the crisis of Yugoslavia, whose dissolution we Europeans have encouraged, but now face with apprehension and ineffectual proposals, and possibly dangerous interventions. Interventions that could aggravate instead of tame the chaos which now prevails in this tormented country. A chaos which, if not confronted with prudence, will surely develop into a permanent area of turmoil in our region."

The caution and pain expressed by the Greek President was stated more trenchantly later in the month by Defense Minister Yiannis Varvitsiotis who told NATO colleagues in Brussels that his country would not commit its navy to a tougher Adriatic blockade of Serbia and Montenegro. "Our position is clear... Greece will not take part, and does not agree with these new rules." He then added that "Athens opposes military intervention (in Bosnia) in any form. Greece will not take part in any military operation and is opposed to the participation of any Balkan nation."

Varvitsiotis, obviously, was referring to Turkey which was becoming increasingly more bellicose and belligerent. Ankara wanted more use of Turkish warplanes to "police" the area. It was seeking a greater role in the northern Balkans as the natural protector of a besieged Moslem community. It was an early advocate of more aggressive military intervention on the part of NATO and in consort with the United States.

And yet, as extraordinary as all this may seem, these calls for further punishment of Serbia were occurring after Milosevic had enacted a blockade against his own ethnic brothers and during an interval in which Bosnian Serbs were placed under severe military constraints by their own leadership. And while the world continued to rail against Yugoslavia, threatening the Serbs with an international war crimes tribunal to settle accounts once and for all, fighting raged in Vitez in central Bosnia and Mostar where Croatian forces were implementing a little "ethnic cleansing" of their own against intimidated Moslem civilians.

This blatant acceleration of hostilities at a time when the United Nations was desperately trying to preserve a peace accord between Serbs and Moslems elsewhere in the country, was almost too much for Danish Foreign Minister Niels Helveg Petersen, also rotating head of the European Community, who finally threatened Croatia with sanctions "unless the attacks ceased". Even Croatia's German patron could no longer be silent. German Foreign Minister Klaus Kinkel arrived in Zagreb with a harsh message, holding Croatia "co-responsible".

Franjo Tudjman responded to mounting European criticism by tacitly offering to use his good offices to arrange a new ceasefire while claiming at the sametime that "Croatia can in no way be held responsible for acts that were committed on foreign territory by persons who are not Croatian citizens". This statement was produced in tandem with a unilateral Croat declaration in Bosnia and Herzegovina that a new Croat state had been declared — Herceg-Bosnia — and that its capital was Mostar. Interestingly, for parallel acts of violence, Yugoslavia had been booted out of the United Nations, openly threatened by the United States, blockaded, boycotted and badgered by NATO and the EC. When Milosevic made the same approximate comments about the Bosnian Serbs, he was ridiculed by the world press and threatened with bombings.

This blatant form of hypocrisy and double-standard dealings were beginning to have a deleterious effect on international relations in general. Russia, that ancient protagonist of the Serbs, was more or less neutralized by the Americans who used all their economic clout to keep Moscow in line. But some of the European nations were beginning to chafe from a barrage of criticism emanating from Washington. "One of the most dangerous aspects of this crisis is that the Europeans are drifting apart from the Americans," said Oxford historian and military analyst Mark Almond.

Another British expert, Jonathan Eyal, explained: "The Americans have an image of a Serbian army crossing frontiers and mauling a small country fighting for independence. The reality is a highly complex civil war and the Europeans know better than the Americans that no immediate solution for this exists."

One of America's most outspoken critics of European

unwillingness to launch a major war against Serbia was Joseph R. Biden, the Democrat senator from Connecticut, who advocated aggressive military intervention from the air by the United States, from the ground by Europe. Appearing on talk shows and TV interviews after a brief visit to Bosnia, the American politician accused the Europeans of being guilty of "indifference, timidity, self-delusion and hypocrisy". As a prelude to the "Battle of the Balkans", Biden and many of his congressional associates were engaged in the less sanguine, but more practical battle for the headlines. A noteworthy sidebar of the controversy, incidentally, was that nearly all congressmen who had actively fought in the American armed forces were against direct U.S. military involvement, their arguments supported and buttressed by the country's top military leaders. While French Foreign Minister Alain Juppe dubbed military intervention "the option of despair", President Clinton (himself a non-soldier) was pumping for bombs over Bosnia (and perhaps Belgrade).

The same Belgrade that certain congressmen would cheerfully have ordered bombed while Croats were ingesting ever larger portions of Herzegovina and Moslems were squirreling weapons for a *Jihad* of their own, had offered a sober warning to the rest of the world over a year earlier about the precipitous recognition of a republic that was yet too vague and fragile to be summoned into existence. Both Serbian Serbs and Bosnian Serbs stated at the outset that the only way to negotiate a lasting and stable peace in the former republic was by first reaching an agreement with all three ethnic groups. Although Belgrade warned that civil strife would be the inevitable price of premature statehood, the EC rushed in to grant recognition, closely followed by the United States, before even preliminary negotiations between three suspicious sides began.

Whether the number of people in Bosnia and Herzegovina who had died by then was 200,000, as claimed by Silajdzic, or "merely" 134,400 as estimated by United Nations' officials, the loss in human life and the suffering of the people was already horrendous. There was blame enough to go around, but still no real solutions.

By the end of that strange month, the Vance-Owen plan was finally pronounced DOA — dead on arrival — and, in a face-saving gesture inspired along the banks of the Potomac, the Security Council called for a war crimes tribunal to be established as quickly as possible, the first such court since the end of the Second World War.

Meanwhile, underscoring the continuing differences regarding Yugoslavia in NATO itself, the commander of the force in Europe, General John Shalikashvili, told five hundred delegates attending a Berlin summit meeting "that the discord within the western policy is as deep as the disagreement between Karadzic and Izetbegovic". Nearly all the delegates were against direct military intervention in Yugoslavia, the most prominent exception being Turkey. Great Britain, France, Greece and a somewhat castigated Germany would have nothing to do with raising the military ante — and without their support, it seemed highly unlikely that Yugoslavia would be attacked.

# CHAPTER VIII
# SOMBER BELGRADE

The 500-dinar bill was lying crumpled and torn — held together by two, uneven strips of scotch tape — just beyond the border of what was once Yugoslavia and now called itself Macedonia. Vlada, who had shared the six-hour journey from Athens to the border with me, kicked deprecatingly at the bill. "Their money is like their country," he said bitterly. "It's new and it's already falling apart. It's worthless from the very beginning."

Serbs like Vlada found it difficult to understand why Macedonia had opted for independence rather than a more liberal form of confederation with what was left of Yugoslavia. "They have nothing going for them," he said angrily. "They have no future. Either the Albanians will eat them up or the Turks will turn them into a satellite or they will start messing around with Greece which will start a new Balkan war or they will just drop dead of hunger and inertia. Everybody wants to be independent, but no one knows how much it will cost."

At that exciting moment, I wasn't sure how to calibrate the trip — in the hours it took to reach the first frontier, in the days of waiting for the travel plans to be finalized, in the weeks and months of gathering old notes and new material, in the elapsed time since I had been in Yugoslavia. There was a war raging not all that far away in Sarajevo and Mostar. There was thunder emanating out of Zagreb about an inevitable new front that would clean the Serbs out of Krajina once and for all. There was restiveness in Kosovo which could ignite at any moment. Later, there was also a great red pennant with a sun and halo trimmed in gold, the battle flag of Alexander and Phillipus, the banner of ancient Macedonia, fluttering in the breeze over the frontier control post of Tabanovci between Macedonia and Serbia. According to agreements and promises made to Hellas, it shouldn't have been there, the Greeks regarding the appropriation of their symbol as provocation, ill will and downright theft. The Sun of Vergina was flapping in the breeze nonetheless, unconcerned with the trivial squabbles of neighbors.

"Do you think the war will escalate?" Vlada asked.

"Mostly wars are not planned," I replied. "They happen because things get out of hand."

"You know why I am asking? My wife is about to have a baby in Belgrade. Our first. That's why I'm here now. And everybody is talking about bombing Belgrade. I don't know what they expect to achieve. We are over ten million people. So they kill a couple of hundred thousand. What have they achieved? They really believe that they will just be able to walk in afterward? They don't understand anything about history."

Maybe I was just pleased to be on my way back to Yugoslavia, but I felt a wee bit hopeful that June 6 day, anniversary of D-Day forty-nine years earlier, start of the Six-Day War in 1967, launching date for Israel's ill-conceived attack against the Palestine Liberation Army in Lebanon in 1982.

Just a few days earlier, Mikhail Gorbachev, as guest of honor of French President François Mitterand at the Elysées Palace in Paris, added his voice to the growing number of critics of unilateral UN actions against Yugoslavia. Critical of the West for precipitously recognizing the independence of Slovenia and Croatia instead of insisting that minority problems be regulated as a prerequisite for acceptance, he said the West should have helped Yugoslavia resolve the impasse with its former constituent states "and sat around a table until an agreement over the different republics was reached".

An important dissension, I thought, but not the only one. After a full year of media recriminations against the Serbs only, a few brave voices were speaking out. Germany's Stern editorialized that "Bonn must finally come out in the open and admit that Croatian President Franjo Tudjman is a nationalist with no conscience who stops at nothing to achieve his goals and that his alleged friendship with Germany is shameful." At the sametime, leading Spanish commentators suddenly reached the conclusion that "all warring sides in Bosnia and Herzegovina have in turn been aggressors and butchers".

Meanwhile, the first film to show the Serbian side of the conflict in Bosnia was shown to Israeli audiences. Haim Yavin, the nation's top TV commentator said: "It is difficult to believe that any plan for dividing Bosnia into a host of ethnic enclaves could resolve the situation in the war-ravaged, former Yugoslav republic because the three nations that lived there together until a year ago now see each other as bitter enemies."

"What are you smiling about?" asked Vlada as both our passports were returned to us which meant that we could proceed at last to the nearby Serbian border.

"Two things," I replied. "The first is that people are beginning to look a little more deeply into the civil war and what has really been inflicted on Serbia. But even better, I've just read that a team of Croatian scholars are trying to prove that the Croats are Aryans who originally came from Persia and had nothing to do with the South Slav migration. I've been expecting this for a long time. Proving that the Croats are really Aryans would complete the circle."

Predictably, Tudjman sent a message of support to the scholars who planned to go to Iran, Afghanistan and Uzbekistan in search of concrete evidence about Croat Aryan origins. This scientific research would have greatly pleased Tudjman's predecessor, Ante Pavelic.

Besides the flag fluttering over Tabanovci, there was another symbol of dispute evidenced at the border crossing. There were UN soldiers peering down into the traffic, watching from their armored personnel cars for signs of illegal fuel shipments into the petrol-starved country. The Scandinavian soldiers were like great, two-legged predatory birds poised to pounce. Their regulation binoculars provided them with the eyes and senses of eagles. Their automatic weapons were a reminder that the world had declared a small war on a small country.

These young boys were performing an invidious task, I thought. They were the instruments for the bullying and the programed enervation of an entire nation condemned by a tribunal of judges more guilty than the defendant. Bush's new world order! Clinton's concept of morality!

Serbian professor and intellectual Dr. Prvoslav Ralic wrote acridly about "a new world order" which victimized and ostracized his country.

"Every well-intentioned person who relies on the truth can easily find out when the conflicts over the secession of Slovenia and Croatia from Yugoslavia started. Who caused and supported these conflicts. Who didn't respect the European Community's original decisions (which were later on forgotten and other completely different decisions were formulated). Why was the Customs war in Slovenia the beginning of the civil war in Yugoslavia? Why did clashes break out in Borovo-Selo between the people and the police? What led to the 'bloody wedding' in Sarajevo's Bascarsija when the first victims were Serbs? Who killed Nikola Gardovic of Serbian nationality and why, and who burned the Serbian flag in the center of Sarajevo? Everyone knows that this was done by Moslem Fundamentalists. Then came the totally irrational and unfounded decision to internationally recognize Bosnia and Herzegovina before the republic's three constituent nations could agree on mutual relations.

"Serbia and the Serbs cannot allow themselves to become a laboratory in which 'the new world order', the West, will do experiments on a democratic state because no one in the West has an exemplary democratic state either."

It was good to pass into Serbia. At the very onset, in the Vardar Valley of Macedonia, the scenery was green and lush, torrents of fast-moving water from the Vardar River spilling over and irrigating the land. Soon afterward, the land seemed parched, less responsive, less happy. Throughout the length of Macedonia, on an excellent road, built in another time by another people, there were idle young men seated in the shade staring listlessly into nowhere. There were damaged and over-tired, over-abused autos perched on the soft shoulders every couple of kilometers. The cars needed first aid in order to continue.

When we finally crossed over into Serbia, Vlada grinned. "Home at last," he said, although we still had hours of driving ahead of us.

Serbia comprised 86.5% of the territory of the new Federal Republic of Yugoslavia which had shrunk to a little over 102,000 square kilometers after losing Bosnia and Herzegovina (51,000), Croatia (56,000), Macedonia (25,000) and Slovenia (20,000). Its population of over ten million consisted of 65.8% Serbs, 17.2% Albanians, 3.5% Hungarians, 3.2% Yugoslavs (usually another way of saying mixed marriages), 2.4% Moslems (probably Turks), 1.1% Croats, 6.8% miscellaneous.

It was still light when we reached Belgrade (the White City), the capital of both Yugoslavia and Serbia. The population of the city, located adjacent to both the Sava River (the longest in Yugoslavia) and the Danube (the biggest in Europe), had swelled to about two million as a result of the influx of refugees from the war zones of the former Yugoslavia.

Certain changes were perceptible from the very beginning. There was hardly any traffic entering into the city and the town center was almost void of private vehicles. There were a few cars and some taxis, but private transportation was down to the same trickle as petrol. In order to drive in Belgrade, you needed a lot of money or a lot of clout. Even black market gasoline was not so easily obtainable and, when it was, the price was nearly $2 a liter, an extravagance that only the very rich could afford.

The trams and buses were running, but they reminded me more of Cairo and New Delhi than the Belgrade I knew less than two years earlier. People were virtually hanging out of the windows. Sanctions had all but done away with replacement parts, so public vehicles were breaking down all the time and they could not be repaired or replaced. I learned also that people simply stopped paying fares because it was too much of a hassle even to move once inside the vehicles.

The shops were still there but the merchandise they offered was sparse and usually of poor quality. The international embargo imposed on Yugoslavia was succeeding admirably.

Tourism was once a major industry, a prime source of foreign currency, employment for tens of thousands of people. Yugoslavia really had a lot to offer from the Alpine scenery of Bled in Slovenia to the Danube frontier with Rumania. Zagreb and Ljubljana were truly beautiful cities boasting splendid accommodations. And then, of course, there was Dubrovnik on the Adriatic which had no peers, no competition. And so on my previous trips, whether in summer or winter, the city was full of foreigners. This time there was no one, except UN personnel and journalists. There were no excursions. No national airline to expedite the movement of tourists. Hotels were open, but mostly empty and shoddy.

In 1990, only a few years earlier, tourism had produced $4 billion in revenue for the old Yugoslavia, $1.3 billion of which was spent in Serbia and Montenegro alone. Nine million foreigners visited the country then amounting to 55 million hotel room nights, a prodigious accomplishment for a relatively small country. Tourism amounted to 5% of the Gross National Product and 4.5% of total employment. In those last quiet days, Germany accounted for 38% of all the tourists, Great Britain 14%, Italy 12%, Netherlands 10%, Austria 10%, France 5% and the United States 2%.

And then suddenly it was all finished!

Unemployment and under-employment were rampant throughout the boycotted country where inflation was the highest in the world, increasing by margins of 200-300% a month and producing economic chaos and instability which were most certainly meant to cause political upheaval. The plethora of weapons available and the lack of both work and prospects had caused violent crime to rise rapidly. Barking guns were killing innocent people as never before in Yugoslavian history. People began going out less at night. Only fools carried large sums of money with them.

Before the embargo and sanctions, professional and administrative salaries in Yugoslavia had been averaging well over $1,000 a month and just about everything was available. On February 15, 1993, a massive devaluation was ordered by the government which plummetted monthly income to $100 or less. Subsequently, this figure was halved and even quartered. So by June 6, when I arrived, there was nothing unusual about a monthly salary in Belgrade of $20. Staple products like coffee and sugar were gone from shelves. The cost of all foreign products was prohibitive and the economy was also sagging under the weight of absorbing 700,000 refugees from Croatia and Bosnia, mostly by friends and families, but also in monasteries, convents and hostels.

Writer Bruce Ralston covered the subject of sanctions against Yugoslavia in a March, 1993 article written for the Delaware Business Review. "The local reaction of sanctions," he wrote, "is that it is hurting the very young, the very old and the very poor. One cannot explain with any conviction that it is the discomfort of the people which is supposed to bring pressure on the politicians to end the war. Among the Serbs, it merely strengthens their resolve."

Ralston also cited the case of the female Serbian scientist who had been working with her husband on a project for the University of Notre Dame at Ann Arbor, Michigan.

"They are both well-known scientists in the field of X-Ray technology. She found, on December 28 last year, that her father was near death in Belgrade. She asked the immigration and naturalization people for assurance that if she flew to her father's, she would not have a problem getting a visa to return

to her husband and twin daughters at Notre Dame.
Assurances were given. She came back home and the USA
has reneged. No visa is being granted. Her father died on
January 4. She can't come back."

Writing from Stockholm, Jan Oberg, a Swedish journalist
and Balkans expert, asked rhetorically and then proceeded to
provide answers. "Why was it a mistake to introduce the
sanctions? There are six simple reasons: (1) They affect the
poorest, the innocent; the leaders are comfortably off; (2)
They create a thoroughly criminalized society and reward the
most criminal elements; (3) They make the economic
development of Serbia more difficult, a development which is
a precondition for peaceful coexistence; (4) They confirm the
Serbian picture that the entire world is against the Serbs; (5)
They favor politicians who take up a negative attitude to the
rest of the world and fight for the Serbian cause (like the old,
proud waitress in the restaurant at Hotel Moscow confides to
me — "Milosevic good man. Everyone don't like Serbs") and
finally (6) They could lead to a civil war in Serbia and thereby
a bloodbath in Kosovo."

If the purpose of the sanctions was to create a new political
reality in Yugoslavia by causing maximal human suffering, it
failed. There was plenty of opposition to the Milosevic
government, but there was also a unanimity of sentiment that
no outside force would determine the future government of
Yugoslavia.

There was, however, another self-evident factor, la-
mentable because of its far-reaching consequences. It would
take years for the Yugoslav economy to recover from the
savage enervation produced by sanctions and embargo.
Smaller, more vulnerable businesses were already destroyed.
An entire international airline, JAT, was petrified. Its staff was
furloughed, aircraft mothballed, offices closed. The tourist
industry was gone. No one in his right mind could or would
think about holidaying in a country under international threat
and virtually isolated from the rest of the world. The

competitive economic edge that Belgrade had worked so hard to hone in the past was over. Even vital industries that somehow continued to subsist were working at half or quarter power, employees reduced to hours instead of days of work.

And how long would it really take for the economy to recover after the sanctions were lifted? One acquaintance estimated ten years; another stated, "the next day".

# CHAPTER IX
# BOJANA'S NIGHTMARE

The same people who proudly recalled the anniversary of the Battle of Kosovo against the Turks, which was a clear, devastating nightmare for Serbia, were observing yet another strange occasion in Belgrade.

Politika, the international weekly published in the capital, recalled the first anniversary of the blockade by conjuring up a "garden party" which included the screening of select films for the specially invited UN guests.

"They first saw twelve dead babies from Banjaluka, whom the United Nations prevented from growing up by depriving them of bottled oxygen. They then saw the hungry and the sick without medicines, children freezing in their unheated schools, empty border crossings guarded by blue-bereted soldiers, hundreds of boats and barges stopped on the Danube, a grounded civilian airplane fleet, frozen fruit melting in cold storage plants without fuel, hundreds of thousands of people without work waiting in front of locked up factories and many other things which gave them immense joy."

I had known Bojana Ivanovic since 1990 when she was a minor, but rising luminary, in the state-owned Putnik Travel Agency. It was a marriage made in heaven — besides Yugoslavia, the two places Bojana loved the most in the world were Israel and Greece.

I spent an entire evening trying to elicit complaints from her, but like her ten-plus million stoic compatriots, the only responses obtainable were in the eyes which could not cover up the suffering of an entire nation with puns and jokes and wistful memories of a more innocent and friendly age.

After fighting fiercely over who would pay for the beer and kebabcici (my defeat was preordained!), Bojana told me the story of a close friend who slashed his hand a few weeks earlier on the shards of a bottle overturned by his son.

"He was bleeding very badly and so we rushed him to a hospital in a taxi (certainly not in an ambulance because those vehicles were paralyzed by the fuel blockade). There was no anti-tetanus serum available in the whole hospital so we had to find a private clinic open at that hour. They had the serum, but the cost was eighty German marks which was more than his monthly salary and far more than I had.

"For the first time, his wife, my childhood friend, sobbed. So we took another taxi and woke my parents. They had just that amount of money in the house — months of savings — and we were able to buy the serum. There was almost no surgical thread in the hospital so we purchased that as well.

"Falling sick or having an accident, either to me or my parents, is my constant nightmare these days. There are almost no medical supplies left in the country. The black market functions, but the prices are usurous. Who can afford them?"

Ask a Serb how he lives and he will smile, shrug his shoulders and invite you for a *rakija* while explaining that the annual inflation rate in 1992 was only 20,000%, a mere bagatelle for a race hardened in the Balkans.

Financial survival in Yugoslavia since the embargo meant a lot of fancy footwork, an increasing level of deprivation, multitudes of odd jobs, exploitation and use of whatever savings might have been left, the fusing of families to better cope with the cyclonic effects of inflation and job insecurity.

"I receive my salary on the first of the month," Bojana explained. "The first thing I have to do is to acquire all the non-perishables required for the month. In my particular case, and in the priority of importance for me, that means cat food, cigarettes, tinned vegetables and fruit. I pay the previous month's debts, if I can, and then appear at my parents' home where I present them with some of the money. If I have anything left after this, I quickly change the dinars into German marks — because that is the only practical currency around here these days.

"My parents are both pensioners and they get their checks about the tenth of the month. So they return the money I loaned them earlier and I then have enough dinars for another week or so — although I must be careful about how I spend the money. Prices move up so quickly that the national sport is racing from shop to shop in order to acquire 'ten-minute bargains'.

"Shopping is the most serious of all activities in Belgrade. People are willing to queue for ten hours in order to acquire something of value at prices they can afford.

"It's hard to explain, but you can walk into a grocery shop in the morning and buy a few items which you leave until the afternoon. When you return later, there is no similarity between what you paid a few hours earlier and the new costs.

"So by the time I finish using whatever dinars left from my parents, I still have a small amount of foreign currency which must tide me over until the next pay check."

The financial acrobatics required for merely staying afloat meant that there was virtually nothing left over for clothes, shoes, cosmetics, entertainment, travel. Sickness, any form of serious illness, was really a disaster although socialized medicine was still theoretically available. The problem, however, was that the hospitals simply had run out of supplies.

The Serbs were not a bitter people and they had been inured to hardship and deprivation before, but the kind of international cynicism prevailing against them remained inexplicable.

Obviously, the concept of imposing a near-total boycott on Yugoslavia as well as an international embargo supervised by the United Nations was directed at one purpose only — creating a sufficient level of human suffering so that the people would bring down their own government which, in turn, would be replaced by an administration more malleable to the political philosophy of the Common Market countries and the United States. But that hadn't happened. Nor was there much chance that it would.

"I am not worried about myself or even my wife," Branislav, a thirty-four-year-old Belgrade mechanic explained to me. "I am only concerned about my two children. We Serbs are a tall people and my children grow like weeds. They need shoes, they need new clothes. They love ice cream. There are books we have to buy them. I don't want the children even to sense we have a financial problem. You are only young once. Why should your mind be scarred by bad memories?

"But I must tell you that my heart sinks each time I must replace the shoes of the older boy or buy new sneakers or a birthday present. Always I must go to my parents for the money and I consider that ignoble for a man my age.

"What will happen in the future? Perhaps it will get worse. But we don't break easily. The world should know this. Serbian politics belong to the Serbian people. We alone will decide if Mr. Milosevic stays in power. I am sorry only that the children have to suffer. It is hard to explain boycotts and embargoes to a seven-year-old boy who wants a football which his father cannot afford to buy him."

Also commemorating the first birthday of international sanctions were two separate, high-level professional meetings of Yugoslav experts in economy and ecology. The former, held in Budra, concluded that "the blockade threatens the very survival of innocent citizens who have been brought to the brink of starvation, endangering health and social care". According to the economists, continuation of the sanctions "will reduce the Yugoslav economy to the level of under-developed countries with a per capita income below $400".

Damage to ecology was, meanwhile, discussed in Belgrade where a terse warning was released. "The UN sanctions are affecting the ecological systems both in Yugoslavia and in neighboring countries because pollution of the environment cannot be stopped by state borders... Sanctions in the area of ecology should never have been imposed because they violate fundamental human rights to clean air, water and food."

Being a resourceful people, the Serbs managed to suck some financial oxygen out of the air through institutions dubbed "private banks". Since the fiduciary situation was so chaotic anyway, the idea was to transform brittle dinars into more acceptable foreign currency, deposit those sums for at least a month at a time and then collect a whopping interest of 12% every thirty days. Almost too good to be true, it was true, for awhile. An initial deposit of $1,000 meant $120 a month additional or a salary much greater than what could be earned from honest toil outside in the real world.

All the private banking institutions suddenly went belly up, almost simultaneously, and large numbers of Yugoslavs, particularly in Belgrade, were ruined.

"The killing inflation we were experiencing," explained Bojana, "had forced lots of people into the private banking scheme. Fortunately, myself excluded, because I felt there was something immoral about it. These people lost everything. All their savings were gone in one day. Can you imagine what this meant for pensioners whose official income was hardly enough to acquire the barest necessities?"

A year after economic warfare was declared against the Yugoslavs, only national pride and Serbian stubbornness kept the dinar even vaguely alive. It might cost more than a million to acquire a soft drink. Zeros were blinding over ten million people whose personal pocket calculators could no longer cope with the legions of numbers glaring at them from wads of bills. All meaningful calculations were translated into German marks which seemed to suit the Serb temperament better than dollars.

One evening, just off the Metropole Hotel in central Belgrade, I watched the gathering in the street of several hundred high school seniors who were about to celebrate graduation. As usual, the students were exceptionally fine looking — beautiful girls, handsome boys, characteristics of all the South Slavs. But they were also very well dressed, as sartorial as their counterparts in Athens, Tel Aviv or New York for that matter.

"Dressing up the girls that way has cost a fortune," I told Bojana afterward.

She agreed.

"Well, in view of what is going on and all the hardships and deprivations, how did their parents get the money?"

Bojana replied with the typical Serb shrug. "Their parents sold things. They borrowed money from other members of the family. They saved for years. They worked on Sundays. Whatever else might happen, they knew that graduation would remain memorable in the minds of their children for the rest of their lives. Nothing would be permitted to spoil that evening because there would not be too many similar, innocent evenings in their lives after that. There are some things we cannot help doing. It is in our blood. Perhaps that is why we are so wild."

In addition to the steady and seemingly inexorable diminution of their purchasing power, "the wild Serbs" inherited yet another awesome economic problem when the nation as a whole agreed to assist 700,000 refugees from Croatia and Bosnia. Whoever had extra living space shared it. Emergency clothing was distributed throughout centers in Belgrade. People with barely enough food for themselves volunteered to support frightened refugee families.

"We donated whatever clothing we could," Bojana explained, "which was the only decent thing to do although we knew in advance that we might never be able to replace the items. Some of my friends parted with baby clothing they were saving for their grandchildren. The Slavs are a very sentimental people. But there was really nothing else to do."

If the air over Belgrade was laden with Slavic stoicism, there was also some bitterness about the inequities in Yugoslav society which were too visible to excuse. While ambulances were immobile and public transportation barely coped with demands, black market petrol kept private Mercedes and BMWs rolling unconcerned over streets and highways. Perhaps 5% of the population continued to enjoy the good life, the dolce vita, no matter how many additional hardships were imposed on the rest of the population.

Some of the promiscuous wealth was simply there before the boycotts and embargoes and was deftly maneuvered so that it swelled rather than shrank during the inflation. Other money, several Serbs I interviewed claimed, was produced by the new lust for arms endemic in a region suffering from civil war, political uncertainty and economic isolation. And evidently quite a bit of the money was the direct result of the gangsterism that was growing almost exponentially in a city once one of the quietest and safest in all Europe.

Literally borrowing pages from the Chicago of the twenties and thirties, Belgrade was suddenly infiltrated by organized crime. It was all rather easy because essential elements were in place. Violence was in the air. Plenty of small-caliber weapons were available. Unemployment, particularly for the young, was rife. Poverty nurtured hopelessness which translated into despair which found a natural outlet in crime.

Without western coercion and with little fanfare, Yugoslavia had been encouraging free market enterprises for years and so plenty of cafés, night clubs and restaurants emerged to satisfy the needs of an otherwise frustrated population. In tandem with their successes, protection gangs suddenly emerged as an unexpected and unwanted corollary to free enterprise. Owners naturally resisted at the beginning although skepticism usually crumbled the next evening in parallel with the bombed out walls of the café. But even simple payoffs were not easy because there were rival gangs in earnest and deadly competition. Tithes to one merely sharpened appetites for others. Of course, the gangsters were killing each other as well as innocent bystanders and intrepid diners, but the miniwar for control of the Belgrade night spots was not encouraging evenings on the town.

Even traveling through the city could be an adventure. One tram was hijacked in midday in central Belgrade. Riders were relieved of jewelry, cash and even eye glasses before reaching their destinations. When the Serbs recounted these stories, they tried making light of them. But there was no humor about murders and muggings, which were keeping people indoors at night, bombs in restaurants and all the other violent acts nurtured by poverty and despair.

For months people at the United Nations had been discussing an international tribunal to establish the guilt and punish war criminals in former Yugoslavia. Pinpointing a rapist or sadistic murderer of prisoners might, indeed, become a plausible undertaking because there were victims, criminals and also witnesses. But a different type of crime was being committed at the sametime that no one seemed to care about. These were the travesties of turning youthful frustration into violent crime or depriving a seven-year-old of a football because there was barely enough cash in the family for food. A moral injustice was being foisted capriciously on an entire people who was guilty of nothing except sympathizing with compatriots and coreligionists who were ethnically identical to them. Was killing children by denying them medicines a solution for the termination of a war in Bosnia and Herzegovina? And would the dreaded fear of illness installed in people like Bojana hasten an armistice in Sarajevo?

Thoughtless people with tremendous power had unconscionably decided to inflict great suffering on a whole people so that their political views would prevail. Yugoslavia was not Iraq. No Yugoslav army had crossed international borders and tried ingesting a foreign, sovereign nation. Indeed, Yugoslavia was a victim of careless promises and thoughtless foreign policies. And so, once again, why couldn't the little boy have the football? Why should it cost more than a month's wages for a simple anti-tetanus innoculation that was available almost everywhere else in the world for almost nothing? Why did Bojana insist, while joking about the economic hardships of her nation, that the tear in her eye was only because of an allergy?

# CHAPTER X
# THE BETRAYAL OF A NATION

Serbian intellectuals and professional political analysts had no trouble understanding western European belligerence against Yugoslavia. The phenomenon was not exactly new. The German role, in the ensuing drama of the disintegration of a sovereign power, was clear from the beginning. On a sentimental level, Bonn felt a distinct kinship for Slovenia which pleaded for recognition and acceptance, and Croatia with which it shared so much recent common history. Adopting the two states meant easy access to the Adriatic, useful new markets for German industry and the materialization of the new trend in Europe of self-determination. After all, East and West Germany were finally reunited by common fiat. The Soviet Union had disintegrated into a large Russia and a lot of smaller neighboring countries by common consent. There may have been a little malice involved as well, however, in the instance of Yugoslavia. The Serbs and Germans hadn't really liked each other for hundreds of years so a little teutonic malice was not too surprising.

Certainly the Vatican, a very important facet of international powerplay, was supportive of Germany for its own clear reasons. Both Slovenia and Croatia were deeply committed to the Church. Relations with Orthodoxy, despite public hand-kissing and joint communiqués, were less than cordial. The disintegration of Yugoslavia not only meant two new independent Catholic countries, but the consequent weakening of an old antagonist.

France, which later expressed second thoughts about what it and its Common Market colleagues had done, found it easier to follow Germany's lead rather than question the significance of what was happening. On a superficial level,

Paris merely saw a cumbersome confederation that apparently wasn't working too well anyway, simply "deconfederating" or breaking up because of strong ethnic differences. So what was so terrible about a little push?

The image of Yugoslavia anyway, at the time, was tarnished. Slobodan Milosevic was not the type of person you would invite to a cricket game. He wasn't sufficiently apologetic about his Communist past. The Serbs, in general, appeared to be a rather backward people, hardly even Europeans, the Croatians assured western friends from Zagreb.

Michel Foucher, editor of the prestigious G.E.O. Newsletter and a close friend of François Mitterand, produced a map in early 1991 under the heading, "Europe – Socio-Economic Borders and Recomposition". A sharp, blue line ran south from Estonia and the other Baltic states to Poland, Czechoslovakia and Hungary, slashing across old Yugoslavia so that Croatia and Slovenia were in the western orbit of Europe while Serbia, Montenegro and Macedonia were consigned to the east. Greece and Albania shared the same fate as Serbia, relegated to a secondary geopolitical role.

This map appeared while Yugoslavia was still very much alive indeed. A year earlier, on January 24, 1990, the Financial Times drew its own European map of the future. The Balkan Union consisted of Serbia, Albania, Macedonia, Bosnia and Herzegovina, Bulgaria, Greece and "southern" Cyprus. Croatia and Slovenia, however, were transferred to Central Europe. The map was supposed to be an exercise into fantasy – or was it prescience? Or astute journalism?

Dr. Predrag Simic, director of the Institute of International Politics and Economics in Belgrade, was, like so many of his colleagues in leading positions in the country, young, around thirty-five.

"For a lot of strange reasons," he explained, "the West really believes that it was the Serbs who killed Yugoslavia. An image of Serbia was created and successfully marketed showing us as little more than Nazis — oppressive, aggressive, dangerous. If the world wanted to avoid a new Hitler, then Serbia would have to be stopped at all cost. After all, one Munich per century was enough.

"The German position regarding Yugoslavia is really not too hard to understand. Bonn has created an image of itself — Snow White and the dwarfs. It likes the idea of client states which rely on it. It is trying to build a new idea of itself, in Germany itself and throughout the West. Germany plans to be a pillar of strength in Europe. It has already shown that it is willing to pay for this privilege by contributing 60% of all the aid that was sent to Russia. It envisages an area of influence that runs from the Baltic to the Aegean and the breakup of Yugoslavia fell well within its plans."

Simic explained that all the old, cogent reasons for a viable Yugoslavia had changed. The country was no longer a barrier between east and west. It was no more a cordon sanitaire between the expansionist designs of Russia on one hand and Germany on the other.

"Strangely, our big problem in the past was not so much Germany as Austria," continued Simic. "The Wehrmacht that attacked us in 1941 was 70% Austrian and the general who planned the attack was from Vienna. But it was the Germans, undoubtedly, who gained the most from the breakup of Yugoslavia. They have now realized an ancient ambition — access to the Mediterranean."

Germany agreed not only to act as the "patron" of the two fledgling countries, but was suddenly morally obliged to protect Slovenia and Croatia from a vengeful and irate Serbia. So it was not just patronage and the promise of economic support that Germany proffered, but a worldwide crusade against Serbia as well. More than any other nation, Germany pushed for the isolation of Belgrade and the tacit commitment of NATO to enter the fray if either of its client states were directly attacked by Belgrade.

In the meanwhile, the press was having a field day with

Yugoslavia.

Unlike the Serbs who treated public relations as an itch, Slovenia, Croatia and later Bosnia and Herzegovina were aware of the investment value of mind manipulation. Reportedly, they hired Washington's Ruder and Finn, one of the world's top public relations agencies, early in the game, long before the split occurred. They also had a couple of other decisive advantages in their favor. The Croatian emigrés were well-organized in the United States and, in particular, in Germany. They had money. They had organization and, unlike their Serbian cousins, they had the good sense to produce the infrastructure for all future scenarios, including war. Also the bulk of foreign correspondents assigned to old Yugoslavia were domiciled in Zagreb, largely because the Croatian capital was more central, more "European" and more accessible to key regions. This provided Croatia with a wonderful opportunity to wine, dine, influence and eventually manipulate some members of the Fourth Estate.

Nonetheless, according to American journalist Peter Brock, who studied the media situation closely, "Belgrade-based correspondents predominated in the volume and quality of reporting done on the civil war until late 1991 when they were 'benched', and wire services imported reporters from western European and American bureaus where anti-Serbian bias was already established."

According to Brock's calculations, there was demonstrable anti-Serb bias of 25.5:1 on all signed articles reporting about the region. Articles without bylines presented almost the same ratio, 25:1. "The combined total of articles with datelines outside Yugoslavia that contained direct or indirect anti-Serb bias or slant was 41:1. (Not surprisingly, these included a significant number of human interest stories about refugees and a large number of resulting editorials, opinions, analyses and interpretive articles by non-Yugoslav writers.)"

The impact of strong editorial opinion, buttressed by atrocity photos that were casually and automatically blamed on Serbs, made Germany's job in the European Community and the United Nations considerably easier. The European press was vigorously mobilized against Serbia while American media was racing quickly toward those same conclusions. Before very long, hatred of Serbs, whether from Bosnia or Yugoslavia, was the only fashionable conclusion for western liberals and intellectuals. That many of the photos were spurious, that the captions were often misrepresented, that one-sidedness prevailed unequivocably, was no longer germane. On top of all the ethnic cleansing bandied about, objective reporting was showered under the shoddiest type of advocacy journalism. All this made it easy for Bonn and impossible for Belgrade. It encouraged and permitted the most colossal, and successful, propaganda campaign since the days of Nazi propaganda chief, Göbbels.

Bonn succeeded in blackmailing, coercing or convincing the rest of the European Community to acknowledge the independence of Slovenia and Croatia at the Maastricht conference on December 16, 1991.

"America initially did not want to see the disintegration of Yugoslavia," according to Simic. "Indeed, the Americans were very upset with Genscher in particular, and the German government in general."

At the time, there was still considerable good will in the United States for Yugoslavia — actually 112 years of friendly relations in which no hostile act ever spoiled the friendship between the two countries. Americans could still recall the valiant struggles of the Partisans. They still owed the memory of Tito some thanks for destroying the monolithic hold of communism over eastern Europe and allowing the first democratic sunlight to filter through the Iron Curtain. Even then though, there was no real absolute consensus in the United States.

Republican senator Bob Dole, for example, had visited the Balkans in the mid-eighties and returned to Washington muttering about "human rights".

"Between the Maastricht promulgation and the spring of 1992," said Simic, "we really felt that the war was almost over and that there were no more surprises waiting for us. There was an exchange of prisoners of war with Croatia. There was a tentative agreement to reopen the Belgrade–Zagreb highway. Our government was making short- and long-time economic plans and then we were hit by an ax.

"On April 6, the very anniversary of the invasion of Yugoslavia in 1941, Germany pushed through official EC recognition of Bosnia and Herzegovina despite all our pleas and warnings that this could lead to a bloodbath if minority rights were not negotiated first. And before we could recover from the initial shock, the impossible happened. America followed suit. We knew that Bosnia and Herzegovina could not survive this premature recognition. Civil war became inevitable, but equally frightening, we knew that we had lost the United States as a trusted friend and ally."

Apparently, the anti-Serb view in America had finally prevailed. Croatian public relations had been adroit while Serbian explanations and rebuttals were tepid. President Milosevic was tarred and feathered in American media. He was a rigid, unsmiling, unconscionable Bolshevik interested in creating a Greater Serbia on the corpses of innocent Moslem and Croatian victims. The term "ethnic cleansing" became a synonym for Serbian racialism and radicalism against innocent civilians. There was a complete obfuscation between Bosnian Serbs who were fighting for their survival at that moment and Yugoslav Serbs hundreds of kilometers away.

"Americans always need villains," explained Simic. "Suddenly, Yugoslavia was made to order. We were Bolsheviks. We were Communists. We were racists and we were Nazis. What more could anyone ask? I think the Americans actually felt betrayed by us. It was as if they were saying, 'Look, we gave you money. We defended your interests. We tried to be your friends. And how did you repay us? You are the last Communists left in the world and everyone knows that the only good Communist is a dead one.'"

Although there was no shortage of domestic problems in the United States at the time, the Bush Administration was moving along with "a new world order" in which petty dictators like Saddam Hussein would be neutralized by a vigorous and reactivated United Nations supported, encouraged and led by America. With the death of communism, the whole world would be transformed into one great free market. Ethnic suppression would no longer be countenanced. The Soviet Union had broken into pieces because the people so willed it and this valuable precedent would be applied to Yugoslavia as well. Also Bush, and Secretary of State James Baker, had very specific ideas about who they liked and who they didn't. Great Britain's Margaret Thatcher had qualified as a valued team member. Israel's Itzchak Shamir, although the head of a friendly government, had not. And Milosevic certainly was not even in the running.

Writing in the Review of International Affairs, Fred Warner Neal of the Claremont Grademont School stated, "National independence obviously was a prerequisite for democracy. Thus the United States had no misgivings when Slovenia, encouraged by Germany, declared its independence from the rest of Yugoslavia and was quick to condemn Belgrade's intervention. The same was true regarding Croatia's declaration of independence. The United States had never really psychologically understood the difference between the Soviet Union and Yugoslavia. Since the breakup of the Soviet Union was considered to be desirable, this attitude affected American reaction to the breakup of Yugoslavia. The United States did not encourage the breakup, but neither did it advise against it. American consultation with the Federal German Republic might well have avoided German encouragement of Slovenian and Croatian independence, but the problems involved simply were not considered."

It was only natural therefore, that the United States would

apply the same moral yardstick to Bosnia and Herzegovina although the ethnic problems were far more complex. "The military conflicts which resulted," according to Neal, "came as a shock to the United States. And as a result, Serbia came out as the 'villain', first in regard to Croatia and then in regard to Bosnia and Herzegovina."

During the 1992 elections in the United States, Bill Clinton, the challenging Democrat, accused George Bush of "timidity" and not formulating a coherent and decisive foreign policy for the Balkans. In effect, Clinton, who had no foreign policy experience at all, was trying to score points against his opponent who had emerged from the imbroglio with Iraq as the world leader.

Even before the November elections, Clinton was more strident and martial than his predecessor. Taking what he considered the moral high ground from the start, he spoke more and more about the possibility of military intervention in the Balkans although top American military advisors counseled against this.

There was yet another important factor essential by then to American foreign policy. If there was one nation in the world which the United States mistrusted and feared, it was Iran, that most implacable of all opponents. Although mellowed a bit at the edges, Tehran still posed a real danger to American interests, as an exporter of Islamic revolution to the rich Arab oil states and as the most violent and unrelenting foe of Israel. Moslem Fundamentalism was also spreading rapidly, capturing parts of North Africa and threatening America, "the Great Satan", throughout the Middle East.

Without wanting any head-on confrontations with Fundamentalism, the State Department was gingerly seeking alternatives to Moslem radicalism. Turkey, a Moslem country with clear western orientation, became an essential ally, no longer against Russian expansionism, but as a modern example of a different, more manageable drift of Islam. Excoriated by the Moslem world for forty-five years over

America's "special relationship" with Israel, the State Department never ceased seeking opportunities to show even-handedness and sympathy for worthy Moslem causes.

And so there it was. Belgrade already branded the bully by Europe and, in particular, that most trusted of all allies, Germany. Wild Serbs attacking tame Croatians who desired little more than an opportunity to live in freedom, enjoy their Roman Catholicism, and meld into the west. Moslems, and even better, docile Moslems, assailed by the black sombreros who pillaged, raped, reinvented the concentration camp and specialized in dropping mortar shells on children. Also, and for the newsreels, those Moslems were good looking, western and often erudite. They spoke on television and in the United Nations with great passion and vigor. They were a commodity that America could understand and merchandise. After decades of frustration and criticism from Arab bloc friends about bias and impartiality, an opportunity to prove the mettle and fairness of American foreign policy finally arose.

Vice President Gore, a relatively mild-tempered man usually, compared the atrocities in Bosnia and Herzegovina with Hitler's crimes against the Jews. With not so much else to concentrate on at the moment, American media became even more rabid about the disintegrating situation in old Yugoslavia, conveniently forgetting all the warnings and all the pleas against premature recognition.

Clinton's clearly enunciated anti-Serb, pro-Bosnian Moslem policy was predicated on a number of conclusions, the first of which was that Belgrade was inspiring and supporting the mess in order to actuate the dream of a "Greater Serbia", an idée fixe by then.

The American President also found it impossible to understand that Bosnian Serbs were not the lackeys of Milosevic, that they had a will of their own, a national independence cultivated over hundreds of years, that they would talk and listen to Belgrade, but that they would not accept orders from anyone.

Seeking a simplistic approach to the new mountain state, American foreign policy applied the same yardstick for Bosnia and Herzegovina as it had previously employed for Slovenia and Croatia, forgetting that Slovenia had been 96% Slovenian and Croatia was 78% Croat. The idea of a country, with 4.3 million inhabitants, of which 43.7% were Moslems, 31.4% Serbs and 17.3% Croats still hadn't penetrated.

There was also the fear, growing all the time by then, that the fire raging in Bosnia would soon spread to other regions of the old Yugoslavia — Kosovo with its restive, large ethnic Albanian population; Macedonia for reasons that no one could explain. And if, as feared, the Balkans were about to ignite because of Serbian intransigence and lust for land and power, then what was to prevent the fire from spreading to Greece, Albania and Turkey, all three of which heartily mistrusted each other — and for good reason?

Commenting again on the situation, Neal had the following to say: "As far as general American public views about Yugoslavia (including Bosnia and Herzegovina) are concerned, there is…an ignorance both political and geographical, so widespread, that foreigners interested in the Balkans find it hard to believe."

Perched in his Institute of International Politics and Economics, Predrag Simic summed up. "Commenting," he said, "on the exact forces, the people, the nations that caused the disintegration of the old Yugoslavian state is a very complex undertaking because there were so many factors involved — historical and political. But if you ask me instead who do I believe is responsible for the death of Bosnia and Herzegovina as a recognizable nation, then I can accuse only one country — the United States."

# CHAPTER XI
# WAR ON CHILDREN

I remembered vividly, several months earlier, the televised after-effects of the mortar shell which had dropped in a Sarajevo school yard while tens of Moslem youngsters were playing soccer. Beautiful children were suddenly transformed into human wreckage. One particular boy, blinded by the ordnance which was programed to explode before hitting the ground in order to maximalize carnage, became the focus for all the senseless brutality and inhumanity that had characterized the civil war in Bosnia. I recalled also the response of the overwrought UN officer who was responsible for evacuating the children to hospitals. He damned whoever had pulled the trigger to everlasting hell.

Never really proven, it was generally reported that the shell had been fired from the Serb-occupied bluffs overlooking the city. It was certainly plausible to assume that that indeed was what happened. It made me feel ashamed and angry — convinced once again that in that unforgiving civil war, there was enough malice and evil to be shared by all the belligerents.

However, young people were not only being killed in Sarajevo. They were being murdered in Serbia as well, only without television cameras to record death rattles. Babies were dying every month — because of lack of basic medical equipment, because of the non-availability of even the simplest drugs, because of the lack of incubators.

Dr. Mima Simic, a thirty-five-year-old psychiatrist in a state hospital, confirmed that the medical situation in the country was more than desperate, it was fatal.

"So many of my patients," she explained, "require drugs merely to function. We have nothing in the hospitals any longer. Instead of ministering to patients, doctors can only comfort and solace them. Most of my colleagues are morally shattered by now. Patients are slipping away from us, dying or retrogressing for lack of the simplest, basic medicines. The weakest are going first — infants, young children, the elderly. But soon it will affect everybody."

A team composed of some of the top medical experts in Yugoslavia prepared a document about the effect of sanctions on the health of a country which had only recently boasted of superlative services. It was a long, sad bit of work. In this instance, the mortar shell was fired by the United Nations, the victims were still often children and the murders continued.

"Is it possible that the world is really ready to coldly implement measures causing a slow death of millions of innocent people? This is a horrible question asked by the population of a country condemned to isolation.

"According to provisions and principles of the international humanitarian law, the right to life and health is a fundamental human right. This right is also guaranteed by the United Nations charter and the World Health Organization constitution. The definition of health accepted by the world is that of the World Health Organization, according to which, health means material, social, psychological and physical wellbeing of the man. It is then needless to ask whether UN Security Council Resolutions 757 and 820 condemned to a loss of life and health citizens of the Federal Republic of Yugoslavia, and together with them refugees and all others receiving health protection in its territory, since they can receive it nowhere else in the former Yugoslavia. And to what are condemned sick people in Yugoslavia by the Security Council sanctions?

"It is a well known fact that Yugoslav health service almost entirely depends on import. About 90% of medicines are produced exclusively on the basis of foreign licences and imported raw materials or half-made products. Other medicines are imported as ready-made products. Over 95% of sanitary material and 90% of medical material are also imported. Almost all medical equipment is imported, as well as spare parts. In order to function, Yugoslav health service needs to import each month thousands of various medical products — drugs, needles, syringes, various surgical sutures, bandages, tubes, catheters, pacemakers, blood testing equipment, infusion systems. If one is familiar with medicine and health, one knows that for various types of surgeries alone, a number of articles such as tubes, catheters and similar equipment is needed.

"The sanctions, introduced in late May, 1992, imposed a procedure according to which each individual foreign trade turnover of these articles requires approval of the United Nations Committee for the implementation of Sanctions. In order to obtain approval, it is necessary to find a partner who is willing to cooperate, and then obtain approval of his government. And this is not enough! There is the second round of the process with the same procedure for carrying out financial transactions for this purpose. And finally the third round, i.e. obtaining approvals for transport of purchased goods.

"Despite the World Health Organization memorandum according to which financial transactions for health products must be excluded from sanctions, 50% of requests for deblocking of financial resources in foreign banks has not been met since September, 1992. Member countries of the United Nations and the World Health Organization that voted at the assemblies of this organization for the two resolutions under which health cannot be subject to sanctions, either for political or for any other reasons, are competing in making purchase and transport of medical products for the needs of the Federal Republic of Yugoslavia as slow as possible or even impossible. Many vehicles transporting humanitarian assistance are even prevented and stopped, thus discouraging those who collect, send and bring this assistance. In the meantime, surgeries for Yugoslav patients are being postponed and some of them die as a result.

"This country, that until recently had first-class medicine and health protection, has abandoned almost all methods of sophisticated specialist treatment. Babies with heart diseases die since surgery is impossible, operating rooms for open-heart surgeries were not heated during the winter, 1993, and there are long lists of patients waiting for kidney transplantation. Some of them die, and for others death is closer and closer. Even if they are lucky enough to be operated on, it is not certain that they are going to live, since their illness deteriorates due to the long delay. And even if they survive this stage, still there is no hope for them, because there are no immuno-suppressive medicines to prevent rejection of the transplanted organ. Neurosurgeons are carrying out the most complex surgeries, e.g. brain tumor surgeries and similar, without X-ray equipment that would better locate the tumor, thus improving the chance of survival. However, it is not only this highest level of health protection that is the problem. Namely for several months now it has not been possible to implement even routine health protection. Due to the lack of tranquilizers, patients with mental disorders are again tied up and treated with electric shocks, although these are not only abandoned, but also banned methods. Death rate of these patients is rising enormously, and increasingly often when having fits of aggression, they attack doctors and other medical staff, who have no means to calm them down.

"Clinics for contagious diseases are full of patients whose blood has been infected since it has not been tested to hepatitis, while shelves for drugs are empty. Patients suffering from allergy cannot be treated with penicillin, cannot receive any help at all at clinics, since other antibiotics are available only occasionally, when they arrive as part of humanitarian aid. Private pharmacies still have medicines, and patients are buying their own anesthetic for surgery, needles, sutures, cytostatics. For one medicine they give their entire monthly salary, and for longer treatment they sell all they have.

"The following are only some of the effects of the sanctions so far:

"The Institute of Oncology in Belgrade does not have even the most fundamental cytostatics. Although three months ago, $500,000 was paid to import these medicines, and although all necessary approvals have been obtained, the bank in London has not released these resources. Four months ago a payment was made to the Siemens' account for spare parts for X-ray equipment. No reply has been received from the Siemens yet.

"At cardiosurgical wards for children in Serbia, 41 babies have died since doctors have not been able to carry out necessary surgeries. Dr. Jadran Magic, a doctor at the Institute of the Mother and the Child in Belgrade, who provided this information, explained how tragic it was to decide which baby was to be operated first, and which one to be sent to death. These babies had heavy heart diseases. Who will take the responsibility for babies that are yet to be born, whose diseases, considered 'most ordinary' by the rest of the world, will be impossible to treat, since there will be no means for that?

"As a response to all appeals of Yugoslav doctors and officials and to the WHO resolutions, the UN Security Council Committee for Sanctions banned the import of raw materials for the production of medicines in Yugoslavia in November, 1992, since it allegedly had information that Yugoslav factories exported medicines to Slovenia. After five months of correspondence, the committee informed competent people in the country that only one small private company from Belgrade carried out export transactions for medicines with some similar Slovenian company from Maribor. Needless to say, not even after this has the ban been lifted. This is despite WHO resolutions 41.31 and 42.24, stating that health industry is not subject to sanctions. Yugoslav doctors, therefore, tried to raise their voice and tell the world that sanctions are seriously endangering the most innocent, children and the sick. Appeals were sent to the world public. In the context of

April 7, World Health Day, our country required the World Health Organization to demand lifting of sanctions in the health sector in the United Nations. Doctors have organized peaceful protests in front of the American, Russian, French and German embassies in Belgrade.

"As a response, it happened that a new Security Council resolution on a complete isolation of Yugoslavia was adopted. The resolution contains a provision that humanitarian aid and medicines are exempted from the ban on import. One can but wonder how 'exempted' health sector will be under Resolution 820, when under the more lenient Resolution 757 it was 'exempted' in such a manner.

"The people of Yugoslavia has become a hostage of the international process of solving the war crisis in Bosnia. Isolation put an embargo on humanity, violated the fundamental human rights, and people in one European country are facing death — out of anyone's sight, without a single offered hand. Doctors of Yugoslavia have the following message: 'We shall find a way to sooner or later charge and condemn those who took the lives of our patients or deteriorated their health.'

"For months now there has been a permanent shortage in this country of a whole range of medicines for basic health care. In the hospitals and pharmacies, there are no drugs for cardiac patients, no drugs for malignant diseases, no antibiotics, no tranquilizers and anti-depressants, no drugs to treat hypertension, no drugs to prevent the rejection of transplanted organs; surgical hospitals have no medical supplies, no anesthetics, no anti-shock therapy drugs, no medicaments for intensive care. The semi-illicit private market, the wares of which are of doubtful origin and quality, is the only source of supply for ill people from which they can buy, for instance, everything that they need for an operation, for doctors to be able indeed to perform one. Not only do chronic patients spend all of their earnings or pensions to buy medicines on this market, but they are frequently forced to sell what little they have, acquired painstakingly, to be able to get treatment.

"Yugoslav doctors have already publicized preliminary surveys which demonstrate a very significant deterioration of the health condition of the population.

"Due to the lack of anti-tetanus vaccines in a hospital in Loznica (on the border between Serbia and Bosnia and Herzegovina) a patient contracted this grave and fatal disease. Another patient had an epilepsy seizure for two days, due to the lack of intravenous anti-epileptics. She survived, but with severe irreversible damage to her cerebral functions.

"In one of the dialysis centers, of the 15 kidney patients whole dialysis was reduced from the needed three treatments to two weekly, four died immediately.

"Over only a year the number of tuberculosis patients in Belgrade has increased by 68 cases. At the Emergency Center in Belgrade, over less than a year, the mortality of injured patients went up by as much as 20% because of the lack of medicines and medical supplies for their timely treatment.

"At the Cardio-Vascular Surgery Center in Belgrade, in 1991, 502 open-heart surgeries were performed, and only 203 in 1992. The number of kidney transplants has been reduced by as much as 50% and in medicine, percentages of even 1 and 2% are significant.

"Epidemics of hepatitis, measles, intestinal and other infections are on the rise. Under the impact of Resolution 820 of the UN Security Council, it is expected that the present situation, difficult as it is, will only deteriorate further."

The tragedy of drug shortages throughout Yugoslavia cannot be fully understood or appreciated by reading a medical report, no matter how factual. The dilemma produced by the shortages grows more poignant and real when observed through patients' eyes particularly little patients.

Dr. Slavko Simeunovic, fifty-three, MD, PhD, vice dean of pediatrics and cardiology at Belgrade's University Children's Hospital, could not estimate how many of his tiny patients had worsened or even died because of the lack of medicines or proper medical equipment.

"There is a terrible antibiotic shortage. Every day there are less cardiotonics available to us. We don't have dieting and nutritional drugs that are essential for the treatment of certain disorders. I have been postponing operating on children with congenital heart diseases because we don't have vital oxygen equipment. And even if the parents locate the $2,000 needed to buy the equipment, where will they find it? How will they import it?

"Once, this hospital, and medicine generally in Yugoslavia, was ranked with the best facilities of western Europe. Now it is not only that I cannot perform the operations here by myself, I cannot even recommend sending the children overseas because there is simply not enough money."

No one will venture to guess how many sick people have already died beause of the sanctions and the consequent lack of medical drugs and equipment. "We are only certain," the cardiologist continued, "that the very young and the very old are the first to succumb."

The ward was full of everything from infants to toddlers to young children. Parents were worried and frightened, incredulous that their children might be permitted to slip away from them, in this day and age of advanced science, because of a lack of medicine.

"I don't want to suggest that we don't have any medicine at all," continued the doctor, "but our supplies are dwindling every day. We cannot schedule anything anymore. As the medicines drop, so do the expectations of our young patients. The longer the sanctions continue, the worse it will be and the greater the suffering."

*Kosovo – Pristina, 24 November, 1988, Albanians rioting.*

*Pristina, 28 March, 1989, clashes between Albanians and the police.*

*Borovo village, 1 May, 1991, Serb defenders of the village after the conflict with Croatia's police.*

*Serbian priest Dragan Glumac watching the debris of the Serbian church in the town of Petrinja.*

*Vucovar in the summer of 1991.*

*Top: Vukovar mayor, Milorad Visic.*

*Bottom: Serbian church damaged in fierce Vukovar fighting.*

*Serb victim in Croatia.*

*Serb soldier mutilated and killed in war with Croatia.*

*Sarajevo, April, 1992, Nikola Gardovic's funeral, killed at the Serb wedding party at Bascarsija.*

*Vasa Miskin Street - The tragedy of Sarajevo citizens queueing for bread.*

*Serbian houses in northern Bosnia burned down by followers of Alija Izetbegovic.*

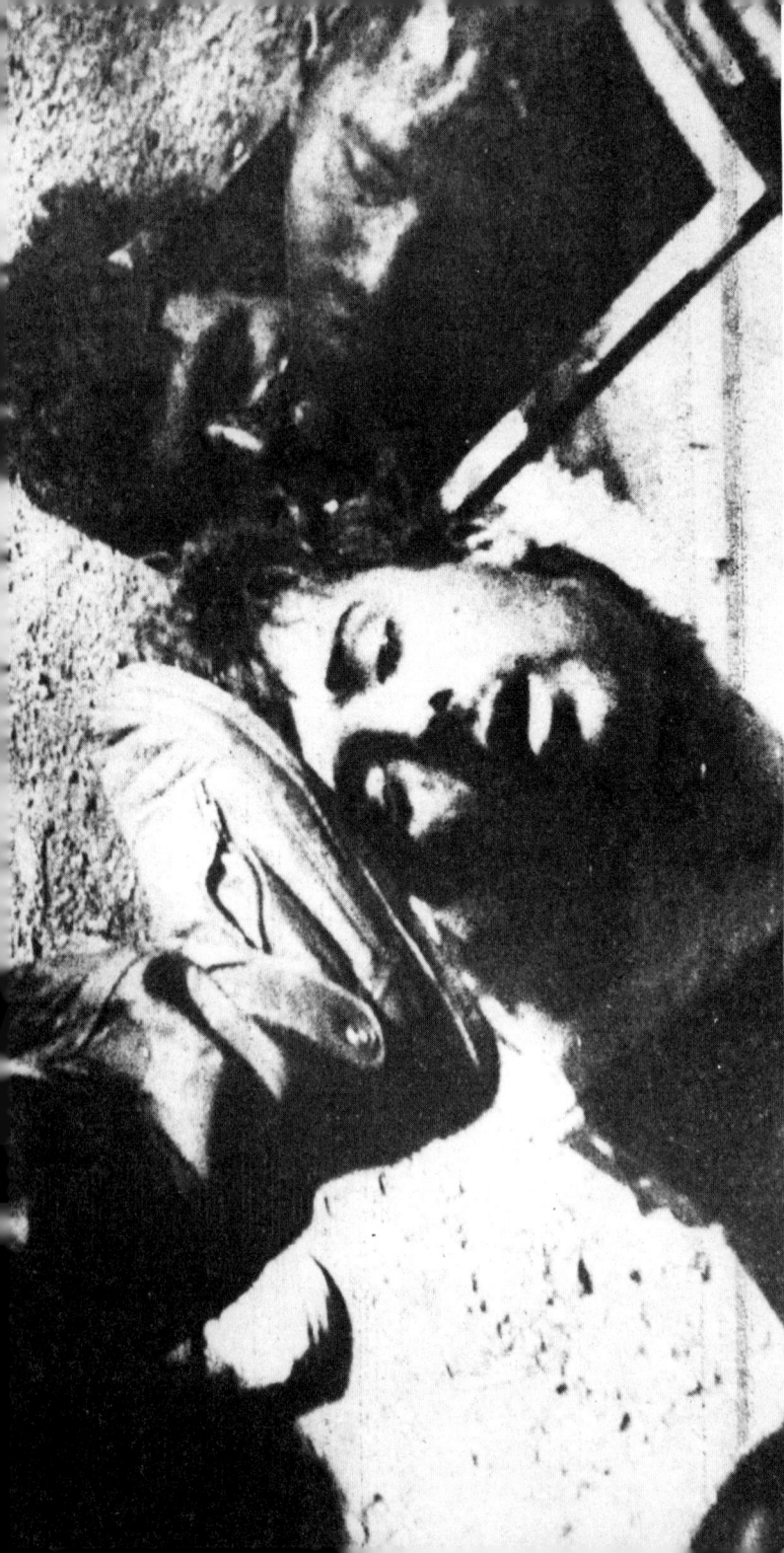

*Heads of Serb soldiers stuffed in ammunition boxes.*

*Massacre of Serbian soldiers in eastern Bosnia.*

The price of warfare in Bosnia and Herzegovina was high. Top photo shows blinded Serb reciting poetry in Pancevo. Woman with author in bottom photo was driven mad after being held captive in Sarajevo for over four months.

*Top: Bosnia - Herzegovina, 1992, a Mujahedeen with the head of a decapitated Serb. Bottom: A Mujahedeen identity card.*

BL-03.LEGITIMACIJA,CRNI VRH,29SEP92 - NA SLICI MEDJU DOKUMENTIMA KOJI SU VAPLENJENI OD MUDZZAHEDINA NA CRNOM VRHU NALAZILA SE I OVA LICCNA ISPRAVA.

*Serbian refugees from Bosnia - Herzegovina.*

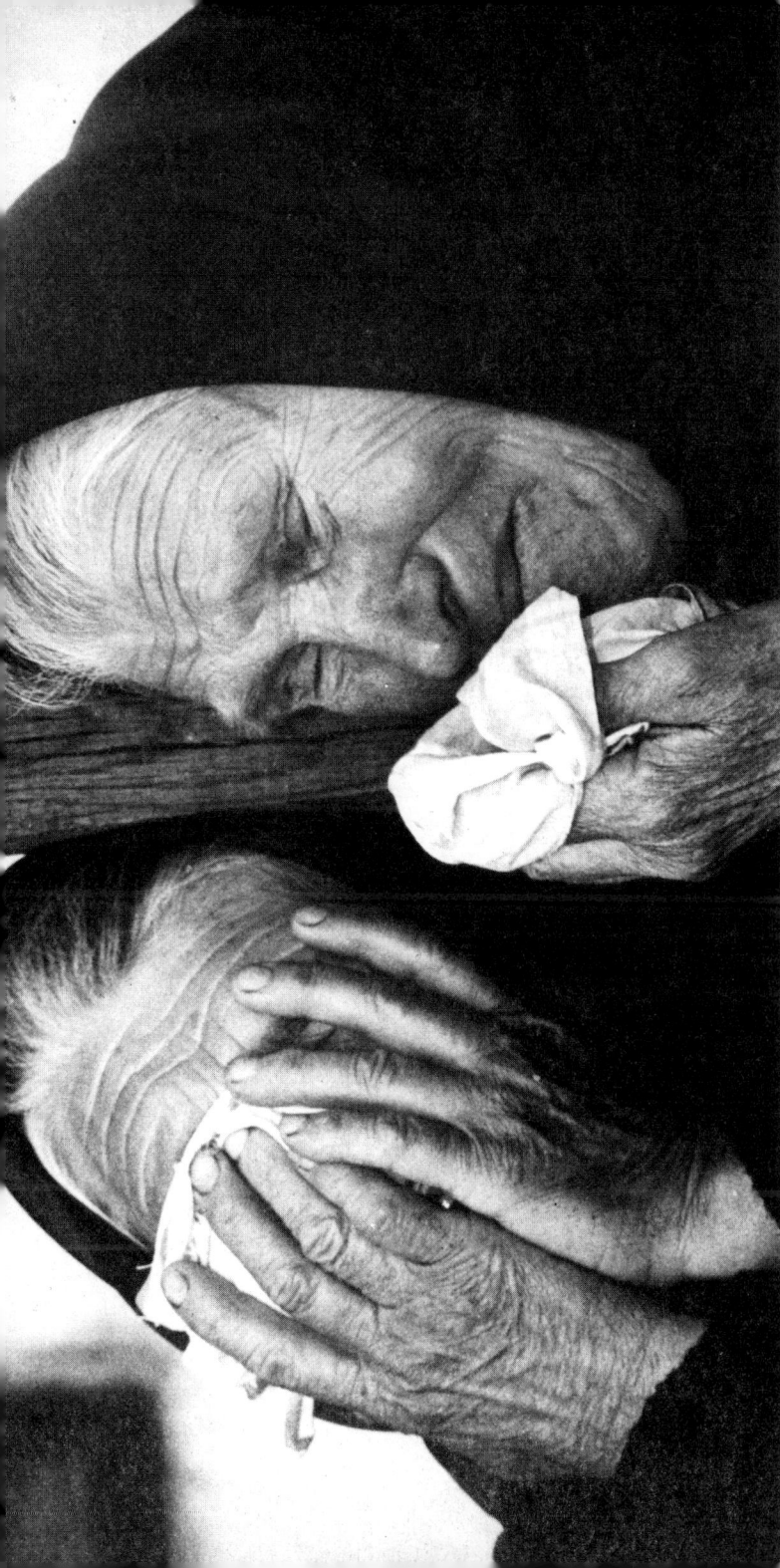

*Old Serbian women from Bosnia - Herzegovina lamenting the death of their next of kin.*

*Serbian refugees from Bosnia and Herzegovina.*

# CHAPTER XII
# SIGHTLESS POETRY

Official refugee statistics indicate, according to Yugoslavia's Commissariat for Refugees and the Red Cross of Serbia, that 587,000 sought haven in the country as a direct result of the war or due to coercion or threats or brutality. The majority of those people, 323,000, came from Bosnia and Herzegovina; another 217,000 from Croatia; 37,000 originated in Slovenia and 10,000 crossed the border from Macedonia.

"These figures are not conclusive," explained Dobrica Vulovic, commissioner of Serbia's Commissariat for Refugees. "Over 76,000 refugees headed directly for Montenegro because of families and friends waiting for them there and they are not included in the total. Also, many professionals from Bosnia and Croatia were 'adopted' by our local societies such as doctors and lawyers and they too are therefore not included. Generally, we suspect that the real number is 700,000 or more."

The overwhelming majority of the refugees, 83%, were women and children up to the age of eighteen. Very few men left because in almost all cases they remained as part of the army or local militia. This made matters even more painful because in addition to terror and loss of property and assets, families were sundered. The bewildered, often numbed women, never knew if they would ever see their husbands alive again.

Serbs naturally comprised the largest ethnic group — 84.2% but surprisingly there were 6.2% Moslems, 1.6% Croats and another 8% consisted of a mixed batch of intermarriages, Albanians, Jews, Gypsies, Bulgarians and Hungarians.

It might have seemed paradoxical that there would be Moslem and Croat refugees seeking safe haven in Serbia, but the war in Bosnia and Herzegovina was a strange one. There were moments when Croats were killing Moslems who had no choice but to flee into the protective arms of Serbs. And then the situation would reverse itself and the Croats would plead for sanctuary. To the credit of Serbia – portrayed as the arch villain in the war by the rest of the world – no Moslem or Croat was ever turned back. In fact, the wife of Bosnian Foreign Minister Haris Silajdzic, was an unusual refugee guest at a Belgrade hotel, according to Vulovic, who called the event "Serbian absurd".

"Perhaps the most important achievement of Serbia in accommodating so many people so quickly," continued the director, "was that 96.9%, or 562,000 people, were immediately accepted by families, friends and persons of good will. People, already suffering from economic hardship, opened up their homes and wallets for those less fortunate. Families were taken in and never questioned about their ethnic origins or religion. It was a high moment for Serbia."

Vulovic said that the people who arrived, particularly from Croatia, were in dreadful condition, many of them having spent months in the woods before they could safely cross over into Serbia.

"They needed everything – from clothing, immediate medical treatment, food, a place to stay. The children required educational facilities and, in some cases, trained psychologists. Many of the people had been terribly brutalized."

Vulovic estimated that his government spent well over one billion dollars in 1992 for refugee relief work. "Because of the condition of the economy, the state cannot absorb all the costs. There used to be help from outside relief agencies, but 75% of this aid was discontinued in 1992 because of increased sanctions. It was strange, but the UN was victimizing the victims."

Vulovic penned an appeal on April 27, 1993, to Mrs. Sadako Ogata, UN High Commissioner for Refugees. He stated that "refugees are being punished merely because they had sought refuge in Serbia".

"Even in instances where humanitarian aid to the refugees was permitted to be assembled," he said, "bureaucracy and bad will often prevented the material from arriving. Many trucks, in fact hundreds, with all the proper documentation, were stopped at the borders of Austria, Germany and Hungary and were forced to return to their points of origin."

About twenty kilometers north of Belgrade, in the autonomous region of Vojvodina where many of the inhabitants were ethnic Hungarians, I visited the refugee center of Pancevo. It wasn't a very impressive complex although everything appeared clean and neat. One building dominated the flat landscape. It had a community sitting room over-shadowed by a television set, barracks-type accommodations with between 8-12 beds per room, a small kitchen and dining room. A year ago, when the center was established, there were 450 people living there. When I arrived, only 170 remained – the rest had somehow managed to find more private accommodations.

Across the road was a sports field. There was no school within walking distance of the center so children were bussed to the town.

Nearly everything, except administrative duties, was performed by the refugees themselves who were responsible for cleaning, hygiene, policing the outside area, preparing and serving food. Although fed and clothed, the refugees received no money at all. If they wanted extras, like cigarettes or chocolate, they had to find part-time work outside – an almost impossible mission because of the high unemployment and paucity of jobs.

I spoke to one dark-haired woman, mother of two children, in her mid-thirties, who appeared particularly sullen. She was seated on her bed alone, staring vacantly at the walls when I intruded. She had a home once and it was gone. She had a brother once and he was dead. She had a husband once, she said, "and he will soon be dead".

"And what do you want?" I asked.

"I want to die," she replied simply.

In another room, I met Branka Jovic who was carrying a particularly handsome young man of four named Alexander. She told me that she was grateful for all the assistance she had received, but there was no hope left in her eyes. She had come from a prosperous Serbian village in Bosnia where her family had been successful farmers for hundreds of years. She described the home that once was, capacious because there were always so many friends and guests dropping over. She confided that she had always had many Moslem friends, "ever since I was a child in school".

Branka didn't want to talk about what happened — only that the house was destroyed and the village razed to the ground, the animals stolen or slaughtered, the church desecrated and then pulled down, the wells poisoned. When she and her husband separated, she knew it might be forever. There was rage in his eyes when they kissed for the last time. His whole life had been taken away from him. The only thing left was to kill Moslems.

"What do you do all day?" I asked.

"I attend to my child. I clean. Sometimes I help with the cooking. Mostly I dream of my home and I worry about my husband."

"How long have you been here?" I questioned.

"Many months. I forget sometimes exactly how long."

"Have you heard from your husband?"

"Two letters. He is not a writing man. He is a farmer. We were all farmers."

"How much longer do you think you will be here?"

"How much longer will the war continue?" she replied.

There was a young man, about twenty-three, who was working in administration in the center. Jura Bugarski was a soldier in eastern Slavonija in Croatia when the European Community recognized Slovenia and Croatia as independent countries.

"I knew there was going to be a lot of trouble," he said,

"and I promised myself that when I was released, I would try to find humanitarian work to perform. There would be enough killing. Someone would have to show mercy as well. So I started working in Pancevo in May of last year. I will continue working with refugees until I find the opportunity to leave my country. There is no future here for me or, for that matter, for any other young man."

I had heard that refrain before. Many young people, including a high percentage of professionals, were leaving Yugoslavia and more were waiting for visas.

"Do you want to leave?" I asked.

"There is no future for people like me," he replied simply.

There was a crew-cutted teenager at the door who was introduced to me as Milan, yet another refugee from Bosnia. It was the same story all over again. Father fighting. Mother subsisting on charity. Home burned. Relatives killed.

"Will you finish high school?"

"No," he replied glumly.

"Then what will you do?"

"I'll go back to my village in Bosnia."

"But your home is no longer there. It was destroyed."

"It doesn't matter."

"Then what will you do?" I repeated.

"I'll kill Moslems."

It took only three minutes to reach the Pancevo Sanitarium for the Blind. I wondered how long it took some of the others to arrive there.

In a large garden, adjacent to several one-storey buildings where the patients were quartered, there was a tight knot of about thirty to forty people. Informed of my arrival, the reception committee began clapping wildly when the director, Ljubica Mucibabic, announced that I was among them.

A tall, splendid-looking man, perhaps about fifty, rose proudly, leaned effortlessly against his cane and then, to the accompaniment of an accordion, began reciting Serbian poetry, aiming his words carefully at the approximate place I should be sitting. Offered a translation, I declined for the moment. There was so much passion and pathos in those words. In his terrible blindness, inflicted on him by a sniper's bullet, the sightless musicologist from Sarajevo spoke about the fate of a people destined always to absorb the first lunge, the first foreign lance, the first cruel attack. He was telling me — all that for him remained of the rest of the world — that although his nation reeled from the wounds of the fields of Kosovo, the spirit of Serbia was never vanquished. Serbia, he said, as his voice rose, was the vanguard of Christian civilization. There was so much blood and so much pain and so much heroism and so many tears. The widows and orphans were endless. But Serbia would never falter, never die.

Even before I was told the meaning of the mysterious words that filled the Pancevo garden that day like a chalice overflowing with dark wine, I knew that I was confronted not with a blind man, but with the indomitable spirit of a nation that would simply never be subdued.

Two women appeared next, singing the folk music taught to them as children in the Serbian villages of eastern Slavonija, a hotly contested region torn from Croatia by the war. They came from different villages, I was informed later by my genial hostess, but fate had conspired that they should end their sightless days together in Vojvodina.

Goran, another Bosnian Serb blinded by a sniper's bullet to the head, left the other patients and sought out my hands so that we could touch. His wound was cruel. There was an uneasiness about his disfigurement.

"You are my only hope," he said as the others tried to hush him.

He would not be mollified, however. There was too much agony burned into the unseeing sockets of his face.

"You are my only hope. You are my last chance. You must tell me why they hate the Serbs. I cannot rest without knowing. With my eyes, my family is also gone so I must know about this hatred so I can sleep again."

He held my arm very tightly, grasping the last flotsam in a turbulent sea.

"Are you treated well?" I asked.

"No," he shook his head. "They are not kind to me. They don't give me enough cigarettes."

"I am sorry to hear that," I commiserated.

"You must tell the President of Serbia that Goran is not getting enough cigarettes. Tell him also that I am not an animal. And tell the Moslems that I have friends. And they will avenge me. But mostly tell the President about the cigarettes."

I promised I would try and so he released me at last.

There was a middle-aged nurse, dressed uncharacteristically in black, who seemed particularly responsive to the needs of the patients. She appeared always to be helping them, touching and caressing them, substituting the warmth of touching for the loss of sight.

I learned later precisely why she was dressed in black. On July 3, 1991, her only son, Vojkan Obradinov, just a little over twenty and performing his compulsory eighteen-month military service at the time in Slovenia, was attacked in his open armored personnel carrier by a band of irregulars. Explosives were thrown into the vehicle, stunning everyone instantly except Obradinov who was conscious, but bleeding badly from multiple wounds.

"I learned later from the testimony of observers," the nurse related sorrowfully, "that my son pleaded for medical attention. His Slovenian attackers laughed at him. They let him bleed to death."

Private Vojkan Obradinov was the first fatality of the war.

Although Slovenia seceded from Yugoslavia with no real warfare and without armed struggle, forty-three Yugoslav soldiers were killed by the Slovenian militia before the army completed its evacuation.

Jura, who had continued with me from the refugee center,

said that his brother narrowly escaped death there as well. "He had to flee across the border into Austria. It took months before he could get back to us."

I sympathized with the nurse for her loss. She smiled thinly and replied, "If they are civilized people, then I don't want to be one of them."

By that time I was a little overwrought, but nothing could persuade the director or her nurse to concede the coffee and cake, especially prepared "for the famous Greek writer".

"You must tell the Greek people," my hostess insisted, "how grateful we all are for their support and friendship. We do not have many international friends these days and the Greeks have proven to be the best."

Well, I promised myself, I will at least tell my wife and family and our friends. Having successfully avoided learning the language after six years in the country, it seemed ironic that I had been so successfully Hellenized in a little Yugoslav hamlet.

Ljubica Mucibabic, who had the polished cheeks and laughing, mischievous eyes of a Slavic princess in a fairytale, said that politics, the war in Bosnia and the threats from Zagreb were very much on the minds of the blind patients. "Some were war casualties as you know. Others were born with congenital blindness and then there were others who were afflicted with tumors and other illnesses that robbed them of their sight."

I asked how the war had affected the institution.

"We are suffering like the rest of Serbia," she answered simply. "There are no drugs in the country and so there are no drugs for us. There is little public money so we have to do with less. And then we have the blind from the war. It is not just medicine they need. They require comforting and love. They must be taught that losing sight does not make them less human beings."

From the expression on his face, I could see that my young friend, Jura was perplexed.

"There is something I don't understand," the emigrant-to-be complained. "No one in Serbia believes that all the right is with us. We know that when guilt must be distributed, we will also get our fair share. Serbs are not angels and Moslems and Croats are not devils.

"But the whole world seems to think differently. The outsiders know nothing about what is happening here and blame us for everything. Can you explain this phenomenon?"

"Not yet," I replied. "But maybe soon. In the meantime, as a representative of your generation, as a soldier who fought for his country and as a Serb who has decided to live elsewhere because of conditions here, I would like to ask you something. Do you hate?"

"Not really," Jura answered. "Certainly, I don't hate Croats or Moslems. Perhaps, if I hate anyone, it is Germans and Austrians. They, more than anyone else, destroyed my country — and my hopes."

Goran was waiting for me as I prepared to leave. "Don't forget to tell the President about my cigarettes," he whispered conspiratorially.

"I won't," I assured him.

# CHAPTER XIII
# THE POLITICS OF EDUCATION

"There is no doubt that the sanctions and the international isolation imposed on us have conspired to negatively affect all aspects of education in the country," according to Prof. Danilo Markovic, Vice Prime Minister and Minister for Education of Serbia.

"The quality of our lectures has dropped," he continued, "because we don't have the ability to obtain external information. There used to be a rich movement of scientists and academicians between Yugoslavia and the rest of the world. This has ceased completely. There used to be a large student exchange program. Now there is none. Yugoslavia was once central to the exchange of ideas and information. And this too is finished now."

Not only an academician of major standing with graduate degrees in both law and economy, Markovic had the dubious pleasure of having survived five major political shakeups in the government. "When I retire," his eyes twinkled, "I'll write a book entitled, 'All My Prime Ministers'."

Author of fifteen books, Markovic said, "I don't see why young people should be made to suffer. There is no connection absolutely between education and politics. In addition to the harm the sanctions have done to our own children, we have had to absorb many refugee children into the school system. Our ability to teach properly is slowly being drained. Classes are overcrowded. Optimally, there should not be more than thirty to a class. Now we have forty. The quality of the education suffers when students have to share desks."

In 1993, there were 200,000 students enrolled in universities and colleges throughout Serbia and another half-million lower grade students.

"I am very depressed by the situation. Whatever we try to do, we are pinned down by circumstance. Our teachers have very low salaries. They can barely manage and yet we expect so much from them. We can't replace learning equipment or buy new laboratory gear. Winters in Belgrade are cold, but last year we had to decrease school heating to 18C because of the shortage of fuel.

"Sanctions forced us to change school schedules so now youngsters are required to learn on Saturdays as well."

Several months prior to my interview with Markovic, Belgrade had vigorously protested UN actions which deleteriously affected the "Rights of the Child". The Federal Republic of Yugoslavia stated: "The social climate in which the children are growing...is laden with fear, anxiety, animosity, hate, sorrow and insecurity. The war conflicts and abrupt and deep social, political and economic changes — the interruption of communications with relatives and friends from other republics, the growing number of pressures, the slow penetration of truth about one's own land and on the genocide carried out against it — all leave grave mental and psychological scars.

"... The right to education is threatened primarily due to the difficult financial situation in this field as well as the total interruption of international cooperation on issues related to education."

One additional, strongly-worded statement to the UN in that same document touched upon an educational issue which had become a bombshell. "Children of Albanian nationality in the autonomous province of Kosovo and Metohija have been denied by the members of their nationality, who lead a nationalistic and secessionist policy, the right to attendance of regular, legally set up schools. There is no objective or real cause for such an action since education in the mother tongue has been provided for and is guaranteed by the Republic of Serbia and, just like everybody else, the members of the Albanian nationality can participate in any level of the drawing up of school curricula as well as in overall school management. The right to education, and the right to education of youth in the Albanian nationality, should be protected from threats emanating from an unacceptable polarization carried out by nationalists and separatists in the ranks of the Albanian nationality."

"And so Prof. Markovic," I asked, "Minister of Education for Serbia, what's happening?"

A heavy set and amiable pedagogue, the Minister sighed deeply before replying. "History is not only the teacher of life. It is also the torturer. Until 1974, there was only one law for all of Serbia. Then new legislation changed all that. (As Tito aged, he became more Croatian and less Yugoslavian!) Kosovo suddenly was granted special rights that went beyond its entitlement as an autonomous region of Serbia. It could have its own national language, for example. All future school training was to be in Albanian. There was a numerus clausus established for the University of Pristina both for pupils and teaching staff. Serbian professors, even if they were born in the region, even if their families had been in Kosovo for generations, were forced to leave higher education. And the way the Albanians were reproducing, Serbian students had almost no chance at all of being accepted. Note the irony! Serbs were excluded from a university in Serbia."

Markovic paused. "This conversation both unsettles my nerves and makes me thirsty. Will you join me in a *rakija*?"

What started as an educational problem in Kosovo was suddenly politicized. The University of Pristina represented more than a mere institution of higher learning for Albanian separatists who despite all of Tito's favors and favoritism, wanted the region melded into Albania. It rapidly became a staging ground where Albanian nationalism could be spawned, where a cadre of new leaders could be educated and then thrust into key and often pivotal positions. The issue was no longer culture or minority status or even nationalism. It was the very future of Kosovo.

Slowly, and in keeping with Tito's strange policies, even training manuals were imported from Albania. Year by year, contact was strengthened with Tirana, weakened with Belgrade. Although the university was originally mandated to meet the regional requirements of the entire area, 90% of the students and nearly all the teaching staff were Albanians.

"This horrible situation continued until 1987," continued Markovic, "when Belgrade finally realized that the situation was intolerable. We Serbians were digging our own graves. Kosovo could have provincial autonomy, but it could not substitute for the State. There could no longer be two standards in Serbia — one for the whole republic and another for a region within the State. The same standards, particularly in the realm of education, had to apply to everyone."

Despite the toughening attitude of Belgrade, however, minority rights in Kosovo and throughout the rest of the Republic of Serbia, were scrupulously preserved. Primary and secondary school education would continue to be in the Albanian language if that represented the desire of most of the people. "But we went even farther," said Markovic who was also Minister of Education at that time. "We agreed that courses in history, language, art and music — in fact all subjects involved with preserving national identity — would be specially tailored to the ethnic requirements of the Albanians. I invited local Albanian officials and academicians to join me in establishing new educational criteria for the university which would be acceptable to all sides. I offered to bring in internationally accepted educators to assist in formulating a program that would fit the needs of Kosovo without abrogating the sovereign rights of Serbia. Despite all the efforts and negotiations to reach a reasonable compromise, the lines hardened. The Albanian position was put in simple terms. They, and only they, would decide on the criteria for education in Kosovo."

The changes passed by Belgrade for uniform standards throughout the republic were enacted into law in 1990. Ethnic

Albanians in Kosovo reacted by breaking off all contact with the central government. Teachers and pupils were withdrawn from primary and secondary schools. The University of Pristina was virtually closed when Albanian students and teaching staff left in a bloc. A shadow system of education was introduced whereby courses and studies were provided in private homes and in club houses by Albanian teachers for Albanian students. And, at the sametime, a war of words and propaganda was launched since the central government in Belgrade was already under siege from the nationalists of Croatia and Slovenia who themselves were pushing vigorously for independence and secession.

The irony here was that both Zagreb and Ljubljana had excoriated Serbia in the past for wasting too much money on the ethnic Albanians in Kosovo and were particularly annoyed over the funds earmarked for the University of Pristina. And so education in Kosovo became the cause célèbre of almost everyone, Croats and Slovenes complaining that too much was being done, ethnic Albanians insisting that they were the victims of cultural genocide.

"The local Albanians formed a bloc. They simply refused to negotiate or talk to us," said Markovic. "They thought that even acknowledging that there was another side to the dispute weakened their position. And, in the meantime, they were illegally and illicitly issuing diplomas signed by the 'Republic of Kosovo' which was what the whole thing was about anyway.

"If for no other reason than the sake of their children, I asked them to reopen the schools. Despite the parallel education, the children were suffering. They were being deprived of a real education. I was even ready to recognize and give credit for the shadow education they had foisted on the population. Again they refused. So there was really not much more I could do. I could not be a minister of the Republic of Serbia and yet countenance the use of education for separatist and political goals. I felt and feel an obligation to the people to resume education as quickly as possible, but this must be done under the law."

There was yet another non-military, non-political area that was hurt, and hurt badly, by the sanctions. All projects in science and technology had been postponed or frozen. Over one hundred joint scientific projects were suspended which resulted in losses of millions of dollars for Yugoslavia, according to Prof. Slobodan Unkovic, Minister of Science and Industry and a professor and former rector at the University of Belgrade.

"Our country has been excluded or prevented from obtaining information from major international installations and data bases. This will no doubt have a significant, adverse effect on the Yugoslav scientific and technological development and make it impossible to integrate successfully into world trends for years to come. It is also not possible to attend international gatherings, receive foreign magazines, exchange publications and other scientific and technological information which makes the protection of patents and licenses very difficult or impossible."

The prevailing situation induced a large number of young Yugoslav technocrats to seek employment elsewhere, causing a brain drain that will adversely effect the economy and the country for years to come. Since the end of 1991, 181 faculty left universities for positions abroad and the number of graduate students accepting foreign offers was growing steadily. Undoubtedly pleasing to the European Community and Washington, the sanctions and boycotts really did work, hurting Yugoslavia more with each passing month.

Since the imposition of restrictions and sanctions, the following damage was reported: Overall industrial production fell by over 40%. The decline was even steeper during the first half of 1993. Exports declined 46% between 1991 and 1992 while sales to developed markets dropped 54% for the same period. The balance of payment deficit multiplied over 2.5 times in the 1991/92 period. Unemployment among the working and educated population increased by a margin of over 22% in 1992 — 60% of those recorded having graduated from universities or completed higher or secondary schools.

If UN Secretary-General Boutros Boutros-Ghali needed further evidence that his sanctions were succeeding in humbling and humiliating a country which had almost fought the Turks to a standstill in 1389 and had stymied the Nazis from 1941 onward and had ripped the first tear in the Iron Curtain, then he should have really enjoyed the chaos, discomfiture and suffering which was inflicted in the most elementary forms of transportation.

All EC members had banned, by special directive, entry into their territories of both Yugoslav buses and foreign registration plates carrying Yugoslav passengers. This had been based on a directive prohibiting financial transactions which had absolutely nothing to do with the transportation of goods and passengers. The most ardent applier of the sanctions was, not surprisingly, Germany, which heaped on limitations that even the most febrile geniuses in the United Nations could not imagine. As a result of the measure, Yugoslav citizens working abroad, either on a permanent or temporary basis, were punished for their lineage.

As mentioned earlier, the embargo put an end to regular air traffic between Yugoslavia and the world, interring the Yugoslav national carrier, JAT. Forty airplanes were mothballed, thousands of employees were thrown out of work, offices throughout the country and in the world were closed. The unhappy consequences of the edict, however, were felt not only in Yugoslavia. In 1991, 646,000 passengers arrived in the country and 692,000 left by air. Yugoslavia was serviced not only by its own national carrier, but by the major foreign airlines. Two years later, if your destination was Belgrade, then your penultimate touchdown was in Sofia or Budapest and hours of excess bus transportation was the reward for stepping over into Serbian soil.

Not that it would really matter, but the Serbian Academy of Sciences and Arts had something to say about what was happening.

"The Academy is concerned about the interruption of scientific and artistic contacts, resulting in numerous acts, such as the refusal of subscriptions to scholarly journals, the purchase of software, or the refusal to accept scientific papers for international journals. Traditional cooperation between the Academy and scientific institutions in the countries of the West, effected successfully for decades, has been completely suspended. This is in total contradiction with a number of documents of commitment signed by the governments of all civilized countries, and also by the highest scientific institutions, on the freedom of scientific communication.

"All this raises the following question: On what moral ground, and in the name of what human principles, is the international community committing this terror against the citizens of Yugoslavia? Is it indeed of great respect to the future of human society that the highest bodies of the United Nations are prepared to disregard, for political reasons, basic principles of international law, even the UN charter, as they have demonstrated by precipitously imposing sanctions, thereby imperilling the existence of an entire state and destroying its prospects for the future? And all this without any seriously founded arguments.

"Convinced that this declaration from the Serbian Academy of Sciences and Arts will have difficulties to penetrate the information blockade, the Academy has decided to send it individually to scientists and scientific organizations throughout the world."

But even in the darkest despair a little humor could emerge and this had to do with a very officious letter from the Walt Disney Co. to the editor of the Belgrade newspaper, Politika.

"As you may be aware, the United States Government, the European Community and the United Nations have all recently enacted embargoes with respect to the conduct of business in the former Socialist Federal Republic of Yugoslavia. Each such embargo imposes penalties on any company which continues to do business in such region and the United States Government embargo provides for very serious penalties for United States' companies which do not abide by such embargo. The Walt Disney Company is affected by all such embargoes.

"Accordingly, Politika is hereby instructed to immediately terminate all activities under the agreement until further notice..."

And so it was that Mickey Mouse too was mobilized in the battle against Serbia.

CHAPTER XIV
# THE FIELDS OF KOSOVO

Certainly the ethnic disputes over Kosovo were not invented in Washington DC or United Nations Plaza. Tito had made his own unique contribution to the destabilization of southern Serbia long before the American State Department was made aware that a toothsome ethnic imbroglio existed in a distant wedge of the Balkans. Serbs and Albanians were exchanging rhetoric and accusations even prior to the new teutonic interest in the region.

One of the more dramatic issues of the dispute centered around education, but substantive differences were much deeper and much wider than whether a syllabus came from Tirana or Belgrade and what courses would be taught in which languages. The problem was politics, pure and simple.

Heartened by the breakup of the former Yugoslavia, encouraged by the venomous, anti-Serb stand adopted by the European Community, the United States and the United Nations, witness to the economic enervation of the central government in Belgrade, the Albanians of Kosovo were almost impelled to act more radically by the welter of events. Claiming a population of almost two million strong, or 90% of the province, the Albanians wanted first an independent state and then merger with the contiguous homeland. All very simple!

The Serbs, however, took another approach to the problem, even more passionate than their Moslem adversaries. Kosovo was Kitchener in Khartoum, Davie Crocket on the Alamo ramparts, the charge of the Light Brigade in the Crimea. It was old Serbia, the cradle of their culture, the first line of defense of Christianity. The fields of Kosovo, just a few kilometers outside of the regional capital of Pristina, were irrigated by Serbian blood 604 years earlier when the Ottomans thrust their long spear into the belly of Europe. Better a cataclysm that would eclipse the entire nation, than the surrender of the holy ground!

If a Serb expounded, there was only a handful of nomadic, unruly Albanians in the area when the battle of Kosovo was fought. Question an Albanian, however, and he will state that his Illyrian ancestors entered the Balkan peninsula sometime between the end of the Bronze Age and the beginning of the Iron Age or about 1,000 BC or 1,600 years before the South Slavs ever finished their migration. And who said the Albanians were the Illyrians, a coastal people, since there were no original Albanian words for sea or fish or anything that had to do with water? countered the Serb. But there was proof, replied the Albanian, that the whole Serbian myth of Kosovo was conjured up in the Nineteenth Century by pseudohistoriography.

So it was better to leave the dark questions to the scholars. Modern history, however, was another matter.

The provincial border of Kosovo was about 350 kilometers from Belgrade, but much closer to Serbia's second largest city of Nis. Pristina lay 30 kilometers deeper, only 100 kilometers from the border with Albania and roughly 200 kilometers to the capital of Tirana. There were no signs, but it was easy to determine the precise moment of crossing into the province — the road was infinitely better. My companion on the journey smiled wryly.

"For years," he said, "this was the problem. Serbia bankrupted itself in order to placate the population of Kosovo. It began with Tito and then the Serbian politicians didn't want troubles with the local Albanians so they spent large amounts of money also. The results, you see. Kilometers of pot holes on one side and a beautiful neat highway on the other."

I really didn't know what to expect as we neared Pristina. There had been gun battles between the local Albanians and the police and army. All the endless rhetoric from the world capitals hadn't helped either, I was sure. Clinton had actually threatened Serbia if it "invaded" Kosovo. Obviously, his advisors on the Balkans were so ill-advised, they were an embarrassment. There wasn't a centimeter of Kosovo uncontrolled by the army. And how do you manage "to invade" your own country?

Like the adjacent countryside, Kosovo was either flat or marked by gentle, rolling hills. The land was mostly arid. There were no rivers or even streams nearby, no lofty mountains to catch the winter snow. And the climate was often extreme – brutally hot in the summer, frigid throughout the winter.

What had changed after crossing the provincial border was the people. The Moslem men and women dressed differently, favoring skullcaps and shawls. There was also a very distinctive look about the Albanian young, something I had noticed in Greece as well. Many were light-haired, but it was a color somewhere between blond and brown. There was also an expression on their faces which seemed characteristic. What was it – weariness, anger, rage? Whatever their origins, the Albanians were something different in Europe, an ethnic branch that bore no resemblance to the rest of the tree. Even the language was strange. Undoubtedly, Indo-European, but unrelated to any other language group on the continent.

At first glance, Pristina, with its approximate population of 200,000, looked a good deal more Levantine than western. There were minarets everywhere and the closely packed homes on the bluffs around the city reminded me of Turkey.

The key to my introduction into the life of Kosovo was a Serb named Bosko Drobnjak, a thirty-year veteran of the area and a well-known journalist and radio and television writer. At that precise moment, he was representing the information services of the province.

"I guess you could define the situation as tense, but quiet," he explained from a chair opposite me at Pristina's Grand Hotel. "The two communities – Albanians and Serbs – live lives that are totally apart, completely separated from each other. Most Albanians simply don't recognize the State of Serbia they are living in. They refuse to take part in any official function or capacity. They boycott secondary schools and institutions of higher learning. They refuse to take part in any census so there is no way of determining their actual numbers. They pay no taxes, refuse compulsory military service, won't pay rent to a Serb. They disregard traffic fines the same way they won't pay state taxes for television sets. If there is a one-way street heading south, they travel on it north."

I was almost incredulous. "And they get away with it?"

Drobnjak shook his shoulders. "If we try to enforce the law, they scream 'genocide', invite the wire services and foreign television and the next day we are accused of 'ethnic cleansing' and warned that the United Nations will take actions against us."

There were certain tacit rules to the dispute over who controlled what. Although illegal, everyone owned guns, lots of them. Albanian radicals could strike out at the police or army but, until then at least, civilian targets were spared. During the last attack against a police station twenty days earlier, two policemen were killed and five others were badly wounded. A later investigation determined that the weapons used were of Chinese manufacture, another way of saying that they were smuggled in from Albania which was a long-time recipient of Chinese military largesse.

"We have a long, open border with Albania," Drobnjak explained, "that is almost impossible to control properly. There is a steady flow of illegal Albanians into Kosovo. We catch a few of them and send them back, but most get away and are subsequently hidden by other Albanians. Because of the steady infiltrations from Tirana, we know that Kosovo has become a major center for illegal drugs and arms. There is an Albanian Mafia distributing major shipments of drugs in New York which is operating as a state within a state here. These criminals have their own laws and their own rules. They try to avoid us, but they terrorize the rest of their people."

Serbs residing in Kosovo felt tense – and with good reason. "People are social creatures," a Serbian woman who had been born in Pristina told me later. "Here we live together, but very much apart also. In Kosovo, people are not people, but Christians and Moslems. We know they don't like us. We don't particularly love them either."

Most Serbs rejected the idea that Kosovo was a powder keg waiting for ignition. Actually, there was never an instance in history where Albanians and Serbs fought each other.

"Of course," continued the journalist, "there is one important qualification to consider – that there are no outside influences or powers trying to worsen the situation. If that happens, all bets are off. Bosnia would be considered a picnic compared with what might happen here."

One politician with some strong views on the subject was Slobodan Ignjatovic, Minister of Information for the Federal Republic of Yugoslavia. A trained journalist and editor, the fifty-six-year-old politician was sure that America had strong economic interests in Kosovo.

"The Americans know more about the natural resources under the earth in Kosovo than our federal government. While the Germans have political interests in our area, the Americans are motivated by economics which is what the United States is all about anyway.

"Kosovo is unraveling because the threads are being pulled elsewhere. Nonetheless, although I anticipate problems and a continuation of the tension, I do not expect a major calamity – yet. Something is happening in Kosovo though, that has never occurred before. Albanians who were traditionally tradesmen, small-time farmers, and drug and arms smugglers are slowly being redirected into industry. For the first time in their history, they are becoming manufacturers. And so what does all this mean?

"It means that Tirana believes that the present generation cannot carry off a revolution successfully, even with some foreign assistance, even with the world press on its side. Albanians need to be better prepared and that is precisely what they are accomplishing now."

There was nothing monolithic about the approximately two million ethnic Albanians, almost all Sunni Moslems, who inhabited the region. Radio journalist Ilijaz Duka, a sixty-two-year-old employee of the state radio and a member of the Executive Board of the Association for Common Life in Serbia and Yugoslavia, would have been branded an "Uncle Tom" if the issue was Mississippi and not a lonely Balkan outpost.

"We are patriots, but we are not chauvinists. We want to live together with the Serbs, not fight against them. If Albanians do what the radicals ask of them, namely to rebel against the sovereign power of Serbia, then there will be a cataclysm for both people. The Albanians will be killed and the Serbs will be blamed."

Elaborating further on his postion, Duka asked, "If the schools and universities were suddenly barred to all minorities in Kosovo, why weren't the others thrown out like the Gypsies and the Turks and why are my children and grandchildren still in school? This is the best refutation to the radicals.

"There are many Albanians living in Greece. Do they have one school in the Albanian language? Do they fly the Albanian flag as they do here? Is the Albanian language recognized? The answers are all 'no' which is why Greece has no Albanian problem."

Duka, born in Tirana, had some hard words for the fatherland as well. "As a child we were taught a poem. I remember it to this day. 'Cry, cry my eyes. For the Kamrija fields of Epirus (Greece). And the fields of Kosovo'. The patriotism we were taught was expansionistic. It is not a very healthy attitude."

The man in charge of the Democratic League of Kosovo, Ibrahim Rugova, was not available for comment at his backstreet headquarters because, I was informed apologetically, "he was busy with the American attaché, and afterward there was a delegation from France waiting to see him and then there was a Dutch photographer who had been promised a meeting days earlier." I was a mite disappointed because I had heard much about the radical leader who was also a writer and academician, but another member of the League's Presidency — Prof. Rexhep Ismajli — a genial, academic host, offered to substitute.

"Yugoslavia does not exist," he said. "It is the figment of the imagination of Belgrade. We have two main missions now and they go hand in hand — the democratization of the society in Kosovo and the liberation of our land from Serbia. Afterward, we would probably like to rejoin with Albania, but that is afterward.

"Kosovo is the last colony in Europe. There are only 400,000 Montenegrins and they have their own state. We are 2,800,000 strong and treated as prisoners in our own country. Fortunately, we are not only democratic, we are non-violent. We can take our time because we will win eventually."

There was a great deal of activity in the little room where we were seated. Phones were constantly ringing — from New York, from Oslo. There was a cadre of young people about, moving like termites from room to room from telephone to telephone. This was the nerve center.

"There is lots of sympathy for us in the United States. Public opinion in Germany and France is completely in our favor. And this is true also of Scandinavia, Holland, Belgium and Austria. They all understand our point of view. They identify with our struggle.

"Almost all of us here are either students or professors. We were all brutally thrown out of the university because the authorities suddenly insisted on preventing teaching in our Albanian national language. In September, 1992, alone, 840 teachers were expelled from the university. Since then we have been conducting private lessons in homes on all levels so that the children will not suffer. There were 450,000 Albanian children effected as well as all the teachers. We teach for nothing. We are not paid."

The ousted professor explained that financial support was obtained from friends in the United States and Europe working under the aegis of a special "Solidarity Council" which provided help through fund raising. He also admitted that there were some contributions from local shopkeepers and businessmen.

These statements were in sharp contrast with the views expressed the day earlier by Drobnjak who claimed that "money was exported back to Kosovo from the drug Mafia in New York for services rendered and that local Albanians were obliged to tithe between 20-30% of their income to the movement — whether they liked it or not".

The Albanian academician stressed that Kosovo was already "quasi-independent" and that the only real control left to the Serbs was exerted through the army and police. He said the league, only three years old, was gaining strength every day, refusing even to comment on Albanians in opposition. "We are convinced that we have a right to our own state. The Serbian authorities understand only force. The two people most guilty for what has happened here are Milosevic and Papovic, the rector of the university."

The rector of the university, Prof. Radivoje Papovic, was a serious, Kosovo-born scholar who had early achieved international stature as a leading biologist.

"If my former students and staff are good at anything these days," he smiled, "it is in the field of propaganda. The problems didn't arise because of any particular edict from Belgrade. There were troubles even before the 1990 boycott. Earlier, for example, the Albanians walked out of the university because we were supposed to have been 'poisoning the air'. All along, they had only one motive — separatism. The 'human rights issue' was and is a simple smoke screen. They were making troubles when the President of Kosovo was Albanian, when the local legislature was almost entirely Albanian, when nearly all the professors were Albanian, when it was virtually impossible for a Serb to obtain tenure or achieve a higher academic standing. About 70% of the population of Kosovo is under seventeen. That means that education is of paramount importance. The young people deserve an education, a real one, and it is available and ready for them. All the Albanians have to do is acknowledge one simple truth — there is one law for everyone."

There were two dates that figured prominently in the Kosovo controversy — 1974 when Tito virtually abrogated Serbian rights to the Albanians and 1988 when Slobodan Milosevic, already a key player in Serbian politics, decided on one law and one republic.

"Before Milosevic," the rector passionately claimed, "the unspoken task of the university was to 'Albanize' all the students. We underwent a period of tremendous national humiliation. New maps were provided which substituted Albanian names for Serbian locations. Churches were identified as mosques. Organized genocide was being applied to the Serbs.

"Of course, the Albanians still love Tito. They virtually worshipped him. He took an illiterate people and gave them the façade of a nation. Just a few simple facts! There are 3.5 times more Albanian Doctors of Science in Pristina than in all of Albania. There are 4.5 times more students here than in Albania. In 1987, when the survey was conducted, our faculty of law had 160 Albanian students. In Tirana, there were only 19. For fifty years we supported our enemies. Serbia provided 100% of the finances for the university. There were 13,000 scholarships. All went to Albanians. Over 90% of all stipends were given to Albanians and the rest was not reserved exclusively for Serbs, but was divided among all the other minority groups."

The good-looking academician, still in his forties, paused for a moment before continuing.

"Tito made us ashamed of ourselves. He tried to rob us of our heritage. With Milosevic, we experienced a new chapter in our history. Suddenly, and for the first time in generations, there was a Serb who represented Serbs. We were suppressed until then, humiliated. And then finally the air was clear. We felt proud of our heritage again, proud to be Serbs."

Since a good deal of the flak about the future of Kosovo was coming from Washington, which was still threatening to do awful things to Belgrade if it "invaded" its own territory, I unearthed an interesting document that perhaps pertained also to the Kosovo impasse. It stated, in article IV, section 3, that "new states may be admitted by Congress into this Union; but no state shall be formed or erected within the jurisdiction of any other state; nor any state be formed by the jurisdiction of two or more states, or parts of states, without the consents of the legislatures of the states concerned as well as of the Congress".

The quote was from the Constitution of the United States of America.

Drobnjak, during a walk through the child-teeming city, said that the biggest of all paradoxes was that the Serbs were accused of being Communists. "An outrage," he spluttered. "Nobody has suffered more from communism than the Serbs. We are the victims and yet Europe is trying to give us a complex of guilt."

Since so many Serbs had fled in the past and because patriotism ran so deep in Kosovo, I was curious about what if any efforts were made to attract Serbs back to the region.

"There were attempts," the journalist stated, "but they were not very successful. There are no jobs here, no homes, still very few opportunities. It is hard to bring people here if you cannot provide them with minimal requirements."

For me it was interesting, perhaps even a little flattering, but both professor and journalist identified strongly with Israel. "The same problem but with different players", according to the rector.

Both sides to the Kosovo conflict had their own statistics and each accused the other, at the very least, of "cultural genocide". However, Pristina Radio and Television broadcasted daily in the Albanian language and there were six local stations doing the same. There was a daily newspaper in the language and at least four periodicals. The ethnic Albanian version, however, was markedly different, claiming that the authorities had virtually eliminated their birthright. "In Kosovo," they stated untruly, "where Albanians constitute about 90% of the population, there is no Albanian-language television or radio."

Prof. Papovic, not one to mince words, said that "violence is the best Albanian export. These are a people who, before 1915, didn't even have an alphabet. The very country was created by Germany and Austria and its first president was an Austrian. Suddenly, the Albanians have become the epitome of civilization. Everyone is concerned about them. Serbia is threatened and intimidated from the European Community and America. If you would really like to know what is the Albanians' most notable achievement, I will tell you. They have become accomplished propagandists.

"For the past fifty years this region hasn't had a single intelligent, brave Serb representing the Serbian people and Serbian interests here. Milosevic has been extraordinary for us. Through him, we know that we will not succumb to terror or threats. We must be free and we must regain our national pride and integrity."

More and more, the deeper I was permitted to delve into the strange mystery of Yugoslavia, a picture emerged in my mind. There was a tree — not all that robust, not yet sufficiently mature, but healthy and alive nonetheless. And then there was a gardener and his name was Josip Broz Tito and he loved the tree and he watered it daily. But this gardener performed a strange ritualistic act along with the water he provided. Around the perimeters of the tree, he placed poison so that life and death, nourishment and

destruction, were simultaneously transferred to the roots. It
was all very simple and a French king had said it earlier, "après
moi le deluge". Tito, most certainly a megalomaniac, could not
envisage Yugoslavia without him. So while loving his country,
he also plotted its death. And what better example could be
provided than Kosovo?

# CHAPTER XV
# ISLAMIZATION OF THE BALKANS

Wise people understand, and less wise people will one day discover, that the implications of events in the Balkans transcend the Balkans. The role of a united, thundering Germany was clear — hard even for Bonn to deny. By performing deft political manipulations in an area traditionally fractionable, client states were established and the old teutonic wish for access to the Mediterranean was achieved. Blameful or blameless, the Catholic Church was happy. Two new countries were under its spiritual aegis and Orthodoxy had been driven back east. Not too much could be said about the European Community except perhaps two hard truths. First, that the spine of the organization was unequivocably German. Next, that it was a band of wimps. And, as for the United States, its real role remained an enigma. Was America impelled by raw economic interests, as suggested by Slobodan Ignjatovic, Minister of Information for Yugoslavia, righteous wrath, as indicated by Elie Wiesel, or just old-fashioned naivety? Deep in the mess, however, was another element which was growing increasingly more pronounced — Islam.

Islamization in Bosnia began in the Fifteenth Century under the Turks. The converts were South Slavs. Their motives were a better life, an easier deal, an extra modicum of security under the mercurial Ottoman masters. Conversion was clean, straight into the Sunni faith, although some sectarian schisms arose later such as the Dervishes, active also, incidentally, in Kosovo.

One of the world's acknowledged authorities on the spread of Islam into Europe, Prof. Darko Tanaskovic, philologist with the University of Belgrade, explained that the West had a very defective picture of what Islam was all about in Bosnia.

"The impression given is a nation of assimilated Moslems, a

moderate European people, living in harmony with Catholic and Orthodox neighbors. This image might have been true fifteen years ago, but it is dangerous and erroneous now."

Although the true faith was still Marxism in 1968, the first visible cracks in the veneer of Yugoslavian communism began to appear. The six republics and two autonomous regions were all heretically and clandestinely developing national consciousness and national movements. Forbidden by the central government and outlawed by Tito, a new national awareness nonetheless arose among Serbs, Croats, Slovenes, Hungarians, Albanians.

There was nothing ethnic about the Moslems of Bosnia, but they too began to respond to the national sentiments. Although separated from Croats and Serbs only by religious differences, the Moslems felt apart and separate for years. Their customs were different. They celebrated other holidays. Islam had instilled different values.

Among the Bosnian Moslems at the time, were two distinct viewpoints. The moderates saw Islam as a religion and were far from anxious to butt heads with the government which was still fiercely anti-nationalist. Others, however, as represented by Alija Izetbegovic, were pronounced Moslem Fundamentalists, already preaching an all-pervasive Islamic way of life to the exclusion of all else.

Illegal Moslem cells had been active in Bosnia since 1939. Tito ordered a general crackdown on the extreme Moslems after the war, however, and, in 1948, Izetbegovic and many of his colleagues were arrested. He was sentenced to three years which probably saved his life because during the next major crackdown, in 1949, all four of the arrested leaders were put to death. Fortunately for him, he was still incarcerated.

Tito, in the mid-seventies, finally gave the Moslems what the majority really wanted by then — recognizable national identity. Although an atheist himself, he courted favor with Third World Moslem powers and, at small cost to himself, was willing to demonstrate good will. For Izetbegovic and his

Fundamentalist cronies, a major victory had been achieved.

Meanwhile, Izetbegovic had already written and printed his famous tract, "The Islamic Declaration", first issued to a few trusted comrades in 1970. The document was the articulation of Moslem Fundamentalist thought that was only then beginning to take hold. "No East, no West. Islam is the Best", was the underriding tenet of the small book which called for a general Moslem reawakening. "...We are announcing to friends and foes that the Moslems have decided to take the fate of the Islamic world in their own hands, and to organize that world as they wish."

"The central government in Belgrade continued to persecute the Fundamentalist Moslems, but in symmetrical proportions with other nationalist outbursts. Serbs, Croats and Slovenes were equally punished," explained Prof. Tanaskovic.

Izetbegovic was arrested again on March 24, 1983, along with twelve other Bosnian radicals. He was sentenced to fourteen years in prison although he was released after six.

"Yugoslavia had its first free elections in 1990," continued the Belgrade academician, "and by then Izetbegovic had established the Party of Democratic Action. Overt nationalism was still forbidden, although this was repealed shortly after, so the party bylaws were carefully prepared. In effect, the Bosnian Moslems had created a dual image. Inside, they were radical Moslems committed to Islamization. But looking westward, they were moderates, they were Europeans, and they were tolerant."

With an exceedingly high birthrate, the tactics of the party were evident. The Moslems of Bosnia already accounted for over 40% of the population. In a very short time, they would obtain an absolute majority and then the right – perhaps even the moral requirement, according to the Islamic Declaration – to apply the Koran to everything.

In keeping with the invaluable lessons gleaned from the public relations experiences of Slovenia and Croatia,

Izetbegovic promptly hired professional help both in the United States and Europe. Establishing the proper image in the West was considered one of the most important early objectives of the party which, from the very beginning, enjoyed the support of between 75-80% of Bosnia's Moslems.

A second Moslem political party evolved – the Moslem Bosnian Organization which later became the Liberal Bosnian Organization. Unlike Izetbegovic, it wanted less religion in government and a higher degree of tolerance for the others in the country. Few, however, were attracted to the party.

Izetbegovic courted favor – and help – from other Moslem countries and organizations from the very beginning. In August, 1991, for example, when Bosnia and Herzegovina was still an integral part of Yugoslavia, Bosnian Foreign Minister Haris Silajdzic participated in the Ministerial Meeting of the Organization of the Islamic Conference in Istanbul. He performed the same role in Dakar several months later when he attended the organization's Summit Conference.

Illustrating the drift of things, Silajdzic paid eight visits to Iran in the course of less than eighteen months while his boss visited Tehran twice and hosted a half dozen Iranian delegations.

Hamid al Ghabid, secretary general of the Islamic Conference, admitted that his organization had been engaged in Bosnia and Herzegovina long before the country was declared independent and confirmed that "a coordinated policy" had been in place since Izetbegovic's visit to Jeddah in December, 1992.

An interesting indication of Islam's growing strength in the region was the almost amazing invitation to Saudi Arabia to participate in the London Peace Conference in 1992 which was convened to find a solution to the civil war in Bosnia. "It showed both Moslem concern and clout," explained Prof. Tanaskovic.

The Bosnian Moslems made no secret of what they wanted from the very beginning – one country under their rule in

Bosnia and Herzegovina. They were outspoken about protecting minority rights in order to mollify Croatia and Serbia, but a single integral government under their control was their aim. Much bloodshed would have been avoided had they not misjudged the reactions of the Serbs and Croats who, together, formed an even larger plurality. Also, it should be recalled that the first bloodshed in the region occurred on March 1, 1992, before the recognition of Bosnia and Herzegovina. During a wedding procession in front of the Serbian Orthodox Church in Sarajevo, the bridegroom's father, Nikola Gardovic, was murdered by a band of raging Moslem nationalists and the officiating clergyman, Radenko Mikovic, was badly wounded. The Serbian flag was pulled down by the mob and burned. The next day the Serbs erected twenty barricades throughout different parts of the city.

"The Bosnian Moslems," according to the professor, "had been receiving practical support from Iran, Turkey and Saudi Arabia since 1990. They were also growing more evident and prominent in worldwide Islamic affairs such as an important meeting in Vienna, in August, 1991, where Moslems from East Europe were represented. The collapse of the Soviet Union had expanded the dimensions of Islam in Europe and Izetbegovic was quick to capitalize on the phenomenon.

"Moslem students were invited to Sarajevo to continue their Islamic studies and to prepare themselves for religious work in the future. Izetbegovic was committed to the idea that Sarajevo would become the stronghold of Islam in Europe, convinced that sooner or later the Serbs and Croats would cancel themselves out of the picture. He calculated that he would have an absolute majority in five to ten years and that with the proper application of pressure, many of the Christians would be encouraged to emigrate."

In order to make points with the rest of the Islamic world and written into his Islamic Declaration, Izetbegovic chastised Jews and Zionists for taking actions against the Palestinians that were "inhuman and ruthless and shortsighted".

"This policy in Palestine has thrown down the gauntlet to all the Moslems the world over. Jerusalem is not only a Palestinian question, nor solely an Arab question. It is the question of all Moslem nations. To keep Jerusalem, the Jews would have to defeat Islam and Moslems and that is — thank God — beyond their powers."

Since Israeli public opinion had, to no small measure, been brainwashed by torrents of one-sided media propaganda, Izetbegovic's next statement on the subject was worth recalling.

"If they (the Israelis) continue along the same road guided by arrogance, which seems more likely under the present circumstances, there will be only one way out of it all for the Islamic movement and all the world's Moslems; to continue the struggle, expand it and prolong it, from day to day, from year to year, regardless of casualties and the time it would take until they are forced to cede every single inch of captured land. Any trade-offs or compromises which might call in question these elementary rights of our brothers in Palestine will be treason which can destroy even the very system of moral values underpinning our world."

"The really dramatic upsurge in Moslem Fundamentalism in Bosnia," said Prof. Tanaskovic, "occurred in tandem with the civil war. It wasn't only the Serbs who were feeling isolated and alone, so were the Bosnian Moslems. Despite international support, the presence of United Nations forces, world opinion, the simple fact was that they were being beaten steadily by the local Serb forces and forced to retreat on almost all fronts. The seeds of Fundamentalism were there for a long time and Izetbegovic was spokesman for radical Islam, but until the pressures of the war most of the local people were still not ardent. That, however, changed very rapidly."

Once it was clear that he wasn't winning the war and, in an attempt to internationalize the dilemma so that the world would impose a satisfactory solution, which for him meant political control over all of the former republic, Izetbegovic increased diplomatic contact with friends and friends-to-be. Even when he was still only the president of the presidency of Bosnia and Herzegovina, in other words, not yet the absolute leader of his state, he engaged in high-level meetings in Libya and Turkey. Subsequently, he visited Austria and then the United States in efforts to increase support.

"Izetbegovic was a very good tactician at the beginning," added Tanaskovic. "His problem was that he lost his nerves quickly. He miscalculated badly, for example, on how much protection he would be getting from the United Nations. He erred as well about how quickly and efficiently the local Serbs would mount their offensive. He was mistaken about the Croats who, he calculated, would remain his ally against the Serbs, even though it was only a marriage of convenience. When the disappointments set in, all the camouflage enacted for the West was dropped. He never used the word himself, but suddenly every mosque was filled with religious leaders calling for a *Jihad.*"

In reply to the Bosnian Moslem appeal for a holy war against the infidels, the Islamic front fractured and unraveled. Yasser Arafat and his Palestine Liberation Organization, for example, were implacably opposed to involvement, experiencing enough troubles with Hamas Fundamentalists who were imperilling authority. Hosni Mubarak of Egypt found himself in an equally difficult position. His own Fundamentalists at home were causing him great grief, having already destroyed the nation's vital tourist industry by assassinating foreigners indiscriminately. Certainly, he was willing to show sympathy for his coreligionists, but little more than that.

Libya, Syria and Iraq, while condemning Serbs and Serbia alike, were willing to provide financial assistance, but made it clear that they were non-supportive of an overt *Jihad* against Yugoslavia. Serious funding was also promised from Saudi Arabia, the Gulf States, Pakistan and Iran, but again, the call for a *Jihad* was politely deferred. Turkey was ambivalent. Although devoted to the cause of the Bosnian Moslems, Izetbegovic was regarded as far from reliable and alluring. Morocco, in the midst of its own territorial dispute, was a strong Bosnian supporter while, at the sametime, completely opposed to the secession of Kosovo.

The strongest support for a *Jihad* came from Malaysia which was also the first country to sever relations with Yugoslavia. Next in line was the Sudan which had adopted a highly visible and militant posture. Actual volunteers in the struggle against the infidels were mostly Mujahedeen from Afghanistan who were first trained in camps in Saudi Arabia as well as Kurds.

Although insisting that it was a secular republic, Turkey's role in Balkan machinations could not be underestimated, particularly since it was the Ottomans who introduced Islam to Europe in the first place.

As Germany pulled from one side, Turkey tugged from the southeast. It was, after all, the late Turkish President Turghut Ozal who proclaimed his official policy as "the fencing in of the Serbs". He also made it clear "that the Moslems in Bosnia and Herzegovina are to Turkey what the Palestinians are to the Arabs".

Expressed at the Istanbul meeting in June, 1992, of the Organization of the Islamic Conference, was Turkey's demand that direct military intervention be directed against Serbia, that the arms embargo on the Moslems in Bosnia be lifted, that a total blockade be employed and that Yugoslavia should eventually be dismantled.

At the sametime, Turkey offered maximal support and aid to Albania, the first European country to become a member of the Islamic Conference. The two countries signed a friendship treaty and a military agreement and Turkey displayed unreserved support for the separatists of Kosovo and their eventual ambition to fuse with the fatherland.

Always deft politicians, the Turks were not only expanding

their influence in Europe by adopting Moslem causes in Yugoslavia, they were also trying to intimidate Greece which had a common border with Albania. This ploy was used artfully again in Macedonia where both a large Moslem population and near economic chaos coexisted. Traditional antagonists for decades, the borders between the two countries were often disputed and unsettling, Turkey seeking "Lebensraum" at the expense of Greece in the Aegean. By increasing tensions in the north as well, Turkey exerted even greater pressures on Hellas.

# CHAPTER XVI
# THE LOST GENERATION

After the possible deaths of a couple of hundred thousand people, the uprooting of millions more, the dismemberment of a legitimate nation that had fought valiantly, U.S. Secretary of State Warren Christopher finally saw a halo of light descend at the Geneva Peace Conference during the third week of June, 1993. He publicly accused Germany of causing much of the Balkan holocaust by prematurely and rashly recognizing the former republics of Yugoslavia. Although Christopher only touched the tassels of Germany's colossal guilt, Chancellor Helmut Kohl responded angrily. How could Germany be so publicly embarrassed by a friend — an associate incidentally which gave tacit support until that very moment?

More, however, emerged from Geneva than a little friendly criticism. The world, and even Lord David Owen, finally reached the unmistakable conclusions that the Vance-Owen Plan was as dead as a dodo and so was Bosnia and Herzegovina. Alija Izetbegovic would have to settle for considerably less real estate and Senator Biden from Connecticut might have to suggest targets other than Bosnian Serbs for American bombers. The new Yugoslavia had somehow managed to endure.

But at what price? Ernest Hemingway once spoke of "a lost generation". If he were alive in 1993, he would have made good use of his talents again.

Golda Meir, Prime Minister of Israel at the time, along similar lines electrified, stunned and saddened an entire nation when she told us that perhaps we might forgive the Arabs for killing our sons, but we could never forgive them for turning our sons into their killers. When my own son came home after three years as a paratrooper, I realized how true and prophetic was her statement. It took a year on a fishing boat between Alaska and the Aleutian Islands for him to rejoin the human race.

For a whole generation of Yugoslavs, however, who were in their prime when their nation began disintegrating, when their economy burst through the ceiling, when the very name of their country became a slander, there was no tundra wasteland to wash away frustration and rage with cool, icy water. They were truly lost, victims of vindictive and foolish people who from far away buried their young dreams.

In 1990, the fates somehow conspired that thirty-two-year-old Pedga Marcus, son of a Montenegrin father and Serbian mother, graduate of the State School for Tourism, owner of a lean, dark body and easy, innocent smile, would accompany my wife and myself on a two-week journey through Yugoslavia.

Over cocktails, many of them, poor Pedga's fate was decided the night before while he slept blissfully and without any premonition of what was in store. When we finally met, he was shaking his head wonderingly.

Pedga had just about everything going for him. He was affable and clever. The Yugoslav tourist industry was burgeoning and the economy was stable and inflationless. He came from a good family, his father having been a high-ranking diplomat. He wasn't spoiled at all, but it was obvious that he knew about the good things in life.

Neither one of us knew it at the time, but we were more than fact-seeking travellers. We were participating in the last pilgrimage to a Balkan shrine called "Yugoslavia". We were breathing the heady air of revolt in Ljubljana which, a year later in July, would account for the first deaths of the war and precipitate the collapse of the country. We were privy to arms collections in Zagreb and the nocturnal arrivals of volunteers. And yet despite the unmistakable signs that there was trouble in the air, there were too many other indications that sanity would eventually prevail and that the worst scenario was a loosening of the bonds of federation.

Drinking beer in Bled, under the massive shadows of the southern Alps, how could anyone believe that Yugoslavia was doomed? Certainly, there was nothing very prescient about Pedga or me. We were sure everything would turn out well.

"It has to," my young colleague smiled. "I have a girlfriend in Zagreb and I go boating every other year off the Adriatic coast. No crazy war is going to spoil all that for me."

Thus I was assured that Yugoslavia would remain inviolate and that quaffing beer was a more intelligent pursuit than analyzing Balkan politics.

Predicting the future of Pedga, however, was easier. Surely, he would marry before long. There would be a child registered as "Yugoslav" because ethnic differences had to vanish, the sooner the better, for the country truly to grow together. There would be promotions in tandem with hair loss and someday he might even develop a pot belly not so different from my own. In other words, he had a good future ahead.

If there was one constant about the Serbian people, it was their refusal to complain. Stoicism was infused into their Slavic genes and it took crowbars or liters of *rakija* or a feather under the nose to pry real information out of them. And Pedga, three years later, was no exception. It took awhile, but eventually words were released, confidences exchanged.

"As conditions grew worse, less people visited the country and tourism was hit very badly. The government agency I was working for began discharging the newer employees after awhile and I was beginning to wonder what would happen to me," he said.

"Well, one day my manager called me in and said that I was to be transferred to a posting a hundred kilometers from Belgrade. There were no apartments available there so I would have to commute. There would be no additional money for the extra travel. In fact, I would have to take a pay cut. They were asking me to quit, so I quit."

Since privatization was the rage at the time, Pedga and his

closest friend invested their savings in a little restaurant about ninety minutes from the capital. It was an inauspicious investment. Political jitters were causing bad economic vibrations. Pedga and his friend lost most of their money.

"I was really short of funds by then and didn't have much choice but to return to live with my mother. She was nice about it, but it was awfully humiliating for me. I felt like a failure.

"There was no work in my field so I had to look for something else. The problem was that nearly everyone else seemed to be looking for work as well. There were a lot of layoffs and closures, particularly after the UN sanctions.

"I finally found a job in a private bank — mostly because of my English. The work though was really not very interesting. The salary was about $60 a month, considered a lot of money these days, but I could never manage if I wasn't living at home. We had to change our whole way of life. People visited friends less because they didn't want to impose. The price of petrol was outrageous so even if you had a car you didn't drive.

"We used to be a night people, but there wasn't very much extra money for cafés or restaurants. Not that we didn't go to them, but we had to be more careful. Also suddenly there was a lot of violence in the streets. Just a few nights ago, my neighbor was on his way home from work on a tram when someone shot someone else. The tram was redirected to police headquarters and the passengers didn't reach home until five hours later. There was a lot of shooting going around. People were on edge and everyone seemed to have a gun. And so you had to be just a little more observant and careful when you went out."

When I asked Pedga if there was any particular woman in his life, he smiled.

"Marriage is not exactly the 'in' thing these days, particularly if it means having children. My friends just had a baby boy and while I know they're happy, I also know that they are terrified. They simply don't have the money. Even with the help that they will get from either parents, it will be very difficult for them. You see, we've learned to manage somehow as long as there are no real expenses besides food. We usually don't buy clothing anymore. We rarely go to cinemas. We pray that we don't get sick and we use our cars, if we have any, only on the rarest occasions."

The Serbian secret for survival was savings, Pedga confirmed along with so many other of my friends. People quickly converted their savings into German marks to augment declining income. Then when they ran out of foreign currency, they sold things — automobiles, country homes, jewelry, furs, clothing, books, anything and everything — so that they could start all over again with foreign currency.

I asked Pedga what was his prognosis.

"Well," he replied, "we Serbs are a pretty resilient people so I guess we'll manage. We always did in the past. As for me, I'll be heading for Canada as soon as my visa comes through. I had to change my profession around a little — I am now a certified cook — but there is really no other alternative here for me. It will be very hard leaving my mother and friends. It will be very hard leaving my country. I just have no hope left. There are no other options. I can't continue this way much longer."

So Pedga who came from a good family, had a fine education and was well qualified in his profession would, in all likelihood, be arriving in Vancouver with virtually no savings and the slender hope that he would be hired quickly as a cook. He would leave his friends and family behind perhaps forever. He would be starting out in a strange, new land at the sametime that most Americans or Israelis or Europeans, residing in saner parts of the continent, were reaching the zenith of their careers. Pedga was not a refugee, nor a war casualty. He wasn't starving and he certainly wasn't complaining. But he was a victim.

And so was thirty-year-old Slavica Marjanovic who might

very well have saved my life.

What should have been the beginning of a good, productive day disintegrated into the worst cramps I had ever experienced. Since the thought of going to a doctor was more odious than dying, I will never know if I was felled by food or water or a microbe specially incubated for me in Zagreb. But sick I was and when a friend visited later in the afternoon, accompanied by radio journalist Slavica, I was reconciled to the painful and undramatic inevitability of my death.

Brown-haired and eyed, quietly pretty, she took charge immediately. Before I knew precisely what was happening, room service was arriving with limitless quantities of herbal tea, mineral water and toast. It worked. I began to feel better immediately. Perhaps, I thought, I would live to finish this book.

Guilty of keeping me alive, Slavica had an obligation to feed my insatiable curiosity and so we met the next day and talked.

A graduate of Oriental Studies, Arabic and Turkish to be precise, she spoke tenderly about her mother and stepfather with whom she continued to live, because she couldn't afford otherwise, and who cushioned her against a hard world.

"I owe them so much and I feel so useless. My stepfather suffers from lumbago and periodically requires injections to relieve the pain. Each injection costs $12 and I earn $15 a month. Sometimes I daydream about buying tickets for them to travel around the world and then I feel miserable because I know that I scarcely have the funds to buy some inexpensive flowers for my mother.

"We don't see people much anymore because of the lack of money. We don't visit each other because we're afraid of imposing. It costs money to host guests even if it represents only colas and crackers. We don't meet outside because that really is too expensive. So we lose contact and everyone is so proud they won't admit why.

"For years, we had a custom here in Serbia. We would

collect little things — tiny, sweet gifts that we would put on a shelf and then slowly give away to friends. I love to give people things. I love to see them smile. But I can't do that either anymore.

"I don't really blame anyone for what happened to Yugoslavia although sometimes I would like to talk directly to younger people of my generation in Europe and the United States and ask them why they permitted this injustice to occur. Why didn't they speak out against the lies? Why didn't they study the Balkans and know a little more of our history before condemning us?

"I voted for Slobodan Milosevic in the last elections. I never regretted that decision. I think he is a fine and honest man, trying to do the best he can for us. We enjoy freedom now that we never had before he came into power. We can talk. We can criticize. There are opposition newspapers. There are multiple television networks that have nothing to do with the government. It is just that the economy is so terrible."

Asked about the future, she took a deep breath before replying. "There are five million Serbs living elsewhere. I guess I will be joining them before long. I can't stay. I can't continue to live on the charity of my parents. There is no way that I can find work here in my profession and I earn so little as a radio journalist. Most of my friends feel the same way. The years are passing and we're not progressing. I should be married now. I should have a child. I should be earning a real income instead of relying so completely on my parents. I don't see a future for me any longer in Yugoslavia. If I don't leave my country, my life will have no meaning."

I thought of Greece and how casual we were about entering into a taverna where we would pay for one meal what Slavica earned in a month or Israel where a young woman of her age and education would most certainly have an attractive apartment and an equally attractive life or the United States with its endless opportunities and challenges. And I felt sad for Slavica and for all Serbia.

"The war has changed everything for us. I had such good friends all over former Yugoslavia once. There is almost no way to contact them. The only way we could communicate was through a postal box in Milan. I sent a few letters, but I never received an answer. Perhaps the letters never arrived. Perhaps my friends are just afraid to reply. Maybe they don't want to.

"There is so much frustration here. I know languages, but I can't travel. I adore good books, but there is no money to acquire them. I can't even afford to buy my own clothing. Isn't that shameful? I never imagined that this is what my life would be like.

"I love my country, perhaps even more than my own life. But I can't live here any longer. We have everything. Really, we have such a rich country — history, culture, mountains, rivers, flowers. And yet if we are so rich, why are we so poor?

"I don't suffer, but that is because of my parents. Many Serbs, however, are suffering terribly. There are people with barely enough money to buy food. Little things terrify us — ruining a blouse because it is so hard to replace, becoming ill because drugs are beyond our reach, losing our jobs because they are irreplaceable. You see, even my $15 a month has become critical to me and I always hated even thinking about money. I already feel like a parasite. How terrible it would be if I had no earning power at all.

"My friends laugh at me because I am an idealist. I want to make the world a better place, but my world, the world of Serbia, I've already lost. It doesn't matter if it will take me a month or a year. I know I must leave my country and seek another way of life so that I will be able to do nice things for my parents and I will not continue to be a parasite."

On May 30, 1992, the United Nations adopted Resolution 757 which called on all member states to "prevent the import into their territory of all commodities and services originating in the Federal Republic of Yugoslavia; prevent any activities by their nationals or in their territories which would promote or are calculated to promote the export or trans-shipment of any commodities or products originating in the Federal Republic of Yugoslavia; prevent the sale or supply of any commodities or products whether or not originating in their territories...."

The last codicil was to have exempted food and medicines which were denied the people of Yugoslavia by other, more subtle means. The Yugoslavian economy was reeling before the UN sanctions. An industrial society was riven. Tourism was dead. Refugees were flowing. Foreign investment was scarce. Inflation was rising. The sanctions merely confirmed to Pedga and Slavica and tens of thousands of others like them that there was no future for them in their own country.

# CHAPTER XVII
## A TALE OF TWO WOMEN

Before leaving Belgrade for the controversial new country of Serbska, better known in its former existence as the home of the Bosnian Serbs, I met two extraordinary women, each of whom was making an indelible mark on history.

Dr. Slobodanka Gruden, fiery and fifty-three, the first lady mayor in the long history of the city, could still find a modicum of humor in what had befallen the capital. "There are no industrial wastes polluting our rivers because there is no industry and there are neither auto emissions nor autos."

Explaining that the middle class of Belgrade society was steadily growing poorer because of the thundering inflation, the strong effects of the sanctions and the cost of providing homes and sustenance for the more than 200,000 refugees who were being accommodated in the city, she admitted that the face of Belgrade had changed drastically.

"The city has fractured into three distinct groups," she explained. "There is a spirit of extreme aggressiveness that was unknown until now. These are the young men who went off to fight and returned full of anger and rage. Usually, they have no jobs, but they do have weapons, plenty of them. They have created an ugly, gray atmosphere in Belgrade which is characterized by violence and unlawfulness. They are extortioners, black marketeers, illegal money changers.

"There is a second group that simply does not understand what has happened. Their pensions have become meaningless, job security imperilled. People in this category are suffering from deep depression. They grow more apathetic and introverted all the time.

"Happily, there is one more category that is responding to poverty and tension through the spirit. These are people of all ages who refuse to be bowed or depressed by circumstance.

They are responsible for an entire new phenomenon in Belgrade — a great outpouring of musical and theatrical work, an amazing number of scientific papers, splendid books. These people understand real values and they know that neither apathy nor violence helps. I support these people with all my heart."

Hopeful that the sanctions would not continue too much longer, Dr. Gruden was making emergency plans nonetheless. "Winter heating is one of our most serious problems," she explained. "Last year, the morning temperatures in my Belgrade apartment were between 5-7C. We had a terrible problem with hospitals, schools, kindergartens, sanitariums. So we are now trying to bring in thermal heating from a powerplant twenty-seven kilometers away which would provide basic heating for 200,000 apartments — not enough for the city, but better than nothing."

The mayor pointed out that standards for public transportation, medical facilities and even street-cleaning equipment were declining because of the boycott. "There is a great deal of hypocrisy in the international community," she said angrily. "The sanctions were not to have affected humanitarian and medical requirements. Theoretically, they didn't. In reality, they have endangered the lives of everyone. Our funds are tied up so we can't pay for the medicines. Our once-thriving pharmaceutical industries have been virtually crippled."

Medicine was a subject even closer than politics. Dr. Gruden was regarded as one of Yugoslavia's leading specialists in blood transfusiology. She was also president of the Red Cross of Serbia.

"The thing that angers me the most about the sanctions," she said suddenly, "is the embargo on knowledge. Denying a whole nation information is almost as bad as depriving a whole nation of medicines. I cannot understand the world's colossal vindictiveness."

The product of a Serb father and a Jewish mother, the

mayor didn't know about her Semitic heritage until she was eighteen. "My mother suffered so terribly during the war, she couldn't bring herself to discuss the subject with me until I was grown.

"The Serbs have always been very proud of 'their' Jews. The main difference between the two peoples is that Jews don't forget, but they do forgive. Serbs, unfortunately, both forgive and forget. It is to our detriment."

The mayor first visited Israel in 1990 under the auspices of the Serbian-Jewish Friendship Society, an organization midwifed and nourished into maturity by yet another female doctor, a dentist this time, fiercely proud of her two great national loves.

Dr. Klara Mandic, an exquisitely handsome woman, spent all but the first nine months of her life in Belgrade. The Second World War claimed sixty-three members of her family including her father who was born in Poland and her mother who came from Spain. A Serbian family brought her to Belgrade from a refugee detention camp in Italy. "They were my family. They were all I had. That's why I adopted their name. I am proud to have a Serbian name."

Describing Dr. Mandic was not the easiest of all tasks. She was considered one of the most attractive — and influential — women in Belgrade. She spoke English with the fractured, sexy lilt of Zsa Zsa Gabor and there was something nervously irrepressible about her, a quality that both excited and exhausted.

"I am very much a Jew, a proud Jew, a proud Serbian Jew and I decided that something had to be done about the lack of relations, and even contacts, between the people of Israel and the people of Serbia. Tito was the first to break off relations with Israel in 1967 because of the Six-Day War, but even after he died, years later, inertia had set in and no one wanted to change anything. Israel had managed to survive without Yugoslavia and Yugoslavia was too busy with its own problems to even think of Israel."

The Mandic credo was revolution and not evolution. She had decided it was time to bring the two peoples closer together and nothing was going to stop her, including the official diplomatic policies of the Federal Socialist Republic of Yugoslavia.

"Of the twenty first founding members of the Serbian-Jewish Friendship Society, sixteen were members of the Serbian Academy of Arts and Sciences. Joining the society soon became a matter of prestige. Before long, there was a membership of 10,000 and, remember, there were only 800 Jews in Belgrade. A year after the society was founded, in May, 1989, I was ready for the next step."

The "next step" was Slobodan Milosevic, the President of the-then Socialist Republic of Serbia. Considering the fact that not even a hint of diplomatic relations had existed between Yugoslavia and Israel for the past twenty-two years, there was something almost zany in the Mandic proposal which, pure and simply, suggested that one of the six constituent republics brazenly establish its own foreign policy in direct contradiction with the federal position taken by the rest of the country.

"I want to launch Serbia Week in Israel as the first stage in my campaign. What I want to know is are you brave enough to stand with me?"

"Against the established policies of the federal government?" Milosevic asked in order to clarify the point absolutely.

"Precisely."

"Klara," he replied, "I give you a blank check. If Israel wants closer relations, Serbia will be more than happy to do its share. With whatever troubles you may have, come to me."

Predictably, Milosevic was criticized fiercely by his colleagues for breaking ranks and initiating a foreign policy of his own. However, he held firm.

"Without Milosevic there would have been nothing," she assured. "The first official group ever consisted of 440 Serbs.

They were politicians, businessmen, tourist operators and artists. We brought an entire children's theater which later performed in the Habimah National Theater in Tel Aviv. We donated a whole collection of some of our best primitive paintings to Tel Aviv Museum and we made presents of 150 valuable books."

Milosevic also sent along six ministers in his government, his own son and the Prime Minister of Serbia for good measure, and he enthusiastically agreed to the twinning of Belgrade and Tel Aviv as sister cities.

Returning to Yugoslavia with members of the society was an Israeli delegation which was immediately and cordially received by Milosevic. When Belgrade television asked to film the event, the ecstatic Dr. Mandic questioned if the publicity was wise.

"Oh, my dear, so you don't want it to be a secret?"

All this transpired eighteen months before formal diplomatic relations were established between the two countries.

The principles of the Serbian-Jewish Friendship Society were founded on five main points — accelerate the process for full diplomatic relations with the only democracy in the Middle East; compile an accurate list of genocide victims irrespective of religion; restore the old Jewish cemetery which had been ruined; build a non-secular monument to the known victims of genocide; return Jewish property rights confiscated during the Nazi occupation.

When I confided that one of the people I wanted to meet in Knin, the capital of the Serbian Republic of Krajina, was a Captain Dragan, a volunteer from Australia who had become a fighting legend over the past two years, her lips betrayed the slightest hint of a smile. When I amplified that I had heard that he was Jewish, thus making him just a tad more interesting for some of the articles I would be writing for Israel, she burst into peals of laughter that caused everyone in the restaurant where we were dining to focus attention on us.

"Why are you laughing?" I asked a little gruffly.

"Because I made him a Jew," she continued giggling uncontrollably.

It appeared that an Australian citizen named Dragan Vasikovic had, indeed, returned to Serbia to volunteer his services as a fighter. Invited to stay at Klara's home for as long as required and until all the formalities could be concluded, Klara decided that Serbia needed an uplift and a colorful character like the Australian was just the right prescription. So she organized a press conference, but moments before the event was to begin, she experienced a flash of genius.

"Here," she told the volunteer as she fitted her own Star of David around his neck, "wear this."

"Why?" he asked.

"Do it for me."

Klara paused while eying me mischievously. "I did it because I wanted Tudjman to have nightmares. I wanted him to see a Jewish Captain Dragan who was standing at the vanguard of Israeli commandos and who would be marching straight from Krajina to Zagreb. I told the story later to Milosevic and he laughed even harder than me. Soon people were writing that his real name was Weinstein. Dragan Weinstein! How do you like that?"

The irrepressible Klara continued. "Sometimes though, I hate the Serbs. They are so forgiving. They don't hate anyone. I hate them because they don't know how to hate. They must learn how to be spiteful. I will give them lessons."

Klara had evolved into a very political creature. "When I watch international television, and had I not known better, I would really sympathize with the enemies of Serbia. You have to feel sorry for the Moslem children. You have to feel sorry for the refugees. But you know, what you see is so often lies. My own cousins have identified the bodies of their own relations who were described as Moslems on television."

Klara Mandic discussed the situation with the same passion that characterized her life. "When the Moslems finally understand what Izetbegovic did to them, that he lost their state, that he must take the responsibility for the deaths of 200,000 people, that he could have had both a nation and peace at the sametime, but chose war instead, they will kill him. This idiot will not die at the hands of Serbs and Croats. His own Moslems will murder him."

By "royal request", I was asked to make an appearance at the Serbian-Jewish Friendship Society (where Klara connived that I would lecture) and where I met an octogenarian, Prof. Andrija Gams, of the Belgrade Faculty of Law and regarded as one of the most esteemed legal experts in the country.

Prof. Gams confirmed that with a few very minor exceptions in the last century, Serbia had no anti-Jewish tradition at all. "The opposite was true. Serbia's rulers were always great friends of the Jews. There was never discrimination. There were no professional restrictions as elsewhere in Europe. Jews attained the highest ranks in government and academia."

The professor vividly recalled "the bad old days" when the Communist Party was completely in the hands of Slovenes and Croats and every criticism was treason. In 1974, he and eight other law professors spoke out against the new constitution which deeply wounded the sovereignty of Serbia.

"We were all punished, but not equally. One of my colleagues was sent to prison for nine months. Another, although he had full tenure at the faculty, was fired. Several were exiled."

Prof. Gams pointed out that whatever were Marshal Tito's political beliefs about Israel, he was always fair to the Jews of Yugoslavia. "Several months after he broke off relations with Israel in 1967, I remember a ceremony in which nine army officers were promoted from colonel to general. Three of them were Jewish, proportionately a very high number."

The prewar population of Jews was 85,000. Current estimates were 1,600, up from a nadir of 1,000 due to the surprising phenomenon that more and more intermarried couples were opting for Judaism.

The exposure to two successful women, both pillars of their community and both proud of their Judeo-Serbian heritage, reminded me again how many similarities existed between the two peoples — victimized and persecuted by the same elements, isolated by similar geopolitics, tortured by a comparable history. If Dragan Vasikovic was not Weinstein, perhaps he should have been.

# CHAPTER XVIII
# THE RIVER DRINA

It took less than three hours from Belgrade to reach the border crossing between Serbia and Bosnia and Herzegovina, part of the latter proudly retitled "Serbska". Midway in the journey, a twenty-one-year-old girl had been crushed under a bus. Death, it appeared, was not inhibited by frontier posts.

The span between the two states was the bridge over the River Drina. Yugoslav author Ivo Andric had written a book by that same name for which he had earned the Nobel Prize for Literature. I remembered a particularly poignant, still-haunting description of a Slav prisoner impaled, skewered and crucified by his Turkish captors who offered the torturer extra pay for every hour the tormented man would continue to live in impalement. I was crossing more than a river. I was entering into a dimension of endless cruelty and historical rage far more turbulent than the Drina at its worst.

In the Serbian part of the city of Zvornik, there was a lazy atmosphere characterized by horse-drawn carts carrying hay, casual strollers, boys swimming along the embankment. When passing the red, white and blue flag of Serbska, however, the atmosphere was more subdued. Nearly all the large apartment houses facing the river were marked by machine-gun fire. There were sandbag emplacements strewn carelessly about everywhere. Men, dressed in shorts and sports shirts, were all carrying automatic weapons. A father and son were strolling hand in hand, the former clutching a rifle with his free hand.

With each kilometer away from Zvornik, the mood worsened, the atmosphere grew heavier, the sense of danger heightened. There were almost no other vehicles on the road and every instinct dictated driving carefully and fast. Soon there was not a single, undamaged building anywhere. Homes were blown to smithereens. There were glass and corrugated metal everywhere along the roadway and yet farmers continued working in the nearby fields — guns cocked and on automatic — but piling hay nonetheless.

In the utterly ruined village of Kasaba, once a Moslem hamlet fifteen kilometers from the sanguine battles around Srebrenica, there was an elderly Serb woman rummaging through the debris. "I have nothing," she explained, "perhaps I can find some pots under these buildings."

"Why do you stay here?" I asked. "There is nothing here but death and ruin."

"There is no other place," she replied.

Although I had been following newspaper reports and watching newsreels of the battle, I wasn't prepared for the extent of the awesome damage. This was Kuneitra on the Golan Heights after it had been reduced to complete ruin; Kantara along the Suez Canal in 1971; Warsaw after Germany completed the final rape.

There was bile in my mouth, a bitterness that would not go away. All this need not have been.

Under the heading of self-determination, it was relatively simple for the European Community and then America to agree hastily to the legitimization of the secession and then declaration of independence of Bosnia and Herzegovina. The same yardstick that applied to the Ukraine, Uzbekistan and then Slovenia and Croatia was used to justify a pitiable comparison.

Although there was an Izetbegovic and 43.7% of the Bosnia and Herzegovina population was Moslem, on April 6–7 when Brussels and Washington joined hands to produce a calamity that could have been avoided, the clear majority in the state was Christian — and it had always been that way. In an 1879 census, the Serbs comprised nearly 43% of the population in contrast to the Moslems with 39%. In 1921, the Serbs were 43.9%, followed by Moslems 31.2% and Croats 23.5%. The demographics changed dramatically only after the Second

World War, only after prodigious numbers of Serbs were slaughtered in a three-way pincer conducted by Moslems, Croats and Germans, and only after tens of thousands more fled the region for their lives.

"We didn't want this war," explained Prof. Aleksa Buha, fifty, Foreign Minister of the Republic of Serbska and formerly instructor of philosophy, just hours before I set out from Belgrade.

"There can be no total winners in this war. All we ever wanted was to free our territory. We do not fight where we don't belong. The Serbs in Serbia comprise only 65% of the population. We, in Serbska, with a population of between 1.6–1.8 million, are 95% Serbs. Sarajevo was not a Moslem city before the war as misinformed people claim. Sarajevo was the second largest Serb city in the world.

"We have a common language, common religion, common history and our 36,000 square kilometers gives us a land mass as large as that of Belgium. So why can't we be a nation like all other nations?

"There has been so much disinformation about us through the European Community. The Serbs of Serbia are not fighting this war. We are. We are not invading anyone, we are defending our homes. We are portrayed as monsters and morons, but all the top posts in our country are occupied by university professors, doctors and poets. Standing next to me is Prof. Radomir Lukic. He is only thirty-six, but a professor of international law and the co-author of our constitution. Throughout our entire government, you will find the same phenomenon.

"This war, more brutal than anyone could have imagined, is not merely a civil war. It is a battle of civilization, a completely new phenomenon. In simple terms, this is a fight between Islam and Christianity."

There were checkposts all along the road to Pale, the mountain aerie just above Sarajevo where the government of Serbska officiated. We were warned by the soldiers to move more quickly. It was darkening. Earlier, to save time, we rejected the concerned offer to leave later as part of a protected convoy so we were alone on the roads, very much so. Several days before, a bus had been ambushed by Moslem infiltrators. Five died. There was a trickle of Moslem soldiers entering also from Srebrenica, killing and then fleeing before they could be stopped.

"Sretno," said one of the soldiers. "Good luck and be careful."

Before Pale became the capital of the new republic, it was the ski capital of the 1984 Winter Olympics and an important tourist center for Yugoslavia. The steeply inclined roofs of hotels and weekend homes indicated the quantity of snow that fell each winter. Nothing, however, prepared me for the sudden cold. It was early summer and yet, as the sun began to dip, my sockless toes were completely numbed.

"We are in the mountains," laughed Miroslav Toholj, thirty-six, Minister of Information, writer, novelist and essayist. "What you need is a little *rakija*."

What I needed, I thought, was a pair of felt-lined boots instead of open sandals.

I liked the young, bearded writer immediately. He wore the title of Minister of Information like a fedora that someone had mistakenly placed on top of his head. If he didn't shake too vigorously, it probably wouldn't fall off, but it felt awfully strange anyway.

"I am really a war criminal," he confided happily. "You see, there were plenty of Serbs still living in Sarajevo even after the unilateral Moslem declaration of independence. No one really knew what was going to happen, but I had a wife and child and everything we owned was in our apartment. So I decided to wait it out for awhile although many of my friends had warned me earlier that staying in the city could be very dangerous.

"I was told, however, not to leave my house under any conditions. The police were indiscriminately rounding up

Serbs in the streets, taking them to points of detention and then beating them severely. Like everyone would later be talking about 'ethnic cleansing', the expression 'war criminal' was much in vogue then.

"On April 23, one of my friends risked his life to warn me that I was at the top of a list of war criminals, that there were 'dead or alive' posters printed with my photo on them and that a list of my 'crimes' appeared also in the German daily, 'Die Tages Zeitung'. I knew perfectly well that my only guilt was membership in the Serb Democratic Party, but I was accused of bombing the city from Pale which would have been quite an achievement since I hadn't dared leave my apartment for days."

"We fled that evening and we were very lucky because the first military vehicle we encountered was a Serbian armored personnel carrier scouting the area for people like us."

One of the paramount issues was war crimes, the subject of worldwide, international condemnation of the Serbs of Serbska and their putative allies in Serbia. Who, therefore, would better answer the accusations than the "war criminal" seated opposite me.

"There were crimes on all sides. This is a civil war, not merely a fight between two opposing armies," he said, suddenly growing serious. "We took out indictments against 2,000 of our people. So far, 500 of them were found guilty and punished. We check every claim, every accusation. If there is evidence, we prosecute.

"Originally, our forces were accused of raping 60,000 women which, considering the size of our army, would have been an Herculean endeavor. Later, the number was scaled down to 30,000 and every international body that came to check objectively the accusation concluded that the figures were ridiculous. We know where these figures originated from. It wasn't even Sarajevo. It was Zagreb.

"Our own investigation has determined that 150 Moslem women were, in all likelihood, actually raped. This number, however, is not outlandish. It compares with figures during peacetime. There is another side to this story as well, however, which has a lot less media interest. We have documents and evidence attesting to the rape of over 200 Serb women by Moslems. Serb girls were taken by force to the Victor Bubanj military barracks where they were compelled to act as prostitutes.

"The whole subject of Serbian rapes and Serbian war crimes was brought up to a fine art by the media. The Manjaca Camp was not a concentration camp as American and European television decided, but a prisoner-of-war camp. Our soldiers were eating only two meals a day then and so were the prisoners, but this was not programed starvation. The other camp at Omarska was again not a concentration camp. Moslem women and children had fled to us from the battle. We kept them in the camp because there was no place else to send them at the time. Also not one international body came. Absolutely no one offered help."

To buttress his point, Toholj related the story of the visit of one of America's best known TV journalists. "He arrived in the evening and left in the morning. Ten days later, 'The Land of the Demons' was screened coast-to-coast."

The young minister shook his head as though trying to dislodge an errant thought. "I believe there is an evil destiny for evil people. Sometime ago, in southeast Bosnia, five of our soldiers entered a POW camp and shot down thirty prisoners. Four months later, three of them died under strange circumstances. One dropped his revolver accidentally and shot himself to death. Another was hit by a stray bullet while driving. The third was driving a truck when it hit a mine. The two survivors were arrested by our military police. They were tried, convicted and given long prison sentences. I relate this story because I believe implicitly that justice will always win and I want the world to know that we don't hide or deny our crimes. When they happen, we are dreadfully ashamed. There have been, however, too many lies and slanders about us. We are not angels. We are not beasts. We are people caught in an ugly civil war."

I asked the Minister to comment on the viciousness and the brutality that characterized this particular civil war from the beginning — the eyes of prisoners gouged out, women murdered after being gang raped, children slaughtered with impunity, churches and mosques desecrated, imams and priests impaled in much the same way as described by Ivo Andric.

"The curse of history," he replied. "The Moslems felt that they were the underdogs here, that they were not treated decently or fairly by the Christians. The Croats blamed the Serbs for standing between them and an independent state for 900 years. The Serbs recalled 600 years of slavery under the Moslems and then the events of the Second World War when our people were massacred both by the Croats and the Moslems.

"I believe, however, that the Moslems are now staging an 'intifada' of their own in the Balkans and that they are being helped, first and foremost, by Germany which is the traditional enemy of all the Serbian people. There was, for example, the famous instance of the 'Serb mortar attack' against Moslem civilians in Sarajevo who were standing in line waiting to buy bread. The whole world condemned us for this atrocity."

According to Bosnian sources, four shells dropped from the skies on May 27 on Vasa Miskin Street in Sarajevo. They landed amidst a large queue of shoppers waiting for bread with the consequent toll of fourteen dead and a hundred and fourteen wounded. Serendipitously, a Bosnian TV crew just happened to be on the spot, photographing the massacre even before ambulances or the police arrived.

Finally having the justification it required, the United Nations Security Council introduced sanctions against Serbia and Montenegro the same night.

After witnessing the carnage on television, America's

President George Bush lashed out at Yugoslavia. "It is hard to believe that in our days, military forces are shelling the center of a city with artillery and mortars, and are killing helpless people, women and children, in the streets. This is beyond anger for it is a barbarian and totally inhuman act."

The presidential statement was followed by the expulsion of the Yugoslav ambassador from the United States, the closure of the Yugoslav consulate in Chicago and the proposal to exclude Serbia and Montenegro from all international exchanges.

The damage to Yugoslavia was irreparable even though UN officers who later checked out the affair were incredulous. As a matter of fact, according to Bosnian Serb military analysts, it was virtually impossible for the shells to have been launched from Serbian territory and reach that target. The trajectory was all wrong and the rows of buildings on either side of the street would have acted as a natural barrier against the shells. The wounds sustained by the civilians were completely not in keeping with the mortar theory, the cuts and lacerations isolated to the lower regions of the body. Had mortars really been used, the victims would have been blown to bits.

"There were also no telltale craters whatsoever on the street indicating that, more likely than not, concealed mines had been detonated which could also explain the chance placement of the TV crew," the Minister stated.

Whatever the truth, however, the Bosnian Moslems had attained their objectives. Public rage boiled against Serbs and Serbia. The UN had the excuse for launching its sanctions. The United States responded with righteous, Yankee indignation.

After the interview with the Minister, I had the opportunity to look around Pale which had swelled to 40,000 inhabitants from an original 5,000 because of the influx of refugees from Sarajevo and the infusion of government offices.

One reassuring factor was that there were children everywhere — escorted and shepherded by teachers, but remarkably unafraid anyway. Presumably all soldiers, the men reminded me of Israel on the eve of war. Battle dress was whatever was nearest in the closet. Some wore fatigues. Others were dressed in camouflage suits. Some of the uniforms appeared new; others might have been mothballed since grandfathers wore them in the Balkan wars. Men were attired half in green and half in blue. Others reversed the colors. If there was nothing uniform about the uniform at least just about everyone was armed. There were assault rifles, automatic submachine guns, Barettas, Colts, even shotguns on display. There was also plenty of military traffic, despite the severe petrol shortage, although movement was somewhat hindered by milk cows who prowled freely from one end of the town to the other.

Most of the government offices were located in an old engine factory which, idled anyway by lack of parts, was sequestered by the various ministries. The President's House, a couple of kilometers away, was a rather simple building snatched from a nearby hotel. It wasn't the White House, but that was where President Radovan Karadzic presided when he wasn't negotiating in Belgrade or Geneva or elsewhere on the Planet Earth. Indeed Karadzic was at that moment on the way back to Pale from Geneva where some headway apparently had been made. The Croats and the Serbs were moving closer to a territorial decision about Bosnia and Herzegovina. The Moslems were riven by those, like Izetbegovic, who feared that the Islamic state was being stolen from him, and realists who acknowledged that without international military intervention, the old idea of united Moslem statehood was merely a fanciful dream.

Many European voices, particularly in France and Italy, were re-examining political positions and even hinting that their nations had been led down the garden path by such luminaries as Genscher and Kohl. More than ever, criticism was being expressed about the German role in the disintegration of the old Yugoslavia and in the bloodbath that was consuming Bosnia and Herzegovina.

Before parting for a hotel farther up on the slopes which had been requisitioned by the army, I met the young Minister for a final drink and a final story. He told me that after visiting the Sarajevo neighborhood of Grbavica, the last Serb citadel inside the city proper, and spending some hours there, he was called to Belgrade.

"I was walking down one of the main streets in the middle of the day. There were children walking about unconcerned. There were trams and food shops. People were walking and not running. And suddenly I started crying. I really couldn't help myself and it was terribly embarrassing. But I just couldn't stop crying. I went back to Pale the next day. It was easier."

## CHAPTER XIX
# THE UNARMED GENERAL

His face was that of a benign cleric. His eyes were those of an eagle. Asked by Time Magazine what he would do if the Allies attacked him, he replied cheerfully that "if they bomb me, I'll bomb London and Washington". He refused to fire a weapon, explaining "my job is to lead men, not to kill men". Gen. Ratko Mladic, fifty, said that he was a simple man. "I rose up from the people. I want to be the same as them. I never want to rise beyond them. Everything emanates from the people — all that is good and all that is bad. I am one with them."

The tall, sturdy professional military officer was born in the village of Kalinovik in southeastern Bosnia on March 12, 1943. His father was slain two years later in a battle with Croatian Ustashe forces. Mladic was promoted to the rank of general in the Yugoslav army on October 19, 1991, one of four who received battlefield commissions.

He shyly admitted that there were moments when he felt aware of his fifty years. "The young are fighting relentlessly. There is no stopping them. They have so much energy and patriotic fervor. It is hard to keep up. However, I decided years ago that if a man gives all of himself to something that he really believes in, he will never grow old. That is the way I feel about myself even if the bones ache sometimes."

The general expressed the sentiment that all the people of Serbska were his soldiers, regardless of who carried weapons and who wore uniforms. The truth of that statement was self-evident.

Men shared their time between work and soldiering. The moment there was tension or trouble in the air they appeared automatically with their weapons. When conditions eased, they knew who could go home and who could not. The soldiers were not only comrades, they were usually neighbors and friends. This was an army of citizens who required no infusions of patriotism to explain what was expected. They were literally fighting for their homes, their property, their families and their survival.

Obviously briefed on who I was and the book I intended to write, the general stated that only the Jews had been exposed to similar dangers and disparities and yet managed to survive.

"You must understand what this conflict is all about. We were attacked by our neighbors, people with whom we had been living together all our lives. Forget about the slanders you read about, written by journalists who rush in and rush out and don't have the slightest understanding of our region. This was a war of neighbors and former friends waking up one day and cutting each other's throat."

There was a mixture of nostalgia and anger when Mladic spoke about Yugoslavia. "There is no merit in creating a new Yugoslavia because twice history showed that primarily the Serbs were victimized. In 1918, one in every three of us was killed, 56% of all the males. And then, during World War II, 11% of the population perished and of those 98% were Serbs.

"From Tito onward, the Serbs were second-grade citizens in their own country. We were ruled by Moslems and Croats because that was what Tito wanted and he used the Communist Party to obtain his objectives. Take a look at what the country was all about before it dissolved. Ante Marcovic, the Prime Minister, was a Croat. The Minister of Foreign Affairs was a Croat. The head of the Communist Party was a Croat and most of his top appointees were Croats. The head of national defense was a Croat, as was the chief of the air force.

"But despite all this, we were then willing to continue as Yugoslavs. It is a defect in our nature. We forgive too quickly. It was the Serbs who kept between sixteen and thirty German divisions confined to the Balkans during the Second World War and, according to a U.S. Central Intelligence study of the victims of the fighting, 78,000 Serbs were killed by Germans, 28,000 by Italians and 750,000 by Croats and Moslems.

"Even the Germans were stupefied by the Ustashe. It wasn't just a matter of killing, but of killing with the utmost sadism. The Ustashe had competitions to determine who could kill the most and in the cruelest ways. They would place a rat on a prisoner's stomach and then cover the rodent with a pot which they gradually heated. The animal had no place to flee but inside the man. It was a favorite recreation.

"There is a document about another Serb. The guards cut his ear off and he refused to cry out. Then they sliced off his second ear and he said nothing. When he was asked if he wanted them to continue, he replied: 'Just do your job. I'm doing mine.'

"Tito tried to conceal all those crimes. He, himself, was a Croat after all. We were not even permitted to remember the shame, the national humiliation, the martyrs. Tito protected the Ustashe criminals all his life. He rewarded the Bosnian Moslems for slaughtering Serbs and actively supporting the Germans by making them a nation. And yet, despite all this, he convinced us to sacrifice our Serbian heritage for Yugoslavia.

"In the 1960 census, I gave my nationality as Yugoslav. I am not proud of that decision. My only excuse was that I was young."

Our meeting together was in the President's House, the penultimate stop before descending down to Grbavica in Sarajevo the next day. Like everything else I had experienced in Pale, the theme was easy informality. While the general and I were speaking, officers arrived and left, curious to see the stranger from the United States, Israel and Greece. Coffee was shunned in favor of *rakija*. A couple of gorgeous young ladies, dressed in camouflage uniforms and armed with awesomely large pistols, entered periodically to whisper something or other to one of the officers. The bond between the Serbs in the room was almost palpable. They were all a part of a common history, sharing a similar fate.

"Mostly," continued the general, "I am a simple person. My mind is not devious and so at the beginning I didn't want to believe that the Croats and Moslems were once again acting as the weapons of Germany. Whatever Tito might have said or done, the Moslems were never a nation and the only one who gave the Croats a state was Adolph Hitler. As far as Franjo Tudjman is concerned, he is a monster. He will end up destroying his own people.

"I see a very complex geopolitical situation emerging in this part of the world and, as usual, the key is Germany. Suddenly, the world is frightened. It sees this terrible, new power re-emerging again and doesn't know how to stop it.

"Of course, America shares lots of guilt for this. It was the United States which arranged for the reunification of Germany and set the stage for what was to happen. After the Soviet Union collapsed, America wanted its own counter-balance in the EC which, if really united, would become the most powerful economic and political force in the world. The United States was willing to give Europe to Germany while it took control of the world. But the Americans are weak historians. Germany will never accept second place in anything for very long. The Germans are a ruthless, aggressive people. How many more wars must be fought before this is realized?

"And while all this political tug-of-war is going on between Europe and America and the Balkans is victimized, the Moslems are moving northward again. The Moslems have no A-bomb yet, but they themselves are a demographic bomb."

Since we had touched upon Islam, I was curious about the role of the Islamic volunteers — the Mujahedeen — in the war. Mladic confirmed that there were probably between 15,000–20,000 Moslem volunteers, mostly engaged in fighting against the Croats in Herzegovina. He added that there were secret training centers in Turkey, Iran, Saudi Arabia and Pakistan, warning that the first was playing a devious role in the Balkans, steadily spreading its influence, constantly promoting divisiveness in the region.

There were also, according to the general, 13,000 mercenaries serving in the army of Croatia, volunteers from Germany, Canada, Argentina, Venezuela, Great Britain, Sudan and Brazil. Their original remuneration was between 3,000–5,000 German marks a month, but that had been cut to 10%. Even with the reduced rewards, however, Mladic speculated, there were plenty of new mercenaries queueing up in Albania, Bulgaria and Rumania.

"Serbska doesn't rely on volunteers. It doesn't need them. There is a fighting tradition among my people that is deep in our blood. For things that we believe in, we are prepared to suffer and ultimately to die if that is required. Our history has hardened us."

There was a tinge of bitterness in the voice of the general when the subject of weapons was discussed.

"Yugoslavia was the sixth most powerful arms producer in the world. We manufactured almost everything here. Four-fifths of all the major arms-producing facilities, however, were located outside of Serbian territories. In Bosnia, nearly all the important plants were left in the hands of the Moslems. In the former Yugoslavia, most of the new factories were consigned to Croatia and Slovenia. Tudjman and Izetbegovic screamed that the Yugoslav army left much of their arms to the Serbs, but you will never hear them talk about the factories and plants to produce those arms."

In the tradition of so many other commanders — from Alexander to Wingate — Mladic had grown increasingly more philosophical about his life and about the role he was playing.

"In 1991, a young man stepped between me and a grenade that was hurled. He was very badly wounded and I was shaken by the experience, not the nearness to death, but the willingness of someone else to die in my place. For a long while, I felt inefficient, not sufficiently mature to understand the real issues. And then one day I realized that it was all very simple. Each man had two mothers — his own and his country. All depended on both mothers. The world was trying to rob me of one of them by abolishing my country, but it would never succeed. Out of the ashes of old Yugoslavia, Serbska has risen. No one will take away this mother."

During his twenty-seven years in the army, Mladic served in just about every conceivable post. "Because I was a Serb, I usually got the dirtiest work and the same applied to my Serbian colleagues. In a way that was good. It hardened us. It made us stronger and more versatile. Because of all the ethnic considerations the old Yugoslav army was a cesspool of intrigue. It was inefficient because a man wasn't judged by his soldiering ability, but by his ethnic identification. This filtered down to everything. All training schools in the country were located in Croatia. The one exception was a military school in Nis, Serbia — for dogs."

The mood was changing. Mladic paused while we toasted twice. There was hurt in his eyes as he prepared to continue.

"The tragedy of the Serbian people is that we have Serbs who are fighting and dying every day and Serbs who are watching from the sidelines. I deeply sympathize with my brothers who are under international blockade and who are suffering due to the sanctions. This was a crime committed against them by an hypocritical international community. But I cannot forgive also my own brothers who are indifferent to the bloody war that has consumed us all.

"In June, 1992, the Bosnian Serbs were dying. More than a hundred villages were burning on our side of the Drina — places that no longer exist like Tegari, Ratkovici, Fakovici, Skelani. Women and children were being murdered. Elderly people were thrown alive into the flames that once had been their homes. We were fighting for our lives.

"I flew over the worst battle areas in a helicopter in order to lead the fight. Even my hardened eyes couldn't believe how terrible it was below. And then, suddenly, I turned my attention to the other side of the Drina — a distance of only seventy meters — and I saw my fellow Serbs playing football.

Spectators were clapping, cheering on their teams. Young men had their arms around girlfriends. It was then that I almost broke my vow not to use weapons. If I had a bomb, I would have thrown it at them.

"I realized in despair that we Serbs have no national program. We are not sufficiently unified. We fought the Turks for six hundred years and then twice the Gemans, but we had never merged sufficiently in our hearts. Go to Belgrade! See the young men and their girlfriends walking happily through the park. See them at the cafés and then ask yourself how this can be.

"Fate has connected the Serbs and the Jews. We too cannot lose a battle because it would mean our extinction. You have asked yourselves the question as I have: 'Do I have the right to my own country? Why am I different from the French or the Welsh or the Greeks or the Italians?' I don't want to deprive the Moslems of anything. Let them have their land. But leave me alone. I have my back to the wall. I am not afraid to fight for what I believe. If I lose this war, I lose everything."

His face took on color as he continued. "Who decides if you are to have your own state or not? The international community! But by what right does anyone else decide my own fate and destiny for me? The question now is whether the Serbian people recognize the international community, and I tell you clearly that this Serb does not. The Swiss were smart enough to stay clear of the EC and they have a better life than all. Are the Germans to tell me whether I live or die? They tried twice. They didn't succeed."

Characteristic of his people, Mladic, the general, was a gifted poet as a young man. Apparently, years of military service had not eroded that talent.

"I am a happy man. I think on earth only woman is sacred. I have my mother, my sister, my wife and my daughter. And equally important, I have my motherland. I invested everything, all that I had and all that I dreamed in this motherland. No powers in the world can destroy Serbska. Someday there will be a common motherland for all the Serbs and then my ultimate dreams will be realized."

It was a little hard to sleep that night, partly because it was really cold and I was completely unprepared for the novel experience of cryogenic numbness at the beginning of July. I was excited about the trip to Grbavica planned for the next morning. Sarajevo was a slaughterhouse. The peace proposals in Geneva had somehow not reached the fighters along the Miljacka River that ineffectively separated the Moslems and Serbs in Sarajevo. I hoped I would not make a fool of myself, that I would somehow manage to reach the most forward positions, that I would honor the pledge I made to my wife before I left Athens to return whole.

But my thoughts were also centered on America that night. About a week earlier, I spent an interesting two hours with Dr. Milan Bulajic who was both an internationally recognized expert on war crimes and a diplomat who had served in the United States for over ten years. He told me that America and Serbia had been strong allies since the Treaty of 1881, that additional pacts had been signed with the Kingdom of Serbia in 1901 and with Montenegro in 1905 and that America was the first country to officially recognize Yugoslavia after it emerged out of the ashes of the First World War in 1918.

The reason I was thinking about America and the interview with Dr. Bulajic, hours before heading down into Sarajevo, was because of the strong impression made on me by Gen. Mladic. With all his Serbian fervor, there was something distinctly American about him. The emotions he felt for his country and people were sentiments instilled in me as a boy growing up in New York. The concept of a motherland as opposed to a mere homeland provided a strange déjà vu, reminiscence of saluting the American flag and praying that I would grow up quickly enough to yet fight the Germans and the Japanese. As Predrag Simic had reminded me earlier, in 112 years of friendship there had never been a single act of hostility between Yugoslavia and the United States.

I wasn't sure if it was Madison Avenue, the influence of the Germans, the strong predilection of the State Department to show more even-handedness to Islam or a lack of historical prospective that had caused the first painful rift between two friendly nations that had twice fought so gallantly side by side. Nor could I rationalize who in good faith in the State Department could have invited Franjo Tudjman to a ceremony commemorating the martyrs to Nazism. I only knew that something sad and baffling had occurred. Mladic was no more a beast than Milosevic was "the butcher of the Balkans", a shameful and derogatory phrase cooked up by American journalism at its absolute nadir.

In supporting Germany, I wondered, which had twice crossed swords with America in a single century, and in sacrificing Yugoslavia which had been betrayed and then dismembered by the rest of Europe, was the United States acting in its own self-interest? There were war crimes — thousands of them — but neither Serbia nor the Bosnian Serbs maintained any sort of monopoly on them. There were documents and testimonials for both sides. Rape, murder and pillage were not confined to either Christians or Moslems. Nobody was blameless. Throat slitting was the expertise of all the belligerents.

And then there was the issue of communism. In all my personal experience in Yugoslavia, there was not one single Serb who said to me, "I was a Communist and I am proud of it." There was something absolutely antithetical about the Serb who was trying to rescue his national identity after years of humiliation and subjugation and communism which was another way of saying Tito, a euphemism for the Croatian appetite for the destruction of Serbia and all things Serbian.

So why didn't America understand? Gen. Mladic was more committed to the ideals of the United States of America than Chancellor Helmut Kohl could ever be. There was a resurgence of Nazis in Germany which had less to do with skinheads and unemployment than in the warnings contained in the poems of Heinrich Heine who, way back in the Nineteenth Century, told the world that the Germans were not really a Christian nation, but were irrevocably committed to Thor.

I slept badly that night because I really wanted to tell Bill Clinton: "Take another look into history before you commit America irrevocably. Don't betray a trust and a love. Don't throw away more than a century of proven friendship and the amity and respect of an entire people."

And then I finally slept, but it still was not a good sleep.

# CHAPTER XX
# THE CAULDRON

I asked Goran if the shrapnel embedded in his left hand still hurt and he replied, as bravely as any twelve-year-old could, that it didn't. Then I questioned why he wasn't in school and he explained that there were no classes for sixth-graders since their teacher was killed.

We were at the very edge of hell, Goran and I. Besides our ages, there was only one subtle difference between us. Goran was a resident and I a tourist.

Protected by concrete on one side and sandbags on the other, we nonetheless winced and moved a trifle closer together when snipers opened fire in our direction from the turret of the Chemistry Faculty of the University of Sarajevo. Between the building in which Goran and twenty-four other families lived on the unexposed side facing the street and not the enemy, there were approximately twenty meters to the Miljacka River which the Greeks would have called the Styx because it was the entrance to the netherworld.

Since there was no school and aimless wandering through Grbavica was a death wish, I asked the sandy-haired, brown-eyed youngster how he occupied his time. Goran merely shrugged his shoulders. The question was not very practical. The answer would have even less meaning. I told Goran that I had a thirteen-year-old girl back in Athens and that her name was Natasha and that she would never believe that Grbavica could exist.

"Then you should bring her," he said simply, without rancour.

Above us, in all directions, were men with mortars and machine guns and grenade launchers. Many of them were armed with rifles equipped with sniperscopes and imported from Singapore. They were very accurate, highly lethal. They fired a 5.6 slug which, properly filed, changed direction on impact, thereby inflicting massive damage. For extra good measure, some of the cartridges were dipped in chemicals so that even a slight wound would produce deadly infections.

The Moslem snipers perched above us were motivated not merely by hatred — although there was plenty of that to go around — but were also rewarded with two packets of cigarettes for every inert victim. In Grbavica, the ultimate equality had been achieved. Men, women or children, civilians or soldiers, elderly or infant — their value was exactly the same.

Sitting on the stoop of the apartment building, wedged between two machine gun nests, I asked Goran if he hated anyone and he nodded his head no. But then I specified the Moslems and he quickly responded affirmitively.

"Why do you hate them?"

"Because they are bad. They kill people."

"But Serbs also kill people."

"But Serbs are not bad."

There was a clatter of automatic rifle fire very close to where we were seated and Goran instinctively burrowed closer into my arms. For a second, I was lost, unsure where I was any longer, reliving a similar episode in another war and in another time.

Goran hadn't changed a bit, the same hair color, the same innocent eyes, only his name was Sami and the firefight in which we were caught was in West Beirut. We were trapped in a murderous exchange between the Christian Falangists and the Palestinians. There was only the rubble and us, hardly a building remained erect and it seemed incredible that Sami and his family could actually have managed to continue living there.

The twelve-year-old waif and the forty-nine-year-old soldier became friends, an understandable phenomenon for those who have survived the ordeal of combat together. Sami asked if I would return to Beirut after the war and I lied that I would. But it was not an intentional lie, just an ignorant statement. I really thought then that there would be peace between Lebanon and Israel and that my family and I would motor from Haifa where we lived and I would watch the child grow into a man and inherit a slightly less tarnished world. I thought that I had lost Sami forever, but again I was wrong. There he was, the same innocent, brave child in Sarajevo.

"What will you do when you are grown?"

"I'll be a pilot."

"And why a pilot?"

"So I can fly away and nobody can hurt me."

I was afraid for myself and I was afraid for Goran and I was not insensitive to the fact that on the other side of the Miljacka were between 300,000–350,000 people who were paying the same mighty tithe to the goddess of death, Kali, as were the frightened residents of Grbavica. Fear was palpable. It smelled. The whole city of Sarajevo stank with it.

Huddled like animals, we rushed from one corner to another, belly as close to the ground as possible, feet paddling frantically, adrenalin released and spewing. Then there was the safety of a shell-eviscerated building and a chance to suck some oxygen before the next sprint. In the middle of the street though, in sublimely indifferent exposure to the snipers above and around us, was a painfully thin woman, black-haired and about thirty-five, who was dancing on the rubble and singing.

"What the hell is she doing?" I asked the Serb officer next to me.

"She's insane. She was held by the Moslems for four months. We finally ransomed her with six prisoners-of-war."

"But she'll get killed!"

"God looks out for her."

Perhaps I was the instrument of God that day because I rushed out to retrieve the dancing woman from the center of the street. Mad or not, she actually spoke some English.

"It rains flowers and bullets," she giggled.

I clutched her hand tightly.

"Do you want to make love to me?"

"Not right now," I replied truthfully, my knees as unsteady as my heart.

"Are you a Christian?" her face brightened.

"No," I replied.

"Then you'll hurt me," she frowned suddenly.

"I am not a Christian and I will not hurt you."

"Then you are a flower," she concluded and skipped away.

People were reduced to animals in Grbavica — all 12,000 of them, mostly Serbs, some Moslems. Homo sapiens, who had learned to stand erect so many millenia ago, was driven back down the path of evolution. They relearned the lessons of burrowing, of crouching, of sprinting with the least of all visible profiles. There was a wildness in their eyes when they stepped into the streets. Everywhere was the scent of danger. There was a primeval quality to life in what had once been a pleasant neighborhood in an attractive, multi-ethnic city. Food was an obsession, bread sometimes a luxury. There were food shortages and bread lines where the fearful and the intrepid queued together because another word for timorousness was starvation.

Why didn't they leave, I thought, but they couldn't. Their homes were there as were their possessions. Their lives were there and so was their pride. Refugees flocked into Serbia from western Slavonija and from the razed villages around Zvornik, but Grbavica was still holy ground, yet undefiled by the infidel, the barbarian.

The situation in the rest of the city, controlled by the Moslems, was equally bleak. People sprinted there also. Incoming machine-gun fire emptied streets on the farside of the river as well. There were food shortages, blackouts, black marketeers. There was hardly any medicine. Trees were firewood, greenery ash. Moslem children perished under Serbian fire, not unlike the small Serbs who were blown to tiny pieces in the Red Cross Clinic that had already sustained multiple mortar hits. Another feature common to both sides of the Miljacka was wartime motoring techniques. A slow, careful, lawful driver was very soon a dead one. No stops. No pauses. No respect for traffic moving from the right or stop signs. The penalty for driving in second gear was very often a slug through the brain.

Drivers of the armored bread delivery trucks in Grbavica were heroes, their life expectancy very short. Over the previous month, four out of five of them were shot dead. Yet people had to eat if the enclave was to remain alive and so replacement drivers were sought — and they too volunteered to die.

On May 27, 1993, the full horror of Sarajevo was graphically depicted in a twin burial in the Bosnian Serb military graveyard. Bosko Brkic, a twenty-five-year-old Serb, and Admira Ismic, a twenty-one-year-old Moslem, were put to rest side by side. Gunned down in "Snipers' Alley" as the two lovers tried to flee from the city, their bodies lay together for days because no one dared enter the killing zone to retrieve them. Finally, an anonymous Serb soldier, sickened by the sight of the two locked in death, twice sprinted a full kilometer through the city, carrying Admira and Bosko home. By common consent, the span near which they were killed was renamed "Lovers' Bridge". Their young lives were worth exactly four packs of cigarettes.

In my haste to find some temporary sanctuary from machine gun fire, I literally collided with sixty-two-year-old Fadilla who was a Moslem woman barely subsisting on a pension, but plucky and hopeful nonetheless. "I don't understand politics," she explained through an almost toothless mouth. "I have been living here all my life and it never bothered me if my neighbors were Christians or Moslems. Do you know how many intermarriages we used to have?

"I am not frightened of being a Moslem in a Serbian area. I am only scared that someone will shoot me or that the bread delivery truck will be blown up.

"I'll never leave here. This is where I have always lived and this is where I die."

So Moslems and Christians did coexist! In Sarajevo center itself, there were still an estimated 65,000 Serbs living the same precarious lives as the Moslems. Some were most certainly hostages; others, like Fadilla, simply refused to leave their homes no matter what might happen.

I still didn't know precisely where we were heading and who I was supposed to meet as we continued cannon-balling from corner to corner, concealing our bodies behind debris, pausing for breath only when safely behind an intricate system of barricades erected so as to conceal us from the voracious snipers waiting for an easy shot.

Reaching the outer edge of Serbska was simple. It took only thirty minutes from Pale to Grbavica and it was like living the crescendo of Ravel's Bolero. First it was green and bovine and there were school children. Slowly, the landscape and peoplescape changed. There were still children, but they walked faster, scurrying rather than ambling. The pretty, neat homes on the sides were no longer unscarred. Gaping holes peeped through roofs. Automobiles were resculpted by artillery shells. But still there was life. There were even flowers and flower boxes.

The deeper we descended into the pit, however, the more sinister the damage, the more feral the children, the more frightened the occupants, the more pronounced the misery. The Bolero was accelerating too quickly for even the adrenalin to keep pace. By then we were precisely four hundred meters from the front and new codes for survival had to be adopted. "Faster, you son-of-a-bitch or we are kebabcici!"

Mica was waiting for us when we slid into the church, a skimpy substitute for the 800-year-old edifice that had been burned to the ground. A journalist by profession when he was not at war — which was almost always — he had the good looks and the good humor to be chosen for the role of military spokesman. Another reason for the less combative, but no less dangerous assignment, was his war wounds. Hit twice by sniper fire from a position seventy meters away, one bullet nearly disembowled him and the other irrevocably shattered his leg. Self-assured, thirty-three-year-old Mica was destined to develop the first hobble-sprint in Balkan history.

"When I woke up in the hospital recovery room about eight months ago, I noticed that there was a four-year-old girl in a cot next to me. She too was hurt badly by sniper fire. I remember thinking, it was understandable if I got shot. I was in uniform. I was a grown man. I was a belligerent in the war. But the girl was only a kid. What had she ever done? Who did she ever hurt? What was the point of the whole thing? When she died that night, I cried a little. I don't do that very often, but I cried a bit."

Mica was very proud of "his" church, almost as pleased as with his newspaper which he called "The City Paper" and which was already six editions old.

"People have a right to the news," he explained cheerfully. "Someday my newspapers will be historical documents. In the meantime, they provide a little local entertainment which is in pretty short supply down here."

The church was a temporary replacement fitted into a partially gutted office building, beamed Mica, an example of the indomitable will of the people. "There is no way that the Moslems are going to break us," he assured. "We've already demonstrated that we can take anything they throw at us."

Only twenty days before my visit, the Moslems had unleashed a sudden, offensive in which thirty guided rockets hit the area where we were talking. This was followed by mortars and grenades. "I wonder what happened to the arms embargo?" Mica grinned. "It's like the ceasefires. The more they're invoked, the more shells land on us."

Snipers, according to Mica, were accounting for an average of two or three civilian deaths every day. "They're up there," he waved his hands, "and it's only a matter of time and patience before they acquire a target. They're helped by the fact that people get a little cocky after awhile. You figure you've survived this long so why not another day? And then you do something stupid, like exposing yourself when you didn't have to, and then pretty soon you're a statistic."

Besides a few hearty flowers, according to Mica, the only thing flourishing in Sarajevo at that juncture was the black market. "The Moslems have got it down to a science. A kilo of coffee is 120 German marks, spices 80 meat 65." The situation was no better across the river where 10 German marks equalled an average monthly salary. Two cokes or four cups of coffee were about as much as the income would buy.

The army was everywhere and everything in Grbavica. In or out of uniform, mobilization was total. You slept more often with your rifle than your wife. You manned your fortification until someone replaced you. And if no one came, you stayed. It didn't matter how long. You simply remained. "Most of us," explained my host, "are fighting 100-200 meters from where we live. Our wives and children are only two minutes behind us. We are locals here. We grew up together. We fight together. And maybe we'll all die together. Professional soldiers account for only 1% of the fighting men here. We don't expect anyone else to defend us. We're Serbs. We can do it ourselves."

It was time to move, Mica explained. There were frontline positions to visit, soldiers stationed deep in concrete and covering an enemy only meters away. There was a legendary priest, I confessed to Mica, who I really wanted to meet, but was elsewhere at that particular moment. A specialist with the mortar, he was asked once how he reconciled his profession with the role of firing weapons. "I shoot only into the sky," he explained, "only in the direction of God. It is he who decides what to do with the shell. Not me!"

There were eight, tightly cramped, curious, good-humored fighters waiting in one cellar-like fortress. They had been together in their underground citadel for fifteen months. All had fled from the center of Sarajevo. All had lost their possessions and their apartments. But none would retreat any farther.

"I could never live with Moslems again," Miodrag explained. "There is too much blood between us now. Once, my best friend was a Moslem. We were really like brothers. I would have had no problem if my daughter married his son. Those were the days when we Serbs were trained to think of ourselves as Yugoslavs. We were told that Yugoslavia was one homogeneous family and that religion and former nationality meant absolutely nothing. But the authorities lied to us because the other side knew differently. They, and the government, bullshitted us for years. While we were being good Yugoslavs our Moslem 'brothers' were preparing for a *Jihad* against us. I don't ever want to live with them again. I don't want to see them. I don't want to hear about them. I don't want to know that they exist."

Miodrag, thirty-four, a machinist from Sarajevo, married with one child, realized his wish. Two hours after we left Grbavica, he was killed by a bullet in the forehead.

# CHAPTER XXI
# THE POET PRESIDENT

Whatever were the eco-political microbes that destroyed the old Yugoslavia and continued to imperil the new Yugoslavia, it was certain that the malady lingered on. Even if Serbska was finally acknowledged and accepted by the international community, even if the Albanians in Kosovo were tranquilized for another ten years, even if Macedonia and Greece did not tear out each other's throat, the ultimate disposition of Krajina still represented a substantial obstacle. So I knew that before returning to Belgrade and assimilating the experiences and sadnesses of Sarajevo, there was one last stop.

But before that there was a man I had to meet. He was a poet. Life had transformed him somewhat into a philosopher. His medical background was the precursor of a distinguished career in psychology. Before mired in politics, he used to enjoy life, particularly time with his family and friends. He was a tall man with bushy hair and an easy smile who would cheerfully have laid down his life for the cause of Serbian freedom. Twenty-two years earlier, when he was twenty-six, his first book of poetry was published. Since then, it was joined by four others.

Appropriately, I met Radovan Karadzic, the President of Serbska, at the President's House in Pale. He was tired, very tired when we met. There were talks in Geneva and discussions in Belgrade and innuendos to be answered from Washington and replies addressed to the European Community. Army officers were waiting to report on the latest military developments. The shortage of petrol was growing into a suffocating problem. There were difficulties with the schools, with the highways, with finance, with industry.

Basically, what really intrigued me was the question of how

to establish a nation in the midst of an ugly civil war that had already evolved into the greatest tragedy in Europe since the Second World War.

"In one sense," he replied, "we were fortunate that communism left us under-developed and economically behind the times because we didn't inherit any big, white elephant companies that were over-staffed and under-worked. Starting from the beginning can sometimes be an advantage because, in tandem with the military operation we are waging, people have to eat, children must go to school, the clinics have to function and the roads must stay open.

"We are concentrating on small, profitable companies — one of them is already exporting $1 million of bauxite a day. Some of the other firms are also slowly earning profits. Our people have always been good farmers so we don't lack for food. We actually have surpluses for sale. In general, our economy is working at 35% of capacity despite war conditions and it will get better as time passes. I see Serbska as a small, but prosperous country in the future."

Dr. Karadzic was quick to admit that Serbska had "inherited" considerable caches of weapons and quantities of fuel from the withdrawing Yugoslav army. The main arms-producing plants, however, in Bosnia and Herzegovina were built in regions populated by Croats, a persistent phenomenon that was contrived by the Croat leadership in both the Communist Party and the Ministry of Defense.

I asked Dr. Karadzic if the war wounds would ever heal. He shook his head sadly.

"Serbs and Moslems cannot live together for the foreseeable future. There has been too much bloodshed, too much uprooting, too much betrayal. This does not mean, however, that we will not protect minority rights in Serbska. Before the war, there were 20,000 Moslems living in Banja-luka. Now there are 40,000. I expect that we will have a quarter of a million Moslems and Croats living in our country when peace is finally achieved. These people shall be protected by the law. Their rights are already guaranteed in our constitution.

"Human rights are one thing, however, and political reality is another. It would be best if we were all autonomous of each other for sometime. There is too much mutual hatred and distrust to overcome with the mere signing of a peace treaty. Unfortunately, the civil war has produced a chasm between the peoples who once lived together in Bosnia and Herzegovina. This will not be bridged for a long time.

"But I'm a realist. The international community currently insists on some form of confederation between Serbs, Moslems and Croats. It represents more political face saving than political reality, but I am not prepared to cause problems over that point if Europe insists that no other alternatives exist. I would sign such a document although I would retain strong reservations. Moslem bias against Serbs did not start in 1992. It is the continuation of a hatred that developed since the Second World War."

Dr. Karadzic paused and closed his eyes for a moment. The fatigue was telling. He had barely slept for four days and he would be leaving for Belgrade and then Geneva the next day. I almost felt guilty over my intrusion.

"You know that Germany won the war in the Balkans. Whatever else the history books may say, the Germans finally realized their objectives in this region. The brutal diplomatic policies of Hans Dietrich Genscher gave back to Germany the diplomatic victory that it had lost in the battlefield. If there will ever be an international tribunal judging crimes in this region, and if the judges are honest men who acknowledge that the causes of the war are no less important than the crimes and the criminals, then Austria's Foreign Minister Alois Mok, Germany's Genscher and Kohl and many, many other West Europeans must be brought to the bars of justice. They violated international laws by supporting secessionary movements. They closed their collective eyes to human rights abuses. And, perhaps worst of all, they established very dangerous precedents which will produce great suffering for many nations in the future."

Some months earlier, at the Athens Conference, Dr. Karadzic had officially signed and thus committed himself to the implementation of the Vance-Owen plan. What brought that about? I wanted to know.

"I was under intense pressure from everyone — including my fellow Serbs in Belgrade — but even as I initialed the document, I knew that my people would not ratify it and I told the world very clearly that without the consent of the people of Serbska, my signature meant nothing.

"When I returned from Athens to Pale, I was morally obliged to recommend to our assembly the adoption of a plan that I knew could never work and understood would jeopardize the security of my whole nation. But I had given my word. I also knew my people and I understood the sentiments of the Assembly. When more than 95% of our voters categorically rejected the Vance-Owen proposal and, in doing so, nullified my own signature, I wasn't the least bit surprised. That document was for war, not for peace. It would have created permanent anxiety and tension in this region which would have exploded time and time again into new wars and steady confrontations.

"The Moslems and the Croats both signed and then immediately lunged at each other's throat. The problem is that too many key players, in the political drama being conducted by Europe and the United Nations, are utterly ignorant of what this area is all about. They have no historical prospective. They never even tried to understand what really caused this civil war. We, representing a third of the nation and owning more than two-thirds of the country, were against secession and, without our agreement, that secession could not be legally enacted. Our absolute veto was abandoned as were all the human rights which were inherent in the laws of the former republic. A constitution was destroyed and nobody cared.

"The crime against the Serbs of Bosnia was premature

recognition which obliterated all chances for a dialogue between people who might have yet settled their differences and established new criteria by which they could live. I pleaded with the world. Milosevic pleaded with the world. All that happened was the acceleration of the process of disintegration under the leadership of Germany, but with the full consent and approval of the European Community."

The war in Bosnia had been divisive for Serbs. The unimaginable occurred. Under heavy pressures from the rest of the world and with America goading for tighter restrictions and perhaps even military intervention, a fissure developed between brothers. Serbia, the blockaded, suddenly became Serbia, the blockader.

"I was sad, not angry, about the position taken by Belgrade. How much pressure could one small nation take? Few countries in the world could have withstood the sanctions imposed on Serbia for more than a year by the international community. When Belgrade decided to impose those same sanctions on us, I understood how saddened Serbia's leadership must have felt. But I couldn't lose track of the fact that the United States, Germany and Turkey were calling for additional sanctions against the new Yugoslavia and were already rattling sabres. I understood, but it hurt anyway. Life was growing very difficult in Serbia, but we were paying a different price — in blood and lives.

"We understood what the world pressures were all about. The international community was trying to coerce the Serbs of Serbia into believing that they were suffering because of us, that if we just went away and disappeared, all the economic problems and political isolation would go away. I was happy that this disruptive attempt at spoiling relations between Serb and Serb never succeeded. I was grateful for the understanding of the people of Serbia who knew that if it wasn't Bosnia, there would have been pressures because of Kosovo.

"We Serbs made one colossal error of judgment in contemporary times. We should have unified two years ago so that we would have been united and stronger and better able to defend ourselves. Once the old Yugoslavia began to dissolve, the most rational of all outcomes was a united Serbia embracing us all."

I couldn't help recalling how the newspapers and a great many political pundits were bandying about the term "Greater Serbia" along with their other favorite cliché, "ethnic cleansing". The very idea of Greater Serbia was an invention of the Austro-Hungarian Empire. The concept simply never was adopted by the Serbs who together with all the Serbs in Serbia and Montenegro, and all their ethnic colleagues in Krajina and Serbska, barely amounted to ten million, nowadays the population of a large city.

Outgunned and outmanned at the beginning, the Bosnian Serbs had performed some incredible military feats and were, as stated before, in control of about 70% of Bosnia. Having met the larger Moslem forces head-on, they managed to roll the enemy back on all fronts. How was that performed? Were the Serbs super-soldiers?

Dr. Karadzic laughed for the first time that evening. His eyes were bright again as he replied.

"Serbs are average, no better and no worse than soldiers anywhere else.

"For us, victory was a desperate act, like the 1914 assassination of the archduke. We were cornered, given no other choice and literally fighting in front of our own homes. We weren't able to deploy our forces from one part of Bosnia to the other. There was never a Yugoslav army to intervene on our behalf. Each house was a battleground. Our wives and children were at stake. There was no other way. We had to win or die.

"I never really appreciated how misinformed the world was about our civil war until the American Secretary of State said that Serb forces would have had 'to roll back' to Belgrade or face international censure. A lot of our people have been living here for five and six centuries."

The Serbska President was realistic about future boundaries and territorial adjustments.

"We don't have many choices," he admitted. "We can stay precisely where we are and formally merge with Krajina. We would then have a strong Serbian state and a good economy and the world will forever treat us as a nation of pariahs. We would be exactly in the shoes of Turkey in northern Cyprus. No one even acknowledges the existence of that puppet state.

"On the other hand, we can seriously negotiate. It means that we will have to give up some land for regional stability and recognized borders. We, and the Croats of Herzegovina, have to ensure that the Moslems have the space and geography for their own independent country. Then they can have Islamic rule as much as they want. We know that the problem will not disappear because of military victories. The military victories were in order that we shouldn't disappear.

"The problem is that usually when you negotiate you need a partner. The Moslem leadership is torn and divided. There are radicals who want to continue fighting, want to import more arms, want to Islamize the conflict and are enrolling more and more Mujahedeen for their *Jihad.* And then there are the saner voices who want to compromise, who want to negotiate, who understand that three peoples must have their complete autonomy and then learn to live as neighbors."

One of the most over-used, ill-used and abused words in the English language was "charisma". It would have been hard, however, and far less precise, to describe Radovan Karadzic any other way. He was a leader and a spokesman and, yes, still a poet.

# CHAPTER XXII
# STALINGRAD IN KRAJINA

The annihilation of the beautiful Danubian city of Vukovar, the pearl of eastern Slavonija, was preordained when the internal maps of Yugoslavia were redrawn by the Communist Party after the Second World War. Regions, where the population had been heavily Serbian for six hundred years and where artifacts and ruins indicated a Serbian presence for more than eight hundred years, were delivered to Croatia irrespective of national considerations. These included the whole fertile valley of Knin, eastern and western Slavonija, Baranja and Zapatini (western) Srem.

Historically, the Serbs were induced to settle the region in large numbers by the Austro-Hungarians to form a human bulwark against the Turkish invaders and to act as the first protective shield of Christianity. There was never a doubt that without these valiant defenders the map of Europe would have changed dramatically. Mandated to preserve the borders of the Hapsburg Empire with their lives, the Serbs were given land and treated as free people, not serfs, from the onset. And yet with one cruel, decisive stroke of the pen in 1945, possibly a million Serbs were delivered permanently to Croatia.

Still, at the time, there seemed to be some sort of rationale for the decision. The regions were populated by both Serbs and Croats from time immemorial and some administrative solution had to be found. War wounds were to be healed and a brave, new society was in the process of being established. Internal rivalries and borders were no longer to be of great importance because one South Slav entity had endured the cauldron of war — Yugoslavia.

This national dream shattered completely on December 22, 1990, when a new constitution was promulgated in Zagreb in which Croatia was proclaimed "the state of the Croatian people". From that moment onward, Serbs were to be merely tolerated as a national minority. On February 28, representatives of the Serbian people in Knin issued their own declaration of independence and announced their formal secession from Croatia. In March, the whole region of Krajina announced it was breaking away from Zagreb control while similar decisions were being formulated in Slavonija, Baranja and western Srem. On May 2, threats matured into hostility. Fighting broke at Borovo-Selo, ten kilometers from Vukovar.

When relating his own experiences in the war, sixty-five-year-old Bozidar Petrovic, tried unsuccessfully to hide his tears. Several times, his voice broke. He would pause and then his blue eyes would stare vacantly out of the window of the building that was the headquarters of the "Serbian Region of Slavonija, Serbian Republic of Krajina". We were exactly 160 kilometers from Belgrade, only 20 kilometers from Croatia. We were in an area referred to as "Stalingrad" by the locals.

"My memories go back much farther than the first half of 1991," Petrovic, the secretary of the local government, explained. "I, and many other survivors from my generation, remember the Ustashe cruelties during the Second World War. There are things that you can put out of your mind, but never forget. What they did to us was inhuman.

"In the spring of 1991, we were working along two parallel courses. Some of our leaders were trying to negotiate with Zagreb, attempting to explain that we could not, and would not, accept second-class citizenship in our own land. We were not like so many of the Croats, recent arrivals. We had been here forever. Simultaneously, we were collecting arms — anything that could shoot and from anyone who would sell them. There were plenty of guns around. What was needed was money and patience.

"When the fighting erupted in Borovo-Selo, we knew that negotiations were over. There would be no peace. In the battle, ten Croat policemen were killed and one Serb. The news spread quickly and we decided to barricade the villages. Each settlement would become an island. Each island would be self-sufficient and responsible for its own defense. If we were overwhelmed, no one could help us. We knew exactly what would happen."

At the time, the Yugoslav national army was still functioning, although already under siege in some of the more remote locations of Slovenia and Croatia. But while the façade remained, the insides were being eviscerated. Reminiscent of the American civil war when southern soldiers marched back to Dixie en masse, Croats and Slovenes were encouraged to desert their posts, taking arms and whatever equipment they could with them. Belgrade, still trying to avoid any major escalations and still hoping for some sort of last-minute reconciliation, ordered the troops to remain passive, to respond only when self-defense required and to try to act as mediators between the two sides.

The villages of eastern Slavonija at the time were either totally Serb or mixed Serb-Croat. Over the years, there had been plenty of intermarriages and ethnic lines were, in many cases, blurred. The situation in cities like Vukovar, however, was different. Many Croats had settled in the region, in response to the prodding of Zagreb, after World War II and they usually moved into urban, developed areas. So when war started, the countryside belonged to the Serbs, while the cities and large townships were occupied by the Croats.

"In response to our barricades," continued Petrovic, "the Croatian police and army sealed off Vukovar completely. It happened very quickly and we were unprepared. The worst part of it was that all the children from the neighboring villages were in school there. They weren't permitted to leave and they were terrified.

"We tried bargaining for them, but that did no good. Finally, we sent a delegation of Croats who had remained with us, mostly from mixed marriages, with a message to the authorities in Vukovar: Release the children unharmed or

Croat blood would begin to spill from one end of Slavonija to the other. They understood the message. It took several days, but the children were released and returned to us."

The situation deteriorated every day. More incidents were reported, additional clashes occurred. From the onset, it became apparent that not only the Serbian villagers had prepared themselves for war. Zagreb steadily and stealthily dispatched police and para-military militias into the region. Large caches of arms were stored in Vukovar and a Croatian commando unit was secreted under the municipal hospital in catacombs hidden beneath the building.

"The whole region was cut off," continued Petrovic. "The Croats couldn't pass our barricades and we were stopped by their blockades. We had food and ammunition, but our most urgent requirement was to evacuate the women and children and elderly because eventually we knew that we would be fighting from village to village, from house to house. This evacuation became even more urgent for us after the Croats broke through our defenses and captured the village of Sarvas. All thirty of the women and children they found there were massacred."

About 1,300 Serbs captured in Vukovar, Osijek, Vinkovci and Borovo-Selo were severely tortured and then executed, usually by slitting their throats. Burial was out of the question so deep gashes were cut in the chests and stomachs of the victims before the bodies were thrown into the Danube. They sank better that way!

A middle-aged Serb farmer, Mijo Krajnovic, recalled his capture by members of the Croatian National Guard. "This is how it all went on... People were screaming from the terrible beatings. They hit us with clubs, iron poles. They kicked us. They used anything they could lay their hands on. You fall down. They trample over you. That lasted the whole night through... With their knives they made crosses on the breasts of some people, later filling the wounds with salt."

For months the bloody war continued, moving from village

to village, hamlet to hamlet. What was left of the Yugoslav national army was fighting with and for the Serbs by then, a high number from the region anyway. Serb volunteers from Serbia joined the fray as the seesaw struggle grew more critical and Croatia countered not only with the full brunt of its own forces, but with an army of superbly equipped mercenaries. The worst battleground became Vukovar itself. Every house was contested. Every meter was fought for.

Born in Vukovar forty-two years earlier, Slobodan Popovic related that "there were 11,000 houses in the city before the war started. Not one of them emerged intact. Approximately 1.5 million shells, rockets, bombs and projectiles landed in the city. That is why Vukovar is called 'Stalingrad'. When the fighting was over, there was nothing left but debris and corpses."

The city was taken on November 23.

The victorious indigenous Serbs who captured the citadel were joined by elements of the army and volunteers. It was, however, a Pyrrhic victory for those who had known and loved the city. Nothing was left, absolutely nothing!

"Prior to the war," continued Popovic who was waiting along with me for the return of the mayor of Vukovar, "there were 84,000 people living in the municipal area and about 45,000 in the city itself. We were the micro of ex-Yugoslavia − one-third Serb, one-third Croat, and one-third minorities. There were over 6,000 mixed marriages recorded in the city.

"Immediately after the war, there were only about 2,500 people left, most of them hiding in cellars. There was no water, no electricity, no telephone, no roads, nothing. All the industry was destroyed. The second largest Danube River harbor in old Yugoslavia was blown to smithereens."

Eighteen months after an armistice was initialed between the two sides in January, 1992, and the subsequent entrance of the United Nations to oversee an unsteady peace, the city center was still totally in ruin.

"Everything was a matter of priorities," Popovic explained.

"No one was going to help us. We had to do everything on our own. The top urgencies were water, food and electricity. This we achieved quickly. Next we had to prevent disease and epidemics. The first building we rebuilt was the hospital. We spared no costs on that building. We bought the best and most modern equipment available. This was the one area where international aid was received, first from Serbian philanthropists living overseas, then from the Red Cross and the organization 'Doctors without Borders'.

"Our population grew to about 23,000-24,000 and then we inherited the new problem of many thousands of refugees who had fled here from western Slavonija which was completely overrun by the Croat army. Nevertheless, and despite all the troubles, we managed to rebuild 6,000 square meters of schools for our 8,000 children."

Popovic acknowledged that the political uncertainties implicit in the region dampened the possibilities of accelerating the renewal. "Industry and construction require investors. We have everything going for us here — rivers, fertile land, a good industrial base, but you need political stability before investors are willing to bring in capital."

Political stability indeed was in short supply. On January 22, 1993, Croatian forces swept across the border and attacked Knin, the capital of the second salient comprising the Serbian Republic of Krajina. The government in Zagreb never concealed its intention of regaining the two regions currently separated by a formidable Croatian military presence in western Slavonija where the Serb revolt was quickly and brutally extinguished. The fate of the Serbs in western Slavonija, incidentally, was ethnic cleansing in its most pristine and undiluted form. Ten cities and 183 rural settlements were completely purged of Serbs while another 87 villages were partially "purified".

Popovic, a member of the local town council and part of the secretariat administering the city, admitted that while there was still political turmoil about the future, "the Croats will never be permitted back here. Three times genocide was applied against us - once during the Balkan Wars and World War I, then by the Nazis and Ustashe, and more recently by Tudjman. The world has to recognize facts as they are. There is no force that could compel us to relinquish our liberty. There is no international guaranty that we would accept for our freedom. Nobody in Belgrade will tell us what to do and nobody in the United Nations is going to dictate terms to us. If there are internationally recognized standards for self-determination, then we most certainly fit them. We didn't steal this land. We didn't take it away from anyone.

"There are few nations in the world that really have a soul. We are one of them. We are not criminals. We are not taught to hate people. We love freedom and we love life. And we know how to defend ourselves. If Croatia is here, under any conditions, then we no longer exist. For us that means genocide. When you are facing genocide, you have to be willing to react desperately."

Mayor Milorad Visic, a thirty-four-year-old Doctor of Medicine, entered the room and added his voice to the discussion.

"I was trained to save lives and yet I carried a rifle during this war. I sent my wife and son away to Bosnia when the fighting erupted, but my mother refused to leave. If someone tried to hurt my mother, I knew I would kill. Fortunately, I didn't have to, but I was ready.

"I am not trained in surgery and yet I had to perform four hundred operations. War not only brings out strange qualities in you, it produces strange reactions. You have to put your priorities into order. You have to accept the fact that maybe you are going to die.

"When I returned to Vukovar, I thought I would feel elation. I looked at my city, at my poor dead city, and all I felt was grief. I too helped destroy Vukovar, but in the heat of battle it is hard to see the whole picture. What I saw finally was only death and ruin.

"Vukovar will remain and will remain Serbian, no matter what happens. We don't accept interference here from anyone, not even Karadzic or Milosevic. They have their own problems. We have ours.

"We have two blockades operating against us now — one from the world and one from our brothers. These blockades produce criminals and terrorists, but the world doesn't want to see that. But whatever happens, we will survive. Even if we have to make bigger sacrifices. Even if we have to sacrifice ourselves."

He paused and then asked. "Do you know why there are so many medical doctors and philosophers in government now? Because the politicians are so bad. Because the Communists have made such a mess of this country. Because people are tired of liars."

Over lunch, later in the day, I met a beautifully radiant young woman named Tatiana. She had big, wondering, brown eyes that seemed perpetually amused. In an area of Serbian giants, she was petite, exquisitely formed, different from the rest. She was about to be married to a local Serb whom she had known and loved for years. The only thing a little different about Tatiana was that she was a Croat, full-blooded and not ashamed or querulous or apologetic.

"My children will be children," she explained. "They will just be good people. They will grow up knowing this is their country. I am twenty-four years old and still an optimist. Isn't that wonderful? Isn't that hopeful?"

*Slobodan Milosevic addressing the Assembly of the Republic of Serbia following the secession of Slovenia and Croatia.*

*Josip Broz Tito in his headquarters on the Island of Vis in 1944.*

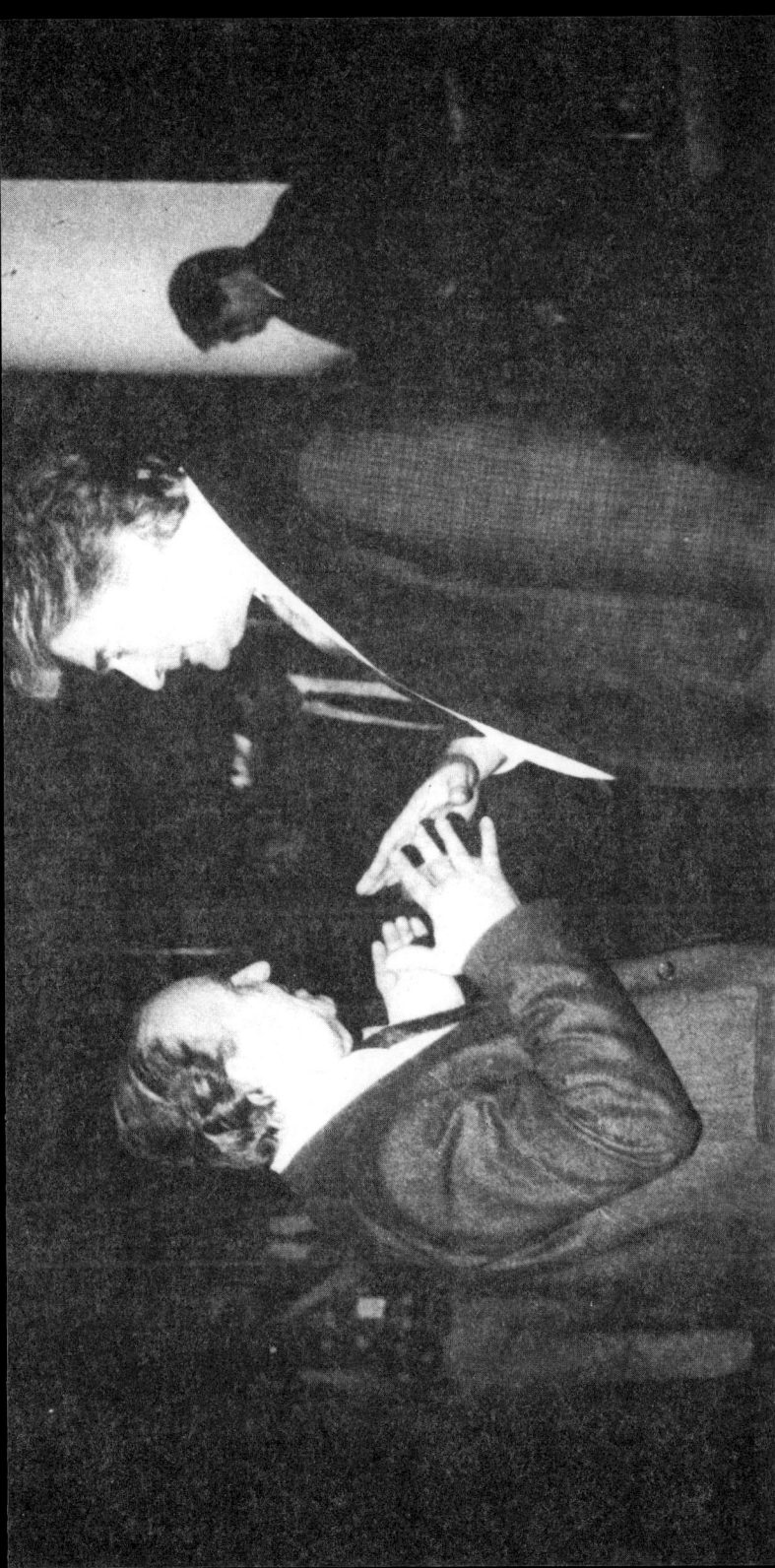

*Alija Izetbegovic and Radovan Karadzic before the war in Bosnia - Herzegovina.*

*Gen. Ratko Mladic.*

*Top: Dr. Slobodanka Gruden, mayor of Belgrade.*

*Dr. Klara Mandic*

Top: Captain Dragan

Bottom: Goran Hadzic - President of the Republic of Krajina.

*Prof. Radivoje Papovic.*

*Bosko Drobnjak in front of Kosovo Memorial.*

*Prof. Rexhep Ismajila,
Albanian nationalist.*

*Ilijaz Duka, Albanian
advocate of moderation.*

# CHAPTER XXIII
# ENDURING SERBIA

Waiting in the foyer of the office of the President of Serbia before the meeting had commenced, I could not recall any world leader villainized more savagely and with less cause than the man I was about to interview. The pejorative expressions used to describe him set a very low tone for serious journalism. And yet, throughout my journey up and down the country, most of the Yugoslavs I spoke to expressed fond views of the man and his policies. In Serbska and Krajina, there were those who thought he was too soft and should have adopted a more aggressive posture against the international community. Speaking to people in Belgrade, there were some who would have advocated a more lenient approach to international relations. No one, however, who I spoke to blamed Slobodan Milosevic for the disintegration of old Yugoslavia, for the economic catastrophe that had been inflicted on the people, for the sanctions and boycotts implemented by the world body.

No one appointed Milosevic to anything. He was elected and, in the last election, despite all the terrible problems facing Serbia, won with a clear, absolute majority — a phenomenon most unusual in Europe or the United States.

This man was an enigma. He was successful banker and proponent of free market economy in the eighties when Slovenian and Croatian economists were attracted by the sound of the words, but uncomprehending of the message. He traveled in all the right international banking circles, was a friend to David Rockefeller, visited America more than a hundred times as the chairman of the largest banking association in Yugoslavia and before that as the managing director of one of the country's most formidable industries, a position he attained at the age of thirty. And yet, in 1983, when he was propounding open and free markets, he was the president of the Communist Party of Belgrade and, three years later, was the president of the Central Committee of the Communist party of Serbia.

Milosevic lost his mother when he was very young and was raised by an austere, conservative priest-father in the town of Pozarevac, near Belgrade. Perhaps the Communist Party, so all-embracing, so all-consuming, so all-demanding was an ideological substitute for a material, irreplaceable loss. Whatever else he might have been or not been, however, no one could accuse him of lacking passion for Serbia — a land he served with an almost obsessive, consuming love. It was he who repealed, in the spring of 1989, as the president of the presidency of Serbia, the oppressive bylaws of the 1974 Constitution which humiliated and shamed the whole Serbian nation. It was he who stopped the further distillation of Kosovo which was inexorably heading to ruin and maybe war. And it was he, although pilloried by the international community, who refused to kneel to outside pressures, and abandon totally the Serbs of Krajina and Bosnia.

I had learned a little about Milosevic from people who knew him well, persons whose judgments and evaluations I trusted. He was deeply introverted, sharing thoughts and pain with almost no one excepting his wife and two children. He was also a strong individualist who appreciated advisors, but found it awkward to accept advice. The greatest of all secrets in Serbia were his real strategic political aims. These he would confide to no one.

My first impression of Milosevic when we met was his eyes. They were small, but incandescent. They were tired and very astute. They were also, I would hazard to guess, full of the loneliness of hard decision-making.

"We wanted to preserve Yugoslavia despite the strong foreign interests that were aimed at our disintegration. We were never against self-determination, but we wanted peaceful solutions and not force. We tried to explain to the world that we had a problem with artificial borders, with historical injustices, but no one wanted to listen. What the Moslems did in Bosnia was unconstitutional. They voided the rights of the other two ethnic groups in that land. How could war have been avoided once the European Community and then America blessed their action?

"The Moslem state that was to have been established made no secret of its intentions to flood Bosnia with citizens who had left and would be enticed to return. They were speaking of altering the demographics permanently by bringing in four million from Turkey. And if they brought only 10% of that number, what would have happened? Millions of Moslems from Algeria and Turkey have already flooded France and Germany. Bosnia was next. We should never forget that the Moslems owned less than 40% of Bosnia. The rest belonged to Serbs.

"And yet," stressed Milosevic, "there can be no peaceful solution in Bosnia and Herzegovina without considering the requirements of the Moslem population. A tripartite agreement must be hammered out between Serbs, Croats and Moslems in order to ensure the future stability of the region."

The upsurge of fighting between Croats and Moslems induced large numbers of Moslems to seek refuge in Serbia. Many of them were already "adopted" by Serbian families, others were living in refugee centers like Pancevo.

I asked for comments on sanctions and I got them.

"Sanctions are just another name for robbery. It's a new kind of genocide. The international community thought we would sell out our national interests. It was wrong. There is nothing we can't buy despite the sanctions. The only difference is that we have to pay three times the normal price.

"Despite the damage done to our economy, it won't take long before we fully recover once the sanctions are lifted. We are one of the most profitable agricultural centers in Europe and we have a surplus of electricity which is a big economic advantage for us. And besides all that, we have an added asset of many skilled and highly educated people because we have always maintained very high levels in our universities. All these factors make Yugoslavia an attractive market for investment.

"Do you know how much Europe has lost because of the sanctions? We were negotiating big contracts for highways and railroad improvements. One large Paris firm told us they will be here one second after the sanctions are removed. I believe them. A healthy Yugoslavia is good business for the West."

We spoke about Germany for awhile which we both knew had played a particularly invidious role in the breakup of old Yugoslavia.

"I don't see Germany as a particular danger to Yugoslavia any longer. It achieved, after all, what it wanted. It has its two client states which are totally dependent on it. It has the access to the Mediterranean it always wanted. But one shouldn't over-simplify and blame only Germany. The European Community is also at fault. In Maastricht, they committed a crime against Yugoslavia. They organized the disintegration of the state. They came to us offering their good services. In innocence, we accepted those offers and then they paid us with perfidy.

"Despite all our setbacks, however, this was the first time in the century that the genocide planned against the Serbian people was not realized. We saved the territories where the Serbs have been living for centuries. If the price for that achievement was the decrease in our standard of living, it was not so terribly expensive. We could not in good conscience opt to maintain our standards when our people on the western bank of the Drina River were fighting for their existences. Who could have done otherwise?"

When I asked how he foresaw the futures of Serbia, Serbska and the Serbian Republic of Krajina, he replied that there was already a process of integration taking place — first in economic matters, later "in other aspects".

I couldn't avoid broaching the subject of Macedonia. The Americans had turned it into a cause célèbre. Greece was obsessed with the topic. There were those who thought Macedonia was a tinderbox waiting for a match. Milosevic was not one of them.

"Creating artificial tensions between Serbia and Macedonia was crazy. We have no reason to quarrel. We have no outstanding differences with each other. Some Macedonians were trying to promote tensions in order to fan the fires of nationalism. What is important, however, is that not one drop of blood was spilled. Unlike Slovenia, Croatia, Bosnia and Herzegovina, Macedonia's transition to independent statehood was entirely peaceful.

"If you ask me whose side I support in the quarrel between Macedonia and Greece, I believe that Athens is right. My friends in Skopje have taken the name and the symbols of a friendly, neighboring country. These acts have caused the Greeks to feel threatened.

"Are you ashamed of being a Slav? I asked Gligorov in our talks and he replied, 'Of course not.' Then go back to the name, I told him, of SR Macedonia. Once you were the Socialist Republic of Macedonia. Now you will be the Slavic Republic of Macedonia."

Inwardly I smiled, wondering how President Kiro Gligorov would sell that name to his very large number of Albanian constituents.

The meeting was concluded on a high, positive note. Milosevic was sure that once the war ended finally in Bosnia and Herzegovina the restoration of links with the rest of the world would take place faster than expected and normal economic and political relations would be achieved quickly. He reiterated that Yugoslavia was a powerful trading partner and that the sanctions had hurt not only his country, but many other European states as well. He shrugged at the media war aimed both at Yugoslavia and him personally. "It was a dirty, well-paid propaganda effort," he said. "Once the focal point of the conflict moved from Serbs and Moslems to Croats and Moslems, the media lost most of its original interest".

"Are you optimistic?" I asked my final question.

"I am a Serb," he replied. "Of course, I am."

Only a fifteen-minute walk from the office of the President of Serbia is the Kalemegdan Park. Located around the walls of a fortress, it looks down on both the Sava and Danube rivers as they touch and merge along the embankments of the "White City".

Geography produced the history of the region, I mulled. The invaders, the conquerers, the mercenaries, the mendicants, they came from north and south; from east and west. Foreign armies marched through the Balkans in heavy boots, trampling each new generation, numbing the earth until a new crop emerged.

I wondered what my young friend Goran was doing that moment in Sarajevo and whether he was being careful and if he still wanted to be a pilot so that he could fly away where no one could hurt him. And then I realized I had committed a dreadful omission with the other Goran, from Pancevo. I had promised that I would tell the President of Serbia about his cigarette shortage. And I had forgotten. I thought of the mayor of Vukovar, wading through the debris and trying to build a city of hope from an aftermath of despair and ruin. I wondered what the future held for Bojana and Pedga and Slavica — if there was a future.

I was not alone that afternoon, staring down at the confluences of the two great rivers. I felt the ghost of Tito mocking and teasing and chortling over the indelible mischief he had produced which simply would not go away. Farther into the haze, I could almost discern the goose-stepping invaders from Germany, stripping Yugoslavia of the thin camouflage of national unity and then disappearing until a more auspicious moment for their emergence two generations later. Where did they bury Miodrag? I questioned. Surely there were no cemeteries in the graveyard of Grbavica.

Although I was extremely pleased with the meeting with Slobodan Milosevic, I felt considerably less optimistic than he. There were still too many shadows, lurking on the sides, too many unanswered questions. Despite my doubts, however, I knew one thing for certain — the Serbs would endure.

# APPENDIX

# YUGOSLAVIA

*Socialist Federal Republic of Yugoslavia (SFRY)*
*territory: 255,804 sq. km*
*population: 23,809,000*

*Federal Republic of Yugoslavia (FRY)*
*territory: 102,173 sq. km*
*population: 10,524,000*

- ☐ **February 21, 1974** - Promulgation of the Yugoslav Constitution which largely made for a confederal state, and greatly contributed to the disintegration of Serbia as both its provinces (Vojvodina and Kosovo) were virtually "states within the state".
- ☐ **November 19, 1985** - Mikhail Gorbachev met Ronald Reagan in Geneva; this marked the beginning of the end of the Cold War and of Yugoslavia's role until that time within the East-West conflict.
- ☐ **November 9, 1989** - Demolition of the Berlin Wall symbolically and virtually marking the collapse of Socialism in Eastern Europe, including Yugoslavia.
- ☐ **January 20, 1990** - The three days long XIV Congress of the League of Communists of Yugoslavia revealed bitter antagonisms between the various republican delegations, culminating in the decision of the Slovenian delegates to walk out. The XIV Congress wound up without the presence of delegates from Croatia and Slovenia on May 26, 1990.
- ☐ **January 19, 1989** - Government of Ante Marković was formed.
- ☐ **August 8, 1990** - The Assembly of the SFRY adopted several amendments to the Constitution of the SFRY enabling the establishment of a multi-party system.
- ☐ **January 17, 1991** - The Assembly of the SFRY stated that there could be no recognition of any of the Yugoslav republics until all points connected with the right to self-determination and secession had been definitely cleared up.
- ☐ **March 21, 1991** - At the expanded session of the SFRY Presi-

dency agreement was reached to start negotiations between representatives of Yugoslav republics on future Yugoslavia.

☐ **March 26, 1991** - The European Community released a Declaration which stressed that a "united and democratic Yugoslavia had the best prospects of becoming integrated into Europe".

☐ **April 23, 1991** - The Assembly of Montenegro elected Branko Kostić as the member of SFRY Presidency from that republic, instead of Nenad Bućin who resigned.

☐ **June 19, 1991** - The CSCE adopted a Declaration upholding the inviolability of Yugoslavia's unity and territorial integrity.

☐ **June 27, 1991** - The Government adopted a decision to man all frontier crossings along Slovenia's borders with Italy, Austria and Hungary, as well as all airports on that republic's territory (following Slovenia's decision to declare its sovereignty and independence).

☐ **June 28, 1991** - The European Community decided to send a peace mission (so-called "Troika") to Yugoslavia. The mission included Jacques Pos, Gianni De Michelis and Hans Van Den Broek. It also decided to freeze all economic assistance to Yugoslavia.

☐ **July 1, 1991** - In the presence of the three-member delegation of the European Community, SFRY Presidency elected Stipe Mesić the President, and Branko Kostić the Vice-President.

☐ **July 7, 1991** - Under the auspices of the European Community the so-called Brioni Declaration on Yugoslavia as an entity was adopted. The decisions of Slovenia and Croatia to declare sovereignty and independence were suspended for a duration of three months.

☐ **July 24, 1991** - The Federal Assembly, in the absence of representatives of Slovenia and Croatia, adopted a decision to suspend these two republics' decision to declare sovereignty and independence.

☐ **September 7, 1991** - The Peace Conference on Yugoslavia began at the Hague under the auspices of the European Community.

☐ **November 29, 1991** - The Arbitration Commission of the Peace Conference on Yugoslavia at the Hague, known as the Badinter Commission, tendered its expert opinion that Yugoslavia was in process of "dissolution", all its republics being considered as successors.

☐ **April 27, 1992** - Promulgation of the Constitution of the Federal Republic of Yugoslavia incorporating Serbia and Montenegro. The Federal Republic of Yugoslavia was declared a sovereign federal state based on the equality of all its citizens and republics.

- ☐ **May 30, 1992** - The Security Council adopted Resolution 757, imposing economic sanctions on Yugoslavia (Serbia and Montenegro).

- ☐ **May 31, 1992** - Elections were held for the Chamber of Citizens of the FR Yugoslavia at which the Socialist Party of Serbia secured 75, and the Serbian Radical Party 33 seats (out of a total of 138).

- ☐ **'June 15, 1992** - Dobrica Ćosić elected first President of the FR of Yugoslavia with a term of office of five years.

- ☐ **July 14, 1992** - Milan Panić appointed Prime Minister of the FR of Yugoslavia.

- ☐ **August 11, 1992** - Yugoslav President Dobrica Ćosić, Prime Minister Milan Panić and the Co-Chairmen of the Geneva Conference Cyrus Vance and Lord Owen released a joint statement on Bosnia-Herzegovina and relations with Croatia.

- ☐ **September 24, 1992** - Patriarch Pavle and Cardinal Kuharić addressed a joint message from Geneva calling for an urgent cease-fire, an end to ethnic cleansing and peace in Bosnia-Herzegovina.

- ☐ **September 30, 1992** - In Geneva a joint Statement was released by the President of FR Yugoslavia Dobrica Ćosić and Croatian President Franjo Tudjman, on the resolution of mutually disputed questions, the issue of the Prevlaka in particular.

- ☐ **December 20, 1992** - Early elections for the Yugoslav Parliament. Results: out of the 138 seats in the Chamber of Citizens there will be 47 deputies from the Socialist Party of Serbia, 34 from the Serbian Radical Party, 20 from DEPOS, 5 from the Democratic Party, 3 from the Democratic Community of Vojvodina Hungarians, 2 from the Democratic-Reformist Coalition and 1 Coalition of Democrats, Reformists and Citizens. The Chamber of Citizens will include from Montenegro: 17 seats of the Democratic Party of Socialists, 5 of the Social-Democratic Party and 4 of People's Party. Twenty deputies each will be delegated to the Chamber of the Republics from the parliaments of Serbia and Montenegro respectively.

- ☐ **January 17, 1993** - The Muslim forces of Bosnia-Herzegovina attacked Bajina Bašta and the Peručac Hydro-power Station, causing numerous casualties; this was denounced at an emergency session of the Yugoslav Government.

# The Yugoslav People's Army

☐ **June 27, 1991** - The Federal Secretariat for National Defense released a statement to the effect that the decisions of Slovenia and Croatia declaring independence unilaterally were illegal and unconstitutional.

☐ The Federal Executive Council passed a decision to the effect that the Yugoslav People's Army should take possession of all airports and crucial strategic points in Slovenia. The Territorial Defense of Slovenia, estimated to number some 30,000 men put up stiff resistance and 39 soldiers of the YPA were killed.

☐ **June 28, 1991** - The Federal Secretariat for National Defense announced that the YPA had taken control of the state frontiers of the SFRY on Slovenian territory.

☐ **July 12, 1991** - The Presidency of the SFRY passed a decision to demobilize all paramilitary forces on the territory of the SFRY with the exception of the Yugoslav People's Army and the regular peace-time police forces.

☐ **September 16, 1991** - A statement was released by the Federal Secretariat for National Defense declaring as unlawful Stipe Mesić's order that the YPA forces should return to barracks and declaring the presence of YPA troops on Croatian territory as unlawful and representing an armed attack by the YPA. Units of the First Military District went into action to break the blockade of military barracks in many localities in Croatia including Vukovar.

☐ **October 12, 1991** - Talks began between representatives of the YPA and Slovenia on the Army's withdrawal from the territories of this one-time Yugoslav republic.

☐ **December 6, 1991** - Under the auspices of the European Community an agreement was reached between the YPA and Croatia to exchange prisoners observing the "all for all" principle.

☐ **July 18, 1991** - The Presidency of the SFRY passed a decision to evacuate all YPA forces from Slovenia within a term of three months.

☐ **October 3, 1991** - The Presidency of the SFRY began functioning under conditions of immediate danger of war.

☐ **October 19, 1991** - By decision of the State Presidency the Federal National Defense Secretary Colonel General Veljko

Kadijević decided to call a cease-fire on the territory of Croatia.

☐ **October 27, 1991** - The last soldier of the YPA pulled out of Slovenia. Part of the armaments, including 100 tanks, to remain in Slovenia until such time as the final balance would be drawn.

☐ **February 28, 1992** - Thirty generals of the YPA were retired, among them Veljko Kadijević, Federal Secretary for National Defense.

☐ **March 8, 1992** - Another 50 admirals and generals were retired, among the Chief-of-Staff Blagoje Adžić.

☐ **March 29, 1992** - Decision adopted to evacuate all YPA troops from Macedonia by April 15, 1992.

☐ **April 26, 1992** - In Skoplje talks were conducted on behalf of the State Presidency by Dr. Branko Kostić and on behalf of the Presidency of the SR of Bosnia-Herzegovina Alija Izetbegović, to discuss the future status of the Yugoslav People's Army in Bosnia-Herzegovina.

☐ **May 3, 1992** - Several soldiers of the YPA were killed when the Command of the II Military District was moved to Lukavica.

☐ **May 5, 1992** - The Presidency of the SFRY adopted a decision to the effect that the Yugoslav People's Army should evacuate from Bosnia-Herzegovina within 15 days, while those members of the Army, citizens of Bosnia-Herzegovina, should remain on its territory.

☐ **June 6, 1992** - The Supreme Command of the Yugoslav Army announced that the presence of the YPA on the territory of Bosnia-Herzegovina had finally been terminated.

☐ **May 20, 1992** - The State Presidency of Yugoslavia passed a decision by which the Yugoslav People's Army would in future be transformed into the Army of Yugoslavia.

☐ **October 20, 1992** - In accord with the agreement reached between the President of the FR of Yugoslavia Dobrica Ćosić and the President of Croatia Franjo Tudjman the Army of Yugoslavia evacuated the Prevlaka.

# SERBIA

*Area: 86,5 per cent of the territory of the Federal Republic of Yugoslavia.*

*Population: 93.9% of the population of the FR of Yugoslavia, i.e. 9,880,000 inhabitants (65.8% Serbs, 17.2% Albanians, 3.5% Hungarians, 3.2% Yugoslavs, 2.4% Muslims, 1.1% Croats, 6.8% miscellaneous).*

☐ **January 24, 1989** - The first major disorders since 1981 erupted in the Kosovo province and went on until early February, their extremist demands being the proclamation of an "Albanian Republic Kosovo".

☐ **February 20, 1989** - Beginning of a political strike of 1300 Albanian miners in Kosovo, lasting until March 1, 1989.

☐ **June 28, 1989** - To mark the 600th anniversary of the Battle of Kosovo at Gazimestan the President of Serbia Slobodan Milošević addressed over one million Serbs rallied from Kosovo and other parts of Serbia and Yugoslavia.

☐ **November 12, 1989** - In the Serbian presidential elections Slobodan Milošević won 65.3% of votes, and Vuk Drašković 16.4%.

☐ **1 July 1990** - Referendum held in Serbia on promulgation of the new Constitution and multiparty elections.

☐ **July 2, 1990** - Albanian members of the Assembly of Kosovo, gathered in front of the Assembly building, adopted constitutional declaration proclaiming Kosovo Republic.

☐ **July 5, 1990** - In view of illegal proclamation of Kosovo Republic, the Assembly of Serbia decided to disband the Assembly of Kosovo.

☐ **July 16, 1990** - Congress of the League of Communists of Serbia at which the Socialist Party of Serbia was founded, and Slobodan Milošević elected its president by 1228 out of 1294 votes.

☐ **July 20, 1990** - The Assembly of Serbia passed a law introducing a multi-party system.

☐ **7 September 1990** - At the secret session in Kačanik ethnic Albanians - delegates of the disbanded Assembly of Kosovo promulgated the Constitution of the Republic of Kosovo.

☐ **September 28, 1990** - Promulgation of the Serbian Constitution defining Serbia as a civic state with a multi-party system.

☐ **December 9, 1990** - First multi-party elections for the Assembly of Serbia at which the Socialist Party of Serbia (SPS) won an absolute majority. Out of 48.06% votes, in the Assembly SPS gained 77.06% seats.

☐ **January 17, 1991** - Serbian government declared that recognition of individual Yugoslav republics could not impair the continuity of Yugoslavia by the standards of international law.

☐ **March 9, 1991** - Violent demonstrations in Belgrade. The protest against the authorities in Serbia were organized by the Serbian Renewal Movement headed by Vuk Drašković.

☐ **February 5, 1992** - In Belgrade representatives of Serbia and Montenegro conducted talks on the organization and functioning of Yugoslavia as a common state. Talks were continued on February 12, 1992 and wound up with the adoption of the principles, competences and organs of the common state.

☐ **19 May 1991** - The Muslim National Council of Sandžak was established and adopted a declaration in which the Council states that it undertakes the protection of national interests of Muslims in Serbia. Sulejman Ugljanin was elected the Chairman of the Council.

☐ **May 24, 1992** - In Kosovo the Albanians organised illegal elections for 130 seats in their Assembly and for President of the Republic. All the seats were won by Ibrahim Rugova's Democratic Union. Rugova elected President by 95% votes.

☐ **August 31, 1992** - The coalition party DEPOS was founded in Serbia within the framework of efforts to unite the opposition; its activities date back to May 1992.

☐ **June 28, 1992** - DEPOS organised the so-called Vidovdanski Sabor (Vidovdan Assembly) in front of the Yugoslav Parliament building in Belgrade. It lasted for several days with thousands of people protesting against the authorities in Serbia and the situation prevailing in national media.

☐ **December 20, 1992** - Early elections for the Assembly and President of Serbia. In the Assembly of Serbia which has 250 deputies there will be 101 from the Socialist Party of Serbia, 73 from the Serbian Radical Party, 50 from DEPOS, 9 from the Democratic Community of Vojvodina Hungarians, 6 from the Democratic Party, 5 from the Željko Ražnjatović group of Citizens, 3 from the Serbian Peasant Party, 2 from the Coalition of Democratic and Reform Party of Vojvodina and 1 from the Democratic Reform Party of Muslims. In the first round of the elections Slobodan Milošević was elected President of Serbia by a majority of 56.21% of votes; 33.95% of votes were cast for Milan Panić.

# MONTENEGRO

*Area: 13.2 per cent of the territory of the FR of Yugoslavia.*

*Population: 6.2% of the population of FR Yugoslavia, i.e. 644,000 inhabitants (61.8% Montenegrins, 14.6% Muslims, 9.3% Serbs, 6.6% Albanians, 4.0% Yugoslavs, 2.7% miscellaneous).*

☐ **January 11, 1989** - Extensive demonstrations in Titograd and other towns, resignation of leadership (Vidoje Žarković, Marko Orlandić, Veselin Djuranović, Miljan Radović and others).

☐ **January 14, 1991** - The government of Montenegro announced that recognition of individual Yugoslav republics could not be permitted to impair the international continuity of Yugoslavia.

☐ **February 21, 1992** - In Titograd the supreme representatives of Serbia and Montenegro continued the talks conducted in Belgrade on February 5, 1992, dealing with the organization and functioning of Yugoslavia as a common state. The principles, competences and organs of this common state were adopted and approved.

☐ **March 1, 1992** - Referendum at which 95.94% of the Montenegrin population opted to remain within Yugoslavia.

☐ **April 27, 1992** - Promulgation of the Constitution of the Federal Republic of Yugoslavia as the common state of Montenegro and Serbia.

☐ **September 30, 1992** - In Geneva the President of Federal Yugoslavia Dobrica Ćosić and Croatian President Franjo Tudjman signed an agreement on the demilitarization of the Prevlaka and UNPROFOR supervision of this peninsula.

☐ **December 20, 1992** - Parliamentary elections in Montenegro. Results: out of a total of 85 seats representatives of the Democratic Party of Socialists won 46, the People's Party 13, the Liberals 13, Serbian Radical Party 8 and Social-Democratic

Party of Reformists 4 seats. In the second round of the presidential elections in Montenegro Momir Bulatović secured 63.29% of votes, and Branko Kostić 36.71%.

# SLOVENIA

*Area: 20,251 sq. km.*

*Population: 1,962,606 (87.6% Slovenians, 2.7% Croats, 2.4% Serbs, 1.4% Muslims, 6.9% miscellaneous).*

- **April 8, 1990** - First multiparty parliamentary elections.
- **May 16, 1990** - Lojze Peterle elected Prime Minister of Slovenia.
- **July 2, 1990** - Slovenian parliament adopted Declaration on the sovereignty of the state of Slovenia.
- **December 23, 1990** - Plebiscite on the sovereignty and independence of Slovenia (88.5% affirmative votes).
- **June 5, 1991** - Slovenian parliament passed a Foreign Affairs Law by which the Slovenian diplomacy seceded from the Yugoslav diplomacy.
- **June 25, 1991** - Slovenian parliament adopted Independence Declaration which was suspended by the Brioni Declaration for three months and confirmed on October 8, 1991.
- **June 26, 1991** - By decision of the Federal Chamber of the Assembly of the SFRY and the Federal Executive Council to protect the territorial integrity of Yugoslavia, the Yugoslav People's Army took measures to occupy airports and other major strategic points in Slovenia and gain control of the state frontiers, in which actions it clashed with the Territorial Defense forces of Slovenia.
- **July 4, 1991** - Red Cross of Yugoslavia stated that 49 persons were killed in armed conflicts in Slovenia.
- **December 23, 1991** - Promulgation of the new Constitution of Slovenia as a sovereign and independent state.
- **December 23, 1991** - Germany formally recognized the independence and sovereignty (known as the Christmas Recognition) of Slovenia, to become effective as from January 15, 1992.

- ☐ **January 15, 1992** - The countries of the European Community recognized Slovenia's sovereignty and independence.
- ☐ **May 22, 1992** - Slovenia admitted to the UN.

# CROATIA

*Area: 56,538 sq. km.*

*Population: 4,760,344 (77.9% Croats, 12.2% Serbs, 2.2% Yugoslavs, 7.7% miscellaneous)*

- ☐ **April 22, 1990** - Parliamentary elections (for the Croatian Sabor) at which representatives of the Croatian Democratic Community won 193 seats, the League of Croatian Communists (Party of Democratic Changes) won 81 seats, and the remaining groups 91 seats, out of a total of 365.
- ☐ **May 30, 1990** - Franjo Tudjman elected President of Croatia, and Stipe Mesić appointed Prime Minister.
- ☐ **July 25, 1990** - At a rally in Srb the Serbian Democratic Party issued a Declaration proclaiming the sovereignty of the Serbian people in Croatia.
- ☐ **August 19, 1990** - The Serbian people in Croatia held a referendum on autonomy.
- ☐ **October 1, 1990** - Proclamation of the Serbian Autonomous Region "Krajina".
- ☐ **December 22, 1990** - New Constitution of Croatia was promulgated declaring Croatia as a state of the Croatian people, in this way the Serbian people was demoted from the status of a constituent nation to the status of national minority.
- ☐ **February 28, 1991** - Representatives of the Serbian people in the Knin region issued a Declaration on independence and secession from Croatia.
- ☐ **March 16, 1991** - At an emergency session of the Executive Council of the Serbian Autonomous Region "Krajina" it was decided that the "Krajina" should break away from Croatia, and only federal regulations and laws of the Krajina be valid on its territory.

- **March 18, 1991** - The following localities decided to join the "Krajina": Knin, Donji Lapac, Titova Korenica, Obrovac, Benkovac, Vojnić, Kostajnica, Vrgin Most, Glina, Dvor na Uni, Pakrac and Gračac.
- **May 2, 1991** - Internationality clashes and Serbian resistance to Croatian authorities in Borovo Selo and other places in the neighborhood of Vukovar, Vinkovci, Osijek.
- **May 6, 1991** - Demonstrations against the Yugoslav People's Army in Split. One soldier killed.
- **May 19, 1991** - Referendum for an independent and sovereign Croatia. An affirmative vote was cast by 93.24% of the participants.
- **June 24, 1991** - Agreement on economic, cultural and informative cooperation signed in Banja Luka between the Bosnian and Knin Krajina. Release of Declaration on Serbian unity as the primary task.
- **June 25, 1991** - The Croatian Sabor (Parliament) adopted a declaration on Croatian independence and sovereignty - the Brioni Declaration, first suspended it for three months and then ultimately confirmed on October 8, 1991.
- **June 25, 1991** - Decision adopted to form the Serbian Autonomous Region Slavonija, Baranja and West Srem.
- **August 3, 1991** - The Croatian Assembly adopted a decision to sever all relations with Serbia.
- **December 4, 1991** - In keeping with Croatia's efforts to meet the demands of the European Community and gain international recognition, its parliament passed a bill on human rights and freedoms, as well as on the rights of national and ethnic communities and other minority groups in Croatia, thus amending the Constitution promulgated on December 22, 1990.
- **December 19, 1991** - Proclamation of the Srpska Krajina Republic. This date to be observed as a national holiday in the Krajina. On this day the assembly of the Serbian Autonomous Region became a constitutional assembly, promulgated a new Constitution and proclaimed the Republic Srpska Krajina with Milan Babić elected its first president.
- **December 23, 1991** - Germany formally recognized Croatian sovereignty and independence (so-called Christmas Recognition), to become effective as from January 15, 1992.
- **December 24, 1991** - The grand national assembly of the Serbian Autonomous Region Slavonija, Baranja and West Srem

decided to join the Srpska Krajina.

☐ **January 15, 1992** - The EC countries recognized Croatian sovereignty and independence.

☐ **February 26, 1992** - The Assembly of the Srpska Krajina Republic amended the Constitution by a new territorial organization of the Republic composed of the Krajina, East Slavonija, Baranja, West Srem and West Slavonija. Goran Hadžić elected President of the Srpska Krajina.

☐ **April 4, 1992** - Grand National Assembly of the Serbian Region Slavonija, Baranja and West Srem adopted its Statute declaring this region as a territorial unit of the Srpska Krajina.

☐ **May 22, 1992** - Croatia admitted to UN membership.

☐ **August 2, 1992** - Early elections in Croatia at which the Croatian Democratic Community secured 43.2% votes, and the Croatian Independent Liberal Party 18.3%, Franjo Tudjman re-elected President with 56.73% votes. Dražen Budiša won 21.87% votes.

☐ **September 28, 1992** - Assembly of the Srpska Krajina Republic adopted a decision to call elections and adopted a protocol on cooperation with the Serbian Republic.

☐ **January 14, 1993** - The five permanent members of the Security Council addressed a protest to Croatia for having violated the Resolution establishing the zone of banned flights in Bosnia-Herzegovina (it had been proved that the greatest number of violations had been committed by Croatian aircraft).

☐ **January 22, 1993** - Croatian armed forces went into action in the region of Maslenica, Zemunik Airport and the Perućac power-station as well as in other regions of the so-called "pink zone" monitored by UNPROFOR. These actions were denounced as acts of aggression against the Serbian Krajina Republic and condemned by the UN Security Council.

# BOSNIA-HERZEGOVINA

*Area: 51,129 sq. km.*

*Population: 4,364,574 inhabitants (43.7% Muslims, 31.4% Serbs, 17.3% Croats, 5.5% Yugoslavs, 2.1% miscellaneous).*

- **July 31, 1990** - Assembly of Bosnia-Herzegovina adopted constitutional amendments by which Bosnia-Herzegovina was declared a democratic state of equal citizens, of the peoples of Bosnia-Herzegovina, Muslims, Serbs, Croats and others.
- **November 18, 1990** - At multiparty elections in Bosnia-Herzegovina the Democratic Action Party (Muslims) won 86 seats in the Parliament, Serbian Democratic Party 72 and Croatian Democratic Union 44.
- **October 14, 1991** - Assembly of Bosnia-Herzegovina adopted a decision to call a referendum on the future status of Bosnia-Herzegovina, however without the participation of deputies of the Serbian Democratic Party.
- **October 24, 1991** - Assembly of Bosnia-Herzegovina adopted a platform defining its stand on the future organization of the Yugoslav community within which sovereign Bosnia-Herzegovina would remain only on condition that the community include Serbia and Croatia.
- **November 10, 1991** - Plebiscite at which the Serbian people in Bosnia-Herzegovina opted for life in a common Yugoslav state.
- **December 21, 1991** - Assembly of the Serbian people in Bosnia-Herzegovina adopted a Resolution to form the Serbian Republic of Bosnia-Herzegovina within the framework of Yugoslavia.
- **February 29, 1992** - Referendum on a sovereign and independent republic in which the Muslim population participated in a vast majority and declared itself in favor of the proposal.
- **March 1, 1992** - During a wedding procession in front of the Serbian Orthodox Church in Sarajevo the bridegroom's father Nikola Gardović was murdered and the officiating clergyman Radenko Miković wounded. The Serbian flag was burned on this occasion.
- **March 2, 1992** - In protest against the incident in front of the Orthodox Church in Sarajevo the Serbs put up 20 barricades in the city.

☐ **March 17, 1992** - Under the auspices of the European Community Alija Izetbegović, Radovan Karadžić and Mate Boban signed a document on the future constitutional order in Bosnia-Herzegovina based on the principle of its three constituent nations.

☐ **April 6, 1992** - European Community recognized the sovereignty and independence of Bosnia-Herzegovina.

☐ **April 7, 1992** - USA recognized the sovereignty and independence of Bosnia-Herzegovina.

☐ **April 7, 1992** - In Banja Luka the Assembly of the Serbian People proclaimed the independent Serbian Republic.

☐ **April 21, 1992** - The Croatian Dinar declared the only legal tender in Western Herzegovina.

☐ **April 26, 1992** - In Skoplje talks were conducted between Vice-President of the SFRY Presidency Branko Kostić, Chief-of-Staff Colonel General Blagoje Adžić and President of the Presidency of Bosnia-Herzegovina Alija Izetbegović to discuss the future status of the Yugoslav People's Army in Bosnia-Herzegovina.

☐ **April 27, 1992** - Respect for the territorial integrity of Bosnia-Herzegovina expressed in the Declaration of the FR of Yugoslavia.

☐ **May 3, 1992** - Several soldiers belonging to the Yugoslav People's Army killed when the Command of the II Military District moved to Lukavica.

☐ **May 12, 1992** - Assembly of the Serbian Republic in Banja Luka passed the decision to form the Army of the Serbian Republic, and colonel general Ratko Mladić was appointed as its commander.

☐ **May 19, 1992** - Yugoslav People's Army began its evacuation of the territories of Bosnia-Herzegovina.

☐ **May 22, 1992** - Bosnia-Herzegovina admitted to UN membership.

☐ **June 6, 1992** - Supreme Command of the Yugoslav Army announced its presence on the territories of Bosnia-Herzegovina as finally terminated.

☐ **June 9, 1992** - In the Security Council Resolution 758 was adopted extending the UNPROFOR mandate to include Bosnia-Herzegovina, for the present meaning Sarajevo and Butmir airport.

☐ **June 21, 1992** - Mate Boban, leader of the Croatian Democratic Community declared that the Croats were in control of almost the entire territory inhabited by Croats and that so-called Herzeg-Bosna accounted for 30% of the territory of Bosnia-Herzegovina.

☐ **June 28, 1992** - Francois Mitterand, President of France paid a visit to Sarajevo and announced the airport there would be opened with a view to continuing humanitarian aid to the population affected by the civil war, and inter-nationality and religious conflicts.

☐ **June 29, 1992** - UN Security Council decided that one thousand UNPROFOR soldiers should be detached to guard the Sarajevo airport.

☐ **July 2, 1992** - The Croatian Community Herzeg -Bosna declared a state of the Croatian people.

☐ **July 22, 1992** - Croatian President Tudjman and Alija Izetbegović, President of the Bosnia-Herzegovina Presidency signed a pact on friendship and cooperation. On September 23, 1992, when they met in New York, an Annex on coordination in the military field was appended thereto.

☐ **August 3, 1992** - Alija Izetbegović asked the Security Council to lift the embargo on arms deliveries to Bosnia-Herzegovina.

☐ **August 13, 1992** - The Security Council adopted a Resolution providing for the use of force as an ultimate measure in enabling the shipment of humanitarian aid. The Resolution was based on Chapter VII of the UN Charter.

☐ **September 3, 1992** - Italian transport plane carrying humanitarian aid crashed west of Sarajevo.

☐ **September 9, 1992** - The Security Council adopted a Resolution banning military flights in the airspace of Bosnia-Herzegovina.

☐ **November 14, 1992** - Seven hundred internees released from Manjača camp.

☐ **January 2, 1993** - In Geneva Cyrus Vance and Lord Owen submitted a plan for a new constitutional order in Bosnia-Herzegovina.

☐ **January 10, 1993** - In Geneva the proposals of Cyrus Vance and Lord Owen for a new constitutional order in Bosnia-Herzegovina were accepted. Radovan Karadžić declared his agreement conditional on the subsequent approval (within 7 days) of the Assembly of the Serbian Republic.

☐   **January 20, 1993** - At Pale the Assembly of the Serbian Repub-
    lic approved the Vance-Owen Plan for a new constitutional
    order in Bosnia-Herzegovina by 55 votes against 15, and one
    abstention.

# MACEDONIA

*Areas: 25,713 sq. km.*

*Population: 2,033,964 (64.6% Macedonians, 21%
Albanians, 8% Turks, 2.7% Gypsies, 2.2% Serbs,
4.7% miscellaneous.*

☐   **November 11, 1990** - First multiparty elections held in Mace-
    donia. After the second round held on 25 November VMRO-
    DPMNE party won most of the 37 seats in the Macedonian
    Parliament.
☐   **January 24, 1991** - The Parliament of Macedonia adopted the
    Declaration on Independence.
☐   **September 8, 1991** - Referendum on the independence of
    Macedonia and its possible association with Yugoslavia. Affir-
    mative vote cast by 74.14% of the participants.
☐   **September 17, 1991** - Macedonian assembly adopted a Decla-
    ration on strict respect for existing frontiers and rejecting any
    territorial claims on whatever neighboring country.
☐   **November 17, 1992** - Promulgation of the new Constitution of
    Macedonia.
☐   **January 6, 1992** - Striving to obtain international recognition
    of Macedonia, considering in particular the stands of Greece,
    the Macedonian Assembly adopted an amendment to the New
    Constitution specifying that Macedonia had no territorial
    claims whatsoever, and frontiers could only be changed by
    agreement, and that Macedonia would not meddle in the inter-
    nal affairs of neighboring states.
☐   **February 21, 1992** - It was agreed in Skoplje by the President
    of Macedonia Kiro Gligorov and the Chief-of-Staff of the
    Yugoslav People's Army Colonel-General Blagoje Adžić that
    the Yugoslav People's Army would pull out of Macedonia by
    April 15, 1992 at the latest.